Theology and Geometry

Politics, Literature, and Film

Series Editor: Lee Trepanier, Saginaw Valley State University

The Politics, Literature, and Film series is an interdisciplinary examination of the intersection of politics with literature and/or film. The series is receptive to works that use a variety of methodological approaches, focus on any period from antiquity to the present, and situate their analysis in national, comparative, or global contexts. Politics, Literature, and Film seeks to be truly interdisciplinary by including authors from all the social sciences and humanities, such as political science, sociology, psychology, literature, philosophy, history, religious studies, and law. The series is open to both American and non-American literature and film. By putting forth bold and innovative ideas that appeal to a broad range of interests, the series aims to enrich our conversations about literature, film, and their relationship to politics.

Advisory Board

Richard Avaramenko, University of Wisconsin-Madison
Linda Beail, Point Loma Nazarene University
Claudia Franziska Brühwiler, University of St. Gallen
Timothy Burns, Baylor University
Paul A. Cantor, University of Virginia
Joshua Foa Dienstag, University of California at Los Angeles
Lilly Goren, Carroll University
Natalie Taylor, Skidmore College
Ann Ward, University of Regina
Catherine Heldt Zuckert, University of Notre Dame

Recent Titles

Milton's Socratic Rationalism: The Conversations of Adam and Eve in Paradise Lost,
    by David Oliver Davies
Walker Percy and the Politics of the Wayfarer, by Brian A. Smith
Romanticism and Civilization: Love, Marriage and Family in Rousseau's Julie,
    by Mark Kremer
Aldous Huxley: The Political Thought of a Man of Letters, by Alessandro Maurini
Sinclair Lewis and American Democracy, by Steven Michels
Liberty, Individuality, and Democracy in Jorge Luis Borges, by Alejandra M. Salinas
*Philip Roth and American Liberalism: Historical Content and Literary Form in the Later
    Works*, by Andy Connolly
Seeing through the Screen: Interpreting American Political Film, by Bruce E. Altschuler
Cowboy Politics: Myths and Discourses in Popular Westerns from The Virginian *to*
    Unforgiven *and* Deadwood, by John S. Nelson
*Beyond Free Speech and Propaganda: The Political Development of Hollywood,
    1907–1927*, by John D. Steinmetz
Politics, Hollywood Style: American Politics in Film from Mr. Smith *to* Selma,
    by John Heyrman
*Civil Servants on the Silver Screen: Hollywood's Depiction of Government and
    Bureaucrats*, by Michelle C. Pautz

The Pursuit of Happiness and the American Regime: Political Theory in Literature,
by Elizabeth Amato

Imagination and Environmental Political Thought: The Aftermath of Thoreau,
by Joshua J. Bowman

The American Road Trip and American Political Thought, by Susan McWilliams Barndt

Flattering the Demos: Fiction and Democratic Education, by Travis Smith and
Marlene Sokolon

Soul of Statesmanship: Shakespeare on Nature, Virtue, and Political Wisdom,
by Khalil M. Habib and L. Joseph Hebert Jr.

The United States Constitution in Film: Part of Our National Culture, by Eric Kasper and
Quentin Vieregge

Short Stories and Political Philosophy: Power, Prose, and Persuasion, by Erin A. Dolgoy,
Kimberly Hurd Hale, and Bruce Peabody

Human Nature and Politics in Utopian and Anti-Utopian Fiction, by Nivedita Bagchi

Wonder and Cruelty: Ontological War in It's a Wonderful Life, by Steven Johnston

Rabelais's Contempt for Fortune: Pantagruelism, Politics, and Philosophy,
by Timothy Haglund

The Coen Brothers and the Comedy of Democracy, by Barry Craig and Sara MacDonald

Popular Culture and the Political Values of Neoliberalism, by George A. Gonzalez

The Final Frontier: International Relations and Politics through Star Trek *and* Star Wars,
by Joel R. Campbell and Gigi Gokcek

Flannery O'Connor and the Perils of Governing by Tenderness, by Jerome C. Foss

The Politics of Twin Peaks, edited by Amanda DiPaolo and James Clark Gillies

AIDS-Trauma and Politics: American Literature and the Search for a Witness,
by Aimee Pozorski

Baudelaire Contra Benjamin: A Critique of Politicized Aesthetics and Cultural Marxism,
by Beibei Guan and Wayne Cristaudo

Updike and Politics: New Considerations, edited by Matthew Shipe and Scott Dill

Lights, Camera, Execution!: Cinematic Portrayals of Capital Punishment,
by Helen J. Knowles, Bruce E. Altschuler, and Jaclyn Schildkraut

Possibility's Parents: Stories at the End of Liberalism, by Margaret Seyford Hrezo and
Nicolas Pappas

Game of Thrones *and the Theories of International Relations*, by Ñusta Carranza Ko and
Laura D. Young

Age of Anxiety: Meaning, Identity, and Politics, in 21st Century Film and Literature,
by Anthony M. Wachs and Jon D. Schaff

Science Fiction and Political Philosophy: From Bacon to Black Mirror,
edited by Steven Michel and Timothy McCranor

Theology and Geometry: Essays on John Kennedy Toole's A Confederacy of Dunces,
edited by Leslie Marsh

Theology and Geometry

Essays on John Kennedy Toole's
A Confederacy of Dunces

Edited by
Leslie Marsh

LEXINGTON BOOKS
Lanham • Boulder • New York • London

Published by Lexington Books
An imprint of The Rowman & Littlefield Publishing Group, Inc.
4501 Forbes Boulevard, Suite 200, Lanham, Maryland 20706
www.rowman.com

6 Tinworth Street, London SE11 5AL, United Kingdom

British Library Cataloguing in Publication Information Available

Library of Congress Control Number: 2019955245
ISBN 978-1-4985-8547-7 (cloth)
ISBN 978-1-4985-8549-1 (pbk.)
ISBN 978-1-4985-8548-4 (electronic)

In memory of my mother, Florence
and my father, Harry

Contents

Preface

The chapters collected here do not stringently conform to an a priori editorial expectation that certain aspects of the novel *must* be tackled. The brief was simply that each contributor write solely on that aspect which motivated them. A different set of writers could well have come up with an equally plausible but different selection of topics.

As things stand, there are many points of contention—and many of confluence. All the chapters were written in good faith by authors with no axe to grind and, at base, have entered into sympathy with the novel.

However one comes to John Kennedy Toole's *A Confederacy of Dunces*, all roads lead to Walker Percy. I can't speak for all of the contributors to this collection, but I suspect that four or five, maybe six (myself included), came to *Confederacy* directly via Percy. Aside from the well-known story of Percy's fortuitous intercession and his Introduction, by definition the benchmark of *Confederacy* scholarship, the clue to the significance of *Confederacy* lies obliquely with Percy himself. The *communion* (in the fullest sense of the word) between these two writers, though touched upon by the late Richard Keller Simon,[1] has yet to be expansively explored.

The tortuous and grim story of Ken Toole and *Confederacy* has been well documented; it stands as a classic case study in the sociology of publishing. With a biopic in the offing based upon Cory MacLauchlin's biography,[2] the story will no doubt become even more widely known. The question often asked is whether *Confederacy* could have been published in our time. The answer is an emphatic "no", at least not by any of the major publishing houses. The reason is twofold.

First, Robert Gottlieb, the then star editor at Simon & Schuster who made such heavy weather of his relationship with Toole, has—even fifty years after the fact[3]—stuck by his original assessment; summarizing the novel as presenting a "sophomoric worldview". Moreover, Gottlieb seemed absolutely blinded by one aspect: that of the Jewish characters, the Levys, and Myrna Minkoff. That Gottlieb "disliked" the way these characters were drawn hardly constitutes substantive editorial guidance, but merely a mealy-mouthed utterance that could be taken as a *tacit* imputation of anti-Semitism toward Toole. Of course, the behavior of Ken's "horrifying mother," Thelma Toole, gave Gottlieb the retroactive justification that he needed. The Levys and Minkoff are recognizable social types and can be found in Park Slope or in St. John's Wood. There is nothing remotely anti-Semitic in Toole's drawing of them. In fact, they come out rather well in the narrative's scheme of things. Gottlieb's underlying failing was that his vague rationale bore the hallmark of that corrosive mind virus going by the misnomer of "political correctness," a groundless hypersensitivity that characterizes those who need to take umbrage where there is none to be taken. Why else would an *uptown* Manhattanite be so irked by two *downtown* New Orleaneans? It is this aspect that undermines any claim to good faith that Gottlieb might have had.

On purely editorial grounds Gottlieb failed miserably. He could not conceptually enter into sympathy with the project (by no means a small failing). He is conspicuously flummoxed regarding the philosophical dimension ("it isn't really about anything"). A derivative consideration, by his own admission, is that Gottlieb is "religion-deaf." This immediately closes off a rich dimension to *Confederacy*, not least because its bawdy and riotous humor is part and parcel of the region's relationship to Catholicism. Gottlieb mendaciously appealed to market considerations when the only way that the market could possibly have been gauged would have been—well, to publish. Gottlieb, at least in the case of *Confederacy* (well into his tenure at Simon & Schuster in 1964) did not abide by his own advice, advice which as of 2016, he still dispenses annually for a publishing course at Columbia and includes the following heuristics: "Try to help make the book a better version of what it is, not into something it isn't";[4] "Every book has its own potential readership—figure out what it is and reach for it, don't try and sell every book to everyone"; and last but no means least, "Readers aren't stupid—their instincts may be sounder than yours." Notwithstanding Percy's assessment, the accolades, the sales, the myriad of translations, the adaptations, the reading groups, the merchandizing, the fan pages, and so on, Gottlieb contravened each one of his own aforementioned nuggets of wisdom. And yet perversely, in a one page gloss Gottlieb *still* stands by his original assessment, flawed as it was.

The Gottlieb fiasco aside, the censorious are always lurking, and this marks the second consideration as to why *Confederacy* might not have seen the light of day, especially in our present climate. There remains the distinct possibility that some epithet or other in *Confederacy* will fall foul of some contrived slight. It used to be that the censorious were typically of the pearl-clutching variety—Mary Whitehouse, Tipper Gore, Susan Baker, &c. Now it is the *Gutmenschen*, or in Ignatius's words, the "liberal doxy" (aided and abetted by university clerisies and state apparatuses) who, in their policing of language, have narrowed the Overton window so much so, they have rein-vigorated the push for blasphemy law within liberal democracies themselves, albeit repackaged as "hate speech". Literary studies has for several decades been given over to theory-saturated "activism masquerading as inquiry." It's self-aggrandizing political and identitarian Newspeak, as the late D. G. Myers put it, is "a caterwaul of screeching, dogmatic 'movements.' Neither method nor logic unites them." Of late, it has become known as "grievance studies."

If, on Auden's account, "satire is angry and optimistic—it believes the evil it attacks could be abolished; Comedy is good-tempered and pessimistic—it believes that however much we may wish we could, we cannot change human nature and must make the best of a bad job,"[5] then *Confederacy* seamlessly weaves these two dimensions. Therein lies John Kennedy Toole's genius.

NOTES

1. Richard Keller Simon, "John Kennedy Toole and Walker Percy: Fiction and Repetition in *A Confederacy of Dunces.*" *Texas Studies in Literature and Language*, Vol. 36, No. 1, Spring 1994.

2. Cory MacLauchlin, *Butterfly in the Typewriter: The Tragic Life of John Ken-nedy Toole and the Remarkable Story of a Confederacy of Dunces,* Boston: Da Capo, 2012.

3. Robert Gottlieb, *Avid Reader: A Life.* New York: Farrar, Straus and Gir-oux, 2016.

4. Toole scholar Jane Bethune, in the documentary John Kennedy Toole: the omega point (2013), is of the view that this is precisely what Gottlieb required of Toole.

5. W. H. Auden (ed.), *George Gordon, Lord Byron: Selected Poetry and Prose* (New York: Signet, 1966), p. xi.

Acknowledgments

As ever, none of this could have been undertaken without the quintuple support of Dave Hardwick, Christian Onof, Charles Ramey, Doug Hardwick and Shannon Selin.

Were I to initiate my own Crusade for Moorish Dignity, the recruits would include Patrick Ashmore (R.I.P.), Sabine Best, Janet Bowman, Marie Helene Chaudonneret-Oudelette, Sandy Del Vecchio, Shaun Hammond, John Jascoll, Klaus Mattar, Alice Onof, Gid Parry, Simon Powell, Charles Ruiters, Richard Selin, Birgit Tafel, Sanne Terhoeven, Geoff Thomas, Hans Vingerhoeds, and Tonnie Wierikx.

The series editor, Lee Trepanier, has proved to be a most responsive, supportive, ecumenical, and a most patient and efficient shepherder. The same can be said of Alison Keefner at Lexington Books and project manager, Hariharan Siva.

Thanks also to the following for their unfussy and helpful service: Ann E. Smith Case, Archivist of the John Kennedy Toole Papers, Howard-Tilton Memorial Library, Tulane University; Samantha Bruner, Archives Processing and Digital Initiatives Associate, Louisiana Research Collection, Tulane University; Kure Croker, Special Collections Registrar & Archivist and Trish Nugent, Special Collections & Archives Coordinator, both at the Walker Percy Special Collections & Archives, J. Edgar & Louise S. Monroe Library, Loyola University New Orleans.

Chapter 1

A Theory of Humor (Abridged) and the Comic Mechanisms of John Kennedy Toole's *A Confederacy of Dunces*

H. Vernon Leighton

INTRODUCTION

As a comic narrative, *A Confederacy of Dunces* (*Confederacy*) by John Kennedy Toole is—like its protagonist Ignatius J. Reilly—a curious beast. Some readers do not find the novel funny, and its reception was infamously rocky.[1] Because of this lack of universal acclaim for its humor, the questions arise: how does Toole generate (or try to generate) the humor in the novel and what sorts of devices does he employ in this effort? Those questions beg a more fundamental question, namely, what is humor? Therefore, a theory of humor (abridged), including some neuroscience, will precede my examination of the novel. Specifically, humor needs incongruities and social tension. *Confederacy* is a traditional Western comedy, and its farcical devices draw their incongruities from the novel's three large-scale, structural contrasts. As for the devices themselves, many readers expect the quick snap of stand-alone jokes or gags, in which one interpretation suddenly replacing the other; by contrast, *Confederacy* generates much of its humor by concurrent incongruities which simmer together as superimposed frames of reference. Ignatius shares qualities with other physical comedians, and these qualities relate the novel more closely to some theories of carnival than others. Finally, Toole may have drawn on concepts of the trickster and fool available at the time he wrote the novel from thinkers in psychology, sociology, and historical studies, particularly from the work of Enid Welsford.

Other critics have discussed the comic mechanisms of *Confederacy*. Michael Kline used postmodern metonymy as a framework for examining the farcical interweaving of the plot.[2] John Lowe studied *Confederacy* in light of the New Orleans carnival tradition and the genre of plays called "ethnic melee." In ethnic melees, characters from various ethnic groups unite to scapegoat and expel a central blocking character, and in *Confederacy* Ignatius provides that unifying plot device.[3]

A THEORY OF HUMOR (ABRIDGED)

One could write entire books about the nature of humor, and many have. Some scholars, such as T. G. A. Nelson, argue that no single theory can encompass the variety and diversity of humor.[4] I disagree. Many of the theories coalesce around similar points, so it is not unreasonable to articulate a single theory, at least for the purpose of creating a framework for investigation. So, just as the Reduced Shakespeare Company offered the complete works of William Shakespeare (abridged) in one performance,[5] I will here present an abridged theory of humor. For the sake of brevity, I will treat humor, mirth, and laughter as synonymous, even though they are distinct.

A quick tour through neuroscience offers an approach toward this theory. Scott Weems, in *Ha! The Science on When We Laugh and Why*, describes recent neurological studies that have identified the anterior cingulate as a critical structure of the brain for humor comprehension and appreciation. One job of the anterior cingulate is to resolve cognitive conflicts coming from other parts of the brain. The dorsal area of this structure focuses on resolving logical puzzles such as grammatical conundrums, while the ventral area deals more with conflicting emotions. When the anterior cingulate registers a contrast as humorous, it triggers a pleasurable release of dopamine in the limbic reward circuit of the brain. This circuit is also the fear response center and the system stimulated by drugs such as cocaine.[6]

Based on these findings and a wide range of other evidence, I posit that humor has two fundamental aspects: (1) an aspect of puzzling over a cognitive incongruity, which could be a conflict among incompatible grammatical constructions, beliefs, and goals and (2) a social aspect, which often deals with conflicting emotions. Some humor has a stronger incongruity aspect, and some humor has a stronger social aspect. These two aspects usually occur within a playful or paratelic context.

To illustrate these two fundamental aspects of humor, it is useful to examine the famous paraprosdokian, "I've had a perfectly wonderful evening, but this wasn't it."[7] The listener begins to interpret the utterance to be a common form of flattery, but the second half of the sentence conflicts with that initial interpretation. It forces the listener quickly to reinterpret the first part and replace the initial interpretation with one that makes sense of the entire utterance. The witticism features both (1) cognitive incongruity—trying to resolve the meaning of the sentence—and (2) a potential social put-down, especially if spoken to the host of a party. And the jokester can escape the potentially dangerous consequences of the social effrontery by playfully claiming, "Just kidding."

Many theorists have circled around these two aspects of humor in the past. In the early eighteenth century, Francis Hutcheson's *Reflections upon Laughter* refuted Hobbes's superiority theory of humor by presenting the first incongruity theory of humor, but he also argued that humor has a social correction function.[8] In 1900, the philosopher Henri Bergson argued that laughter was generated by a special type of incongruity, an incongruity between the vital and the automatic, but he also insisted that, "[Laughter] must have a social signification."[9] In 1964, Arthur Koestler argued that an event is humorous when it is associated with two incongruous frames of reference, a bisociation, but he added that there must also be an element of aggression. He defined aggression so broadly, however, that it could encompass many emotionally charged social situations.[10] In 1992, Wyer and Collins offered a schema theory that focused on incongruity, but they did so within the context of social communication.[11] Some theories, such as the "false committed belief" theory of Hurley, Dennett, and Adams (2011), focus on the cognitive aspect of humor;[12] some theories, such as Freud's first theory of humor, focus on the emotional release of the resolution;[13] and some theories focus on the social context within which humor operates.[14]

Within the cognitive incongruity aspect of humor, at least two potential interpretations of the event or utterance must be readily available to the mind, the first being the interpretation toward which the listener is being initially directed, and a second interpretation readily available in the listener's mind. For the witticism above, the listener begins to assign the "had" to the present evening, but the alternative—that the "perfectly wonderful evening" was far in the past—is readily available. Comedians often rely on shared knowledge with the audience to provide the second interpretation toward which a joke will pivot. Stereotype jokes rely on shared cultural characterizations of groups of people, but the shared knowledge could come from the known character traits of a famous politician, a well-known comic persona, or a common fictional character. Within small, stable social groups, such as a family, group members know each other well and can draw on an abundance of shared experience to provide the second interpretation for humorous incongruity. The dynamics of the small group should be understood as the original context for humor, because as a species Homo sapiens have existed for about a quarter million years, and for most of that time such small group interactions were our primary social context.

One can divide the cognitive incongruity aspect of humor into two categories. As the paraprosdokian above illustrates, in some humor events, the brain begins tentatively to assign the event to one interpretation but then is forced in surprise to reassign the event to a second interpretation. Let's call this the "interpretation replacement" type of humor.[15] Because stand-alone jokes are experiment-friendly, this replacement type has been the focus of humor research. It is also possible to hold two or more interpretations in continuous and playful ambiguity—let's call this the "interpretation concurrence" type of humor.[16] This long-running incongruity relates to teasing, nonsense humor, and children playing make-believe. Because this humor is more difficult to create in a lab, the neuroscience of interpretation concurrence is not well studied.[17]

As for the second fundamental aspect of humor, the social aspect, because our distant ancestors were dealing with social status hierarchies and pecking orders since they had fur and lived in burrows,[18] it should come as no surprise that one of humor's common functions is to negotiate social status. What is a pompous person but someone who claims a higher status than the group is willing to grant? Vanity and pretentiousness are perennial targets for humor because the downward status readjustments of those judged to warrant them resonate emotionally. In 1974, Zillmann and Bryant found that the intensity of humor was not related to the listener's sense of superiority, but was greatest when the target of the put-down was perceived to have deserved it.[19] That downward adjustment of social status can range from the open aggression of slapstick to George Meredith's cautionary "silvery laughter."[20] Humor can also function to increase the feelings of social bonding.[21] Chapter Five of Rod Martin's *The Psychology of Humor* provides a good catalog of the social functions of humor.[22] This social aspect of humor suggests a path for the evolution of laughter and humor as a mechanism for the maintenance of pro-social behavior in our species.[23]

This theory of humor frames my study of *Confederacy*, because, as I will show below, many of the comic devices in *Confederacy* are of the form of interpretation concurrence rather than the more traditional comic form of interpretation replacement. They also rely heavily on the status diminishment of members of the social group, a common social function of humor.

GENRE AND PLOT

The Oxford English Dictionary defines comedy as "a drama written in a light, amusing, or satirical style and having a happy or conciliatory ending. More generally: any literary composition or entertainment which portrays amusing characters or incidents and is intended to elicit laughter."[24] This definition describes a wide variety of theatrical and literary genre including sentimental comedies, which do not necessarily aim at being funny per se, and dark comedies, which aim to generate mirth without a conciliatory ending. Much of the comedy in the western theatrical tradition follows from the Greek New Comedy of Menander and includes both humor and a conciliatory resolution in a domestic situation.[25] While these features are specifically describing theatrical performances, many comic novels exhibit similar features and can be characterized using the same concepts. In this context, *Confederacy* can be seen as a traditional western comedy, because it uses humor and resolves to a happy ending for most of the characters.[26] With its many elements of physical comedy, it is a farce.

A plot common in western comedy ever since Greek New Comedy is the attempt by people with lower status to rise within the story's social group. They are prevented from rising in status by a blocking character.[27] The comic climax involves the overthrow of the blocking character and the release of the suppressed. The characters who are blocked are often young lovers, and the blocking character is often an older adult preventing their union. The lowering of the status of the blocking character within the social group—often with a climactic surprise when schemes are exposed or hidden identities revealed—triggers humor. That comic event allows the formerly blocked characters to take enhanced roles within the group. In some comedies, a trickster character causes confusion, which, when resolved, leads to the social lowering of the blocking character.

In *Confederacy*, Ignatius blocks his mother. He has spent all their money, demands that she care for him, and tries to prevent her from making friends or seeking new romantic relationships. The novel has two other blocking characters: Mrs. Levy blocks Gus and Trixie, and Lana Lee blocks Darlene and Burma Jones. The character who starts Ignatius's downfall is "the fly in everyone's ointment," Patrolman Mancuso,[28] but once Ignatius is launched, he is the source of the chaos and disruptions that cause the downfall of the other blocking characters. So Ignatius is both a blocking character and a character who unblocks, he is both tricked and trickster.

In the aftermath of the farcical climax, all three blocking characters lose the status they need to continue to control their social groups.[29] With Ignatius's downfall, his mother can marry the financially secure Claude Robichaux; without Mrs. Levy, Trixie can retire and Gus can rebuild his company, and with Lana in jail, Darlene and Burma both have new opportunities. This constitutes a traditional comic happy ending.

CHARACTER AND STRUCTURAL INCONGRUITIES

To produce humor, a story needs to have incongruities that allow events to be associated with more than one meaning or frame of reference, that is,

Koestler's humorous bisociation. *Confederacy* features three major structural incongruities. First, aspects of Ignatius's character conflict with one another. Second, Ignatius characterizes himself in ways that sharply differ from how his actions reveal him to the reader. Finally, the philosophical context underlying the story provides competing frames of reference that contain the potential for humorous contradiction.

Tim Ferguson, in his sitcom writer's manual *The Cheeky Monkey*, advises the budding comedy writer to focus on character. Audiences of comedy accept far-fetched plots and implausible story compression "because the audience's enjoyment stems from the characters, not the illusion of reality."[30] In *Confederacy*, Ignatius's overriding character trait is being immature and self-centered. As Patteson and Sauret describe in their excellent character study of Ignatius, "He is essentially a grossly overgrown, self-indulgent child."[31] His self-indulgence makes him profoundly lazy. Emotionally, he reacts toward those to whom he is close by heaping abuse and disparagement, belittling his mother, and trying to "deal with" Myrna Minkoff.

Ferguson advises that a character's conscious desires and unconscious needs should be in conflict for the character to be funny. An example he gives is the character of Dorsey in the movie *Tootsie*. Dorsey consciously wants professional success, but he unconsciously needs love. His need for love drives him to ruin his career by unmasking himself. In *Confederacy*, Ignatius consciously prefers, as Patteson and Sauret point out, to remain in the womb of his mother's house, but he is driven by an unconscious need to gain respect from Myrna. Once obtaining employment at Levy Pants, he could have remained there as a negligent employee; instead, he is provoked by Myrna's dismissive letters to demonstrate his superiority to her by starting a worker's revolt, which gets him fired. Later, her letters provoke him to start his political campaign for Peace through Degeneracy, again with catastrophic results. Walker Percy described *Confederacy* as a tragicomedy,[32] but if one views Ignatius's effort to "deal with" Myrna as an unconscious cry for help, then that effort does succeed, the cry is heard, and Myrna rescues him.

For Ferguson, comic heroes must have hope. A hero in a serious drama has both hope and the ability to handle the plot's challenges. For the comic hero, however, "the more forlorn the hope, the more feeble the attempt, the funnier the situation becomes."[33] Upon seeing the pornographic card with a shapely woman's body hiding behind his very own copy of Boethius's *Consolation of Philosophy*, Ignatius imagines that there is a beautiful Boethian scholar to be rescued. He hopes to rescue her, and he fears humiliation. His hope is misguided, his attempt is feeble, and humiliation is what he gets.

The second structural incongruity is the distance between how Ignatius sees himself and how he is portrayed to the reader. With regard to action in the world, Ignatius describes himself as a crusader for Taste and Decency against the corruptions of the modern world,[34] but his actions reveal him to be incapable of leadership. When he and the workers of Levy Pants confront the office manager, the workers abandon Ignatius because he will not give Mr. Gonzalez the opportunity to speak, much less to meet their demands.[35] At the rally for Peace through Degeneracy, Ignatius tries to inspire his audience, but they heckle him, then shove him, and then eject him from the party.[36] Lowe demonstrates that the scene where Ignatius enters the French Quarter with his hotdog cart and pirate costume is a parody of Spenser's Red Cross Knight entering the Woods of Error.[37] Ignatius is a cowardly knight with a plastic sword.

Another clash of conflicting frames of reference that generates humor in *Confederacy* relates to the philosophical context of the story. As I detailed in an earlier paper, "Dialectic of American Humanism,"[38] among medieval Arab astrologers, a person under the planetary influence of Saturn could be either devoted and deliberate or impudent and clumsy. The Renaissance philosopher Marsilio Ficino turned that claim into a theory where the child of Saturn was either a melancholy genius or a misfortunate brute. Ignatius sees himself as a genius among dunces, but the narrative portrays him as fulfilling all the negative qualities of the child of Saturn. *Confederacy* forms a dialectic, satirizing modern humanism as the thesis, satirizing Renaissance humanism as the antithesis, and then suggesting a synthesis. At the practical level of humor, the reader is repeatedly confronted by the contrast between Ignatius's claims to genius and his clearly brutish and ludicrous behavior.

COMIC DEVICES

Comic devices invoke the puzzle aspect of humor by exploiting contrasting interpretations of utterances and actions. Some devices trigger interpretation replacement, while others employ interpretation concurrence. For example, joke punchlines and straightforward comic gags typically rely on speed and reversal. The second interpretation is sprung before the audience expects it. Other devices such as mistaken identities and deception schemes create situations where events have multiple ongoing interpretations. These confusions and schemes are often in the end exposed for an eventual replacement, but for extended periods the audience enjoys the building tension of superimposed frames of reference.

Although most of the incongruity in *Confederacy* is in the form of interpretation concurrence, it uses some devices of interpretation replacement. One replacement device Toole does use is what I would call "the underwhelming reveal." An early example of this is when Ignatius cites his own scholarly work, which the reader begins to interpret as a signal of academic prestige, but then Ignatius reveals that the work in question was two pages written in pencil on lined paper and mailed to the Tulane University Library, which negates its original claim to status.[39] As is usual in the social aspect of humor, the reveal in this case lowers his claim for respect.

Another type of interpretation reversal in *Confederacy* is when Ignatius begins to refute a negative assessment of him only to reconfirm it strongly. For example, in describing his only foray into teaching, he disputes the students' complaints that he was defending the pope. He doesn't reject their claims because he had not brought religion into the classroom; rather, he did bring religion into the classroom, but the current pope is too liberal for Ignatius. He further describes how his students had a committee to organize protests. Instead of protesting war or injustice, though, they protested the fact that Ignatius never graded their papers.[40]

Toole typically uses devices of interpretation concurrence, such as ongoing incongruities between a character's self-image and the image the narrative presents to the reader. In Chapter Two, Patrolman Mancuso knows he is being watched by the Reilly neighbors, so he tries to strike an impressive pose, while the narrator describes his sallow figure and spindly legs. Likewise, Ignatius characterizes the office at Levy Pants as exhausting, but the narrative has shown that he does no productive work there.[41]

The contrasting visions of Ignatius as genius and Ignatius as grotesque underlie many of these incongruities. For example, Ignatius tells his mother he is praying, but he is praying to Fortuna to spin him higher on her wheel, rather than praying to a Christian God to liberate him from that wheel. Then his religious ecstasy turns out to be a vision of his deceased dog, to which he masturbates. This scene of sexual disparagement then provides the background knowledge for a later incongruity. When Ignatius leads the attempted worker's revolt, he declares, "I am holding before you the proudest of banners, an identification of our purpose, a visualization of all that we seek." He sees "FORWARD" in block letters and "Crusade for Moorish Dignity" in elaborate script; everyone else sees an old sheet covered in masturbation stains. What purpose the banner identifies has continuous and opposing interpretations.[42]

Another source of contrasts comes from Ignatius repeatedly criticizing modern consumerism, but then obviously enjoying it. In Chapter One, he declares he will not eat food from cans, which would save his mother labor, but he then asks his mother if he can have a hot dog from a street vendor, which she considers disgusting. He heaps abuse at *The American Bandstand* on television, but he won't miss it, and he has an almost orgasmic experience watching movies, even as he heckles the screen and disrupts the theatre.[43] Ignatius's relationship to consumerism is like his relationship to individuals to whom he is emotionally close: an outward hostility but a secret need.

Ignatius's attempts to communicate with Myrna Minkoff likewise feature parallel frames of reference. Myrna does not believe anything Ignatius writes. She dismisses the existence of Levy Pants, and she does not believe that he tried to lead either a worker's revolt or a peace movement of sodomites. To her, all these events are the imaginings of his isolated and deluded mind. In the final scene, Ignatius can only convince her to rescue him if he falsely confesses that his letters were all fantasies and that she is rescuing him from his delusions.[44]

Confederacy sometimes uses stereotypes to provide the second interpretation for its humorous incongruities, but in most instances, the shared knowledge comes from the reader's knowledge of the characters, especially Ignatius. The narrator cues the reader early in the book that Ignatius is immature and not to be taken seriously, so even some devices that might seem like interpretation replacement are not. Ignatius often declares that he will call his lawyers, or the mayor, or the police, only to immediately back down when challenged. This does not amount to a true comic reversal because the reader never believed the initial claim. It amounts to a display of Ignatius as a braggart coward, which the reader was anticipating—again, incongruity without replacement.

Toole uses the interweaving nature of the multiple storylines to cause a knowledge gap between the reader and the characters, and that gap also leads to comic incongruities. For example, Burma Jones looks out a bus window and sees an altercation in which someone is hitting a man in a beard and Bermuda shorts. From the description the reader knows what Burma does not, that Patrolman Mancuso is suffering yet another slapstick humiliation.[45] As Lowe points out, a quality or fact will appear early in the book, then reappear in the climax to become comical.[46] The initial appearance establishes a second interpretation toward which the narrative gag then pivots. However, the second interpretation does not replace the first; the first is in the mind of the character, while the second is superimposed on it by the reader.

PHYSICAL COMEDY AND CARNIVAL

Physical comedy is often considered the lowest form of comedy. It generally lacks cleverness, and it features physical, sometimes violent contact between actors. The original acts that used the name "slapstick" featured performers with sticks that were designed to generate a slapping sound rather than seriously injure. In physical comedy, even the laws of physics can be suspended. Before movies had sound, physical comedy was their dominant comic genre, and, although the characters in the films were portrayed as clumsy, actors such as Charlie Chaplin and Harold Lloyd embodied that clumsiness with acrobatic skill.[47]

The documentary "Laughing Matters" starring Rowan Atkinson and directed by Robin Driscoll details the qualities of protagonists in a physical comedy, and Ignatius Reilly fulfills them all. The qualities are the following: (1) the protagonists are alienated from the society around them; (2) they are childish; (3) they have to fight with ordinary objects; (4) their bodies can be humorous by themselves; (5) they are uncivilized and cannot or will not conform to social rules; (6) they are a threat to respectable people; (7) they mock authority and politeness; (8) they spread confusion; and finally (9) they cannot be killed, no matter how much those around them try.[48]

In this novel, Ignatius embodies all nine qualities: he lives with his mother, thinks she should support him at age thirty, cannot manage to ride on a bus, is regularly described with animal attributes, hits a policeman in the book's first scene, scares away ladies hosting a street art show, shouts abuse in movie theatres, causes the book's climactic chaos, and finally tricks Myrna into rescuing him from the insane asylum. He shares most of these qualities with other great physical comedy characters such as Rowan Atkinson's Mr. Bean and Peter Sellers's Inspector Clouseau.

New Orleans is famous for its celebration of carnival, the period of license and festivities between New Year and Ash Wednesday. Those who interpret carnival have used a variety of theories of its meaning and nature (despite the fact that it has a rich, complex, and multicultural history).[49] In the late nineteenth and early twentieth centuries, the most prominent theory of carnival was that it is a form of the ancient Roman Saturnalia. This tradition culminated in the anthropological study *The Golden Bough* by James Frazer.[50] Beginning in the late-1960s, the ideas of Mikhail Bakhtin were embraced as the proper framework through which to interpret carnival.[51] Toole wrote *Confederacy* at a time when Frazer's theory was dominant, but his critics interpreted *Confederacy* after the ascent of Bakhtin's theory. Of the two, Frazer's theory offers a superior explanatory framework for understanding *Confederacy*.

Frazer's anthropological theory centers on a scapegoat, an individual who represents the god of agriculture. That god dies at the end of each year and is reborn after the winter solstice, renewing life to the earth for the next planting. In Roman Saturnalia, a young man was selected by lot as the Lord of Misrule, and he oversaw a festival inversion of the social order and was finally put to death. Other similar traditions feature a scapegoat who is subjected to mock death or who is expelled from the community in order to renew it. In my earlier study, *Evidence of Influences*,[52] I point out that Frazer's theory was the one used by popular accounts of New Orleans Carnival which were available to Toole when he wrote *Confederacy*, and in fact Ignatius identifies himself as a scapegoat,[53] and he is expelled at the end of the book as the community is renewed. By contrast, Bakhtin's vision of carnival has all of the participants mutually cursing and abusing each other in an inverted ritual of abasement and transgressive renewal, and using Bakhtin causes the critic to pass over *Confederacy's* central feature: the expulsion of Ignatius as a carnival demon.

Saturnalia and physical comedy relate to one another through the figure of the scapegoat protagonist. Frazer specifically identifies the Christian passion and resurrection as an example of the scapegoat story. Likewise, Alan Dale identifies the slapstick hero as a redemptive figure: instead of the tragedy turned comedy which is salvation, the slapstick hero is "a comic martyr, suffering the compromises of dignity that we're spared for the duration of our sit in the theater."[54]

THE FOOL

At the time Toole wrote *Confederacy*, theories from the realms of psychology, sociology, and historical and literary scholarship about the nature of the fool and the trickster were available to Toole which may have provided him with material for Ignatius. In psychology, Carl Gustav Jung's writings on the trickster archetype had just been published. In sociology, one of the early studies toward a sociology of humor was on the social role of the fool. Finally, in historical and literary studies, Enid Welsford's *The Fool: His Social and Literary History*[55] cast a long and powerful influence over Toole's generation. In my earlier study on Toole and Ficino, I argued that Toole had created a dialectic between two forms of humanism. What was the point of the dialectic? Welsford's writing provides an answer.

While today Jung's theories might not be taken seriously as psychology (to say nothing of their racism), they were at the time influential and helped support the era of myth criticism in literature.[56] Jung's essay "On the Psychology of the Trickster-Figure" was first published in English in 1956 and then reissued in his *Collected Works* in 1959. On the essay's first page, Jung describes the trickster as "half animal, half-divine." Although Jung claims to be studying the trickster of American Indian (specifically Ho-chunk or Winnebago) mythology, he argues that the trickster archetype is universal and connects it to relevant aspects of Christianity and the fool traditions, carnivals, and grotesque masquerades of the European Middle Ages.[57] Jung's trickster can be gender ambiguous, and at his lower end, he is lower even than the animals "because of his extraordinary clumsiness and lack of instinct." Jung fits this archetype into his system thus: "In his clearest manifestations, he is a faithful reflection of an absolutely undifferentiated human consciousness."[58]

Jung's study fits well with the interpretation that Ignatius, through his immaturity, is one of Ficino's lower saturnine types. Jung connects the trickster archetype to Renaissance clowns and buffoons and to the modern physical comedy.[59] He even mentions the medieval mock religious ceremony called the "Feast of the Ass" where the congregants bray (and Ignatius does bray when Miss Trixie falls on him[60]). Jung interprets the path of the trickster as a path of the human mind maturing from an unconscious state to a reasoning state.

Early attempts to articulate a sociology of humor included the 1949 essay "The Fool as a Social Type" by Orrin E. Klapp. Like Henri Bergson in 1900, Klapp argues that one of the functions of humor is to enforce the social norms of the group by ridiculing the deviant. "Whereas the hero represents the victory of good over evil, the fool represents values which are rejected by the group: causes that are lost, incompetence, failure, and fiasco." Klapp provides a catalog of fool types: "1) the antic fool, 2) the comic rogue, 3) the rash fool, 4) the clumsy fool, 5) the deformed fool, 6) the simple fool, 7) the weak fool, 8) the comic butt, 9) the pompous fool, and 10) the mock hero."[61]

To ascribe to any member of the group the role of fool is a collective imputation which threatens that member's rights and role in group leadership. However, an effective strategy for status enhancement is to assume the fool role, and then turn the tables on group opponents to pass on the role to them. "Activity, aggressiveness, or 'fight' may transform a fool into a hero, particularly when he picks a larger opponent or identifies himself with a social cause. By choice of a larger opponent there is a double chance of heroic status, since victory will make the person a 'giant-killer.'"[62] A literary example here is Shakepeare's Prince Hal.

Ignatius fulfills many of Klapp's overlapping fool types. He does not consciously take on the fool's role, but through his aggressive disruption, he makes fools out of Mrs. Levy and Lana Lee. In this way, he takes on some heroic qualities. "The status of the fool presents a paradox in that it is both depreciated and valued: It is at the same time despised and tolerated, ridiculed and enjoyed, degraded and privileged." His trickster role is as a fool who makes others foolish. "As butt or scapegoat [the fool] receives indignities which in real life would be mortal insult or conflict-creating."[63]

Enid Welsford published in 1935 a still unparalleled study of the historical and literary fool. Written in the depths of the Great Depression, one can sense in the book her awareness of liberalism's economic failures and of the specter of authoritarian responses to that failure from Hitler and Stalin. If Toole did not read Welsford himself, he certainly was part of the culture that valued her work. One can find her possible influence in both details of *Confederacy* and in its overall meaning.

Welsford studies a wide range of mythic, historic, and literary fools in many different cultures, from ancient Egypt's Danga to classical India's Vidusaka, Tibet's King of the Years, Arabia's Nasr-ed-Din, Ireland's Comgan Mac-da-Cherda, Renaissance Italy's Il Matello, Germany's Till Eulenspiegel, France's Mère Sotte and Brusquet, and English fools such as Archy Armstrong and Falstaff. She finds that the role of the fool was often mixed with that of the poet and the saintly hermit who channels messages from the gods or foretells the future. Fools are either natural—deformed, developmentally disabled, mentally ill, or some combination of these—or they are artificial—persons in possession of their wits who act foolishly or who can create extemporaneous jokes and humorous rhymes, predecessors perhaps to the modern stand-up comedian.

Welsford investigates the motivation for supporting fools. In many cultures, to praise oneself or to be praised by others risks attracting cosmic jealousy, an evil eye, and the surest way to evade this misfortune is to be mocked by others. Those who do the mocking then take on the risk of misfortune, and who better to do so than "someone who is either too stupid or too helpless to decline the undertaking?" Welsford discusses Frazer's scapegoat, who takes on the sins and misfortunes of others and who is then killed or expelled from the community. She acknowledges the difference between the ritual scapegoat and the court-fool, but she argues that they may be related: "Why not employ a permanent scapegoat whose official duty it is to jeer continually at his superiors in order to bear their ill-luck on his own unimportant shoulders?"[64]

Common among court-fools of the Renaissance are some actions featured in *Confederacy*. In *Confederacy*, Ignatius forges a letter from Gus Levy which opens Levy up for a possible lawsuit. According to Welsford, in the Renaissance "the writing of familiar burlesque letters seems to have been a speciality of every kind of buffoon." For example, one fool wrote to the sons of a duke to inform them that they would be cut out of their inheritance because he had been recognized as the true heir. Fool societies engaged in absurd mocklawsuits, and Ignatius often threatens lawsuits on equally absurd grounds. As for Ignatuis's ludicrous attempts at scholarship, in Germany after the Thirty Year's War it was common to have a pedantic court-fool who was also a professor at the university and who would mock academic forms. In reflecting on the passing of the fool, Welsford even decries what she sees as the contemporary worship of money, which is a major theme in *Confederacy*.[65]

As Welsford concludes her section on the court-fool, she reflects that the decline of the divinely anointed king and the court-fool occurred together. "The King, the Priest, and the Fool all belong to the same regime, all belong essentially to a society shaped by belief in Divine order, human inadequacy, efficacious ritual; and there is no real place for any of them in a world increasingly dominated by the notions of the puritan, the scientist, and the captain of industry." This observation could almost have been written by Ignatius. She then asks the question that I believe Toole was trying, through his narrative dialectic, to answer: "Who is to present our humanists and dictators with the Cap and Bells?"[66] For the humanists at least, Toole's answer seems to be Ignatius Reilly.

CONCLUSION

In this chapter, I presented a theory that humor has two aspects, cognitive incongruity and a social aspect. To produce humorous incongruity, an event needs to be associated with two different interpretations. One interpretation can replace the other, as is common in joke punchlines, or the two interpretations can be superimposed and concurrent. I argue that much of the humor in *Confederacy* comes from devices that use interpretation concurrence.

The novel's structural contrasts that produce its dual and opposing interpretations come from three main sources: contrasts within Ignatius's character, contrasts between how Ignatius sees himself and how others see him, and contrasts between the philosophical systems behind the novel's ideas. I then survey some of the comic devices in *Confederacy*, showing that most feature interpretation concurrence. Further, Ignatius can be seen as a physical comedian and a carnival scapegoat. Finally, I show how Toole may have used the comic potential of the trickster and the fool to give the humanists of his day the cap and bells.

There are many reasons why a reader might not care for the humor of *Confederacy*. This was the first novel Toole sent to a publisher, and the execution is sometimes wanting. The reader might not accept some of the stereotypes Toole relied on in the early 1960s. The reader might see through Ignatius's outrageous childishness and pity him too much. Or the reader might have expected interpretation replacement, such as verbal wit, and may not appreciate the novel's use of interpretation concurrence.

NOTES

1. The first and most important rejection was by Robert Gottlieb, who after a year of working with Toole declined to publish it at Simon and Schuster. Perhaps a dozen other publishers rejected it before Louisiana State University Press published it with the encouragement of Walker Percy and with help from a grant from the National Endowment for the Arts to publish novels which contain local dialects. René Pol

Nevils and Deborah Hardy, *Ignatius Rising: The Life of John Kennedy Toole* (Baton Rouge: Louisiana State University Press, 2001), 200. Acknowledgement: Thanks for assistance with this research to Susan Byom, John Kerr, Carol Slade, Lauren Leighton, and Jean Leighton.

2. Michael Kline, "Narrating the Grotesque: The Rhetoric of Humor in John Kennedy Toole's A Confederacy of Dunces," *Southern Quarterly* 37, no. 3–4 (1999): 283–291.

3. John Lowe, "The Carnival Voices of A Confederacy of Dunces," in *Louisiana Culture from the Colonial Era to Katrina*, ed. John Lowe (Baton Rouge: Louisiana State University Press, 2008), 186.

4. T. G. A. Nelson, *Comedy: An Introduction to Comedy in Literature, Drama, and Cinema* (New York: Oxford University Press, 1990), 17.

5. Jess Borgeson, Adam Long, and Daniel Singer, *The Reduced Shakespeare Company's the Complete Works of William Shakespeare (Abridged)* (New York: Applause Books, 1994).

6. Scott Weems, *Ha! The Science on When We Laugh and Why* (New York: Basic, 2014), 30–47, 69.

7. This witticism has been falsely attributed to Groucho Marx, see "I've had a perfectly wonderful evening, but this wasn't it," Quote Investigator, last modified April 2016, http://quoteinvestigator.com/2012/07/02/wonderful-party-not/.

8. Francis Hutcheson, *Reflections upon Laughter* (Glasgow: Baxter, 1750, but originally published serially in 1726).

9. Henri Bergson, "Laughter," in *Comedy: An Essay on Comedy*, ed. Wylie Sypher (Garden City, NY: Doubleday, 1956), 65.

10. Arthur Koestler, *The Act of Creation* (London: Hutchinson, 1964), 35, 52.

11. Robert S. Wyer and James E. Collins, "A Theory of Humor Elicitation," *Psychological Review* 99, no. 4 (1992): 663–688.

12. Matthew M. Hurley, Daniel C. Dennett, and Reginald B. Adams, *Inside Jokes: Using Humor to Reverse Engineer the Mind* (Cambridge, MA: MIT Press, 2011).

13. Freud's first theory of humor, originally published in 1905, deals with the release of desires from the id that were forbidden by the superego, and it is found in Sigmund Freud, *Jokes and Their Relation to the Unconscious* (New York: Norton, 1963). His second theory of humor, originally published in 1928, sees humor as a tool used by the superego to help the ego deal with stress. See Sigmund Freud, "On Humour," in *The Standard Edition of the Complete Psychological Works of Sigmund Freud*, v. 21, ed. Anna Freud and James Strachey (London: Hogarth Press, 1961), 160–166.

14. A recent study on the social functions of laughter is Adrienne Wood and Paula Niedenthal, "Developing a Social Functional Account of Laughter," *Soc Personal Psychol Compass* 12 (2018): e12383, https://doi.org/10.1111/spc3.12383. For a review from the field of sociology, see Gary A. Fine, "Sociological Approaches to the Study of Humor," in *Handbook of Humor Research, Volume I, Basic Issues*, ed. Paul McGhee and Jeffrey Goldstein (New York: Springer, 1983), 159–181.

15. Interpretation replacement or the "Incongruity-Resolution Model" was best described by J. M. Suls, "A Two-Stage Model for the Appreciation of Jokes and

Cartoons: An Information-Processing Analysis," in *The Psychology of Humor: Theoretical Perspectives and Empirical Issues*, ed. Jeffrey Goldstein and Paul McGhee (New York: Academic Press, 1972), 81–100.

16. Koestler refers to this as "a continuous state of mild amusement" in *Act of Creation*, 37.

17. Scott Weems, personal communication, September 26, 2018. A factor analysis of humor conducted by Willibald Ruch divides jokes and cartoons into two classes based on structure. One is the incongruity-resolution class, INC-RES, and the other is the class of nonsense humor, or NON, which is often zany and does not feature a resolution to the incongruity. Interpretation replacement maps to INC-RES, while NON is similar to interpretation concurrence. See Willibald Ruch, "Assessment of Appreciation of Humor: Studies with the 3 WD Humor Test," in *Advances in Personality Assessment*, v. 9, ed. C. D. Spielberger and J. N. Butcher (Hillsdale, NJ: Lawrence Erlbaum, 1992), 27–75. The third statistical factor from Ruch's study is sexual humor, which is related to humor's social aspect, sexual relations being highly emotionally charged social relations.

18. For a review of interpersonal status theory see Denise Cummins, "Dominance, Status, and Social Hierarchies," in *The Handbook of Evolutionary Psychology*, ed. David Buss (Hoboken, NJ: Wiley, 2005), 676–697.

19. Dolf Zillmann and Jennings Bryant, "Retaliatory Equity as a Factor in Humor Appreciation," *Journal of Experimental Social Psychology* 10, no. 5 (1974): 480–488.

20. George Meredith, "An Essay on Comedy," in *Comedy: An Essay on Comedy*, ed. Wylie Sypher (Garden City, NY: Doubleday, 1956), 48. Wyer and Collins argue that all humor features some form of diminishment; I would argue that even abstract diminishment derives from interpersonal status adjustment.

21. Jenepher L. Terrion and Blake E. Ashforth, "From 'I' to 'We': The Role of Putdown Humor and Identity in the Development of a Temporary Group," *Human Relations* 55, no. 1 (2002): 55–88.

22. Rod Martin, *The Psychology of Humor: An Integrative Approach* (Burlington, MA: Elsevier Academic Press, 2007).

23. Human laughter and humor evolved from the pant-hoots that other primates utter during youthful mock aggression. Some theories about this evolution are part of the effort to explain why humans can be altruistic despite our selfish genes. A proposal by Gervais and Wilson comes from "multilevel selection theory." In that theory, human groups use low-cost social mechanisms for promoting altruistic behavior, and humor is one such low-cost mechanism. See Matthew Gervais and David Sloan Wilson, "The Evolution and Functions of Laughter and Humor: A Synthetic Approach," *The Quarterly Review of Biology* 80 (2005): 395–430. Another evolutionary theory is that of the altruistic punisher. An altruistic punisher is a group member who through personal cost enforces group cooperation. Other group members then must support and compensate this punisher in order for the dynamic to be evolutionarily stable. William Flesch describes a theory of tragic heroes as altruistic punishers in *Comeuppance: Costly Signaling, Altruistic Punishment, and Other Biological Components of Fiction* (Cambridge, MA: Harvard University Press, 2007). In comedy, both the group member who uses humor to lower the status of other group members and the comic role of the trickster can be seen as altruistic punishers, and the laughter provoked by

their efforts can be seen as second order support for them. These two theories are not incompatible. The question of altruism was also part of the early discussions of humor; Hutcheson criticized Hobbes for basing his worldview on selfishness, "Now natural affections and kind instincts are banished from philosophy," Hutcheson, *Reflections on Laughter*, 7. Hurley, Dennett, and Adams use an evolutionary framework for their theory, but they neglect the social function of humor to their detriment.

24. "Comedy, n.1," *Oxford English Dictionary Online*, accessed July 1, 2018, http://www.oed.com/.

25. Eric Weitz, *The Cambridge Introduction to Comedy* (New York: Cambridge University Press, 2009), 50; Nelson, *Comedy*, 19.

26. By contrast, *Confederacy* is not a picaresque novel, which is more episodic and unresolved. For an investigation of this question, see Greg Giddings, *The Picaresque Element in A Confederacy of Dunces* (MA Thesis, Wichita Falls, TX: Midwestern State University, 1993), 13, 85.

27. The earliest use of the phrase "blocking character" appears in Northrop Frye, *Anatomy of Criticism* (Princeton: Princeton University Press, 1957), 166–168, but the concept is much older.

28. Toole, *Confederacy*, 137.

29. In this regard, the act of damning seems to be significant, as only the blocking characters in the book are damned. Gonzalez damns Mrs. Levy, George damns Lana Lee, and Ignatius's mother eventually tells him to go to hell. Toole, *Confederacy*, 112, 190, 365.

30. Tim Ferguson, *The Cheeky Monkey: Writing Narrative Comedy* (Strawberry Hills, NSW: Currency Press, 2010), line 2547, Kindle.

31. Richard F. Patteson and Thomas Sauret, "The Consolation of Illusion: John Kennedy Toole's 'A Confederacy of Dunces,'" *Texas Review* 4, no. 1–2 (1983): 83.

32. Walker Percy, "Forward," in Toole, *Confederacy*, ix.

33. Ferguson, *Cheeky Monkey*, line 2418.

34. Patteson and Sauret perceptively argue that Ignatius's situation is more complex than a simple contrast. To them, there are three versions of Ignatius in the book. First, he sees himself as a crusader against the corruption; second, the other characters see him as a selfish buffoon; however, the third Ignatius has retreated into a world of illusion after a painfully awkward childhood in order to avoid being humiliated by rejection and alienation. Ignatius's outrageously childish behavior insulates the reader from feeling too much pity for him, but this third Ignatius gives the reader some sympathy for him, even as the reader laughs at his humiliations.

35. Helga Beste, *"What's that, Crazy?" Zur Funktion Verrückter Charaktere bei John Kennedy Toole, Joseph Heller, Marilynne Robinson und Leslie Marmon Silko* (Trier, Germany: Wissenschaftlicher, 2003), 138.

36. Toole, *Confederacy*, 320–325.

37. Lowe, "Carnival Voices,"165.

38. H. Vernon Leighton, "The Dialectic of American Humanism: John Kennedy Toole's A Confederacy of Dunces, Marsilio Ficino, and Paul Oskar Kristeller," *Renascence* 64, no. 2 (Winter 2012): 200–215.

39. Toole, *Confederacy*, 28. While some readers may dislike *Confederacy* because they do not appreciate its style of humor, others might dislike it because the comic

devices are not always well executed. In this instance, Ignatius reveals unnecessarily that his previous work was written in pencil; the reversal would have been funnier had another character revealed this fact.

40. Toole, *Confederacy*, 51.

41. Toole, *Confederacy*, 37, 74.

42. Toole, *Confederacy*, 30–31, 138.

43. Toole, *Confederacy*, 24, 42, 57.

44. Toole, *Confederacy*, 387.

45. Toole, *Confederacy*, 54.

46. Lowe, "Carnival Voices," 186.

47. An excellent study of physical comedy is Alan Dale, *Comedy Is a Man in Trouble* (Minneapolis: University of Minnesota Press, 2000).

48. Robin Driscoll, Rowan Atkinson, et al., "Laughing Matters" in *Funny Business* (London: Tiger Television, 1992).

49. For a good overview of the complex threads of New Orleans Carnival, see Reid Mitchell, *All on a Mardi Gras Day* (Cambridge, MA: Harvard University Press, 1995).

50. James Frazer, *The Golden Bough: A Study in Magic and Religion* (London: Macmillan, 1913), especially part six, *The Scapegoat*.

51. Mikhail M. Bakhtin, *Rabelais and His World* (Cambridge, MA: MIT Press, 1968).

52. H. Vernon Leighton, *Evidence of Influences on John Kennedy Toole's "A Confederacy of Dunces," Including Geoffrey Chaucer*, Version 2.0. (ResearchGate, 2011), 30N16.

53. Toole, *Confederacy*, 362.

54. Dale, *Comedy*, 14.

55. Enid Welsford, *The Fool: His Social and Literary History* (London: Faber and Faber, 1935).

56. A search of the JSTOR database September 21, 2018, set to "all content" for the phrase "myth criticism" yielded 861 results. For the search "myth criticism" AND Jung, there were 161 results for approximately a one-fifth ratio.

57. Carl Gustav Jung, "On the Psychology of the Trickster-Figure," in *The Archetypes and the Collective Unconscious*, v. 9 pt. 1 of *Collected Works*, ed. R. F. C. Hull (New York: Pantheon Books, 1959), 255, 259, 261–264.

58. Jung, "Trickster-Figure," 264, 259.

59. Jung, "Trickster-Figure," 262.

60. Toole, *Confederacy*, 86.

61. Orrin E. Klapp, "The Fool as a Social Type," *American Journal of Sociology* 55, no. 2 (1949): 157, 158.

62. Klapp, "The Fool as a Social Type," 160.

63. Klapp, "The Fool as a Social Type," 161, 162.

64. Welsford, *The Fool*, 67, 68, 74. One could argue that the real source of supposed cosmic jealousy is in fact the spiteful envy of lower status individuals within the social group.

65. Welsford, *The Fool*, 136, 209, 188, 270.

66. Welsford, *The Fool*, 193, 194.

BIBLIOGRAPHY

Bakhtin, Mikhail M. *Rabelais and His World.* Cambridge, MA: MIT Press, 1968.

Bergson, Henri. "Laughter." In *Comedy: An Essay on Comedy,* edited by Wylie Sypher, 59–190. Garden City, NY: Doubleday, 1956.

Beste, Helga. *"What's that, Crazy?" Zur Funktion Verruckter Charaktere bei John Kennedy Toole, Joseph Heller, Marilynne Robinson und Leslie Marmon Silko.* Trier: Wissenschaftlicher, 2003.

Borgeson, Jess, Adam Long, and Daniel Singer. *The Reduced Shakespeare Company's the Complete Works of William Shakespeare (Abridged).* New York: Applause Books, 1994.

Cummins, Denise. "Dominance, Status, and Social Hierarchies." In *The Handbook of Evolutionary Psychology*, edited by David Buss, 676–697. Hoboken, NJ: Wiley, 2005.

Dale, Alan. *Comedy Is a Man in Trouble.* Minneapolis: University of Minnesota Press, 2000.

Driscoll, Robin, Rowan Atkinson, et al. "Laughing Matters." In *Funny Business.* London: Tiger Television, 1992.

Ferguson, Tim. *The Cheeky Monkey: Writing Narrative Comedy.* Strawberry Hills, NSW: Currency Press, 2010. Kindle.

Fine, Gary A. "Sociological Approaches to the Study of Humor." In *Handbook of Humor Research, Volume I, Basic Issues*, edited by Paul McGhee and Jeffrey Goldstein, 159–181. New York: Springer, 1983.

Flesch, William. *Comeuppance: Costly Signaling, Altruistic Punishment, and Other Biological Components of Fiction.* Cambridge, MA: Harvard University Press, 2007.

Frazer, James. *The Golden Bough: A Study in Magic and Religion.* London: Macmillan, 1913.

Freud, Sigmund. *Jokes and Their Relation to the Unconscious.* New York: Norton, 1963.

Freud, Sigmund. "On Humour." In *The Standard Edition of the Complete Psychological Works of Sigmund Freud*, v. 21, edited by Anna Freud and James Strachey, 160–166. London: Hogarth Press, 1961.

Frye, Northrop. *Anatomy of Criticism.* Princeton: Princeton University Press, 1957.

Gervais, Matthew and David Sloan Wilson. "The Evolution and Functions of Laughter and Humor: A Synthetic Approach." *The Quarterly Review of Biology* 80 (2005): 395–430.

Giddings, Greg. *The Picaresque Element in a Confederacy of Dunces.* MA Thesis, Wichita Falls, TX: Midwestern State University, 1993.

Hurley, Matthew M., Daniel C. Dennett, and Reginald B. Adams. *Inside Jokes: Using Humor to Reverse Engineer the Mind.* Cambridge, MA: MIT Press, 2011.

Hutcheson, Francis. *Reflections upon Laughter.* Glasgow: Baxter, 1750, originally published serially in 1726.

Jung, Carl Gustav. "On the Psychology of the Trickster-Figure." In *The Archetypes and the Collective Unconscious*, v. 9 pt. 1 of *Collected Works*, edited by R. F. C. Hull, 255–272. New York: Pantheon Books, 1959.

Klapp, Orrin E. "The Fool as a Social Type." *American Journal of Sociology* 55, no. 2 (1949): 157–162.

Kline, Michael. "Narrating the Grotesque: The Rhetoric of Humor in John Kennedy Toole's A Confederacy of Dunces." *Southern Quarterly* 37, no. 3–4 (1999): 283–291.

Koestler, Arthur. *The Act of Creation.* London: Hutchinson, 1964.

Leighton, H. Vernon. "The Dialectic of American Humanism: John Kennedy Toole's A Confederacy of Dunces, Marsilio Ficino, and Paul Oskar Kristeller." *Renascence* 64, no. 2 (Winter 2012): 200–215.

Leighton, H. Vernon. *Evidence of Influences on John Kennedy Toole's "A Confederacy of Dunces," Including Geoffrey Chaucer.* Version 2.0. ResearchGate, 2011.

Lowe, John. "The Carnival Voices of A Confederacy of Dunces." In *Louisiana Culture from the Colonial Era to Katrina,* edited by John Lowe, 159–190. Baton Rouge: Louisiana State University Press, 2008.

Martin, Rod. *The Psychology of Humor: An Integrative Approach.* Burlington, MA: Elsevier Academic Press, 2007.

Meredith, George. "An Essay on Comedy." In *Comedy: An Essay on Comedy,* edited by Wylie Sypher, 1–57. Garden City, NY: Doubleday, 1956.

Mitchell, Reid. *All on a Mardi Gras Day.* Cambridge, MA: Harvard University Press, 1995.

Nelson, T. G. A. *Comedy: An Introduction to Comedy in Literature, Drama, and Cinema.* New York: Oxford University Press, 1990.

Nevils, René Pol and Deborah Hardy. *Ignatius Rising: The Life of John Kennedy Toole.* Baton Rouge: Louisiana State University Press, 2001.

Oxford English Dictionary Online. "Comedy, n.1." Accessed July 1, 2018. http://www.oed.com/.

Patteson, Richard F. and Thomas Sauret. "The Consolation of Illusion: John Kennedy Toole's A Confederacy of Dunces." *Texas Review* 4, no. 1–2 (1983): 77–87.

Quote Investigator. "I've had a perfectly wonderful evening, but this wasn't it." Last modified April 2016. http://quoteinvestigator.com/2012/07/02/wonderful-party-not/.

Ruch, Willibald. "Assessment of Appreciation of Humor: Studies with the 3 WD Humor Test." In *Advances in Personality Assessment,* v. 9, edited by C. D. Spielberger and J. N. Butcher, 27–75. Hillsdale, NJ: Lawrence Erlbaum, 1992.

Suls, J. M. "A Two-Stage Model for the Appreciation of Jokes and Cartoons: An Information-Processing Analysis." In *The Psychology of Humor: Theoretical Perspectives and Empirical Issues,* edited by Jeffrey Goldstein and Paul McGhee, 81–100. New York: Academic Press, 1972.

Terrion, Jenepher L. and Blake E. Ashforth. "From 'I' to 'We': The Role of Putdown Humor and Identity in the Development of a Temporary Group." *Human Relations* 55, no. 1 (2002): 55–88.

Toole, John Kennedy. *A Confederacy of Dunces.* New York: Grove, 1987.

Weems, Scott. *Ha! The Science on When We Laugh and Why.* New York: Basic, 2014.

Weitz, Eric. *The Cambridge Introduction to Comedy.* New York: Cambridge University Press, 2009.

Welsford, Enid. *The Fool: His Social and Literary History.* London: Faber and Faber, 1935.

Wood, Adrienne and Paula Niedenthal. "Developing a Social Functional Account of Laughter." *Soc Personal Psychol Compass* 12 (2018): e12383, https://doi.org/10.1111/spc3.12383.

Wyer, Robert S. and James E. Collins. "A Theory of Humor Elicitation." *Psychological Review* 99, no. 4 (1992): 663–688.

Zillmann, Dolf and Jennings Bryant. "Retaliatory Equity as a Factor in Humor Appreciation." *Journal of Experimental Social Psychology* 10, no. 5 (1974): 480–488.

Chapter 2

The Literary Foolishness of Ignatius Reilly

Jessica Hooten Wilson

In *A Confederacy of Dunces* John Kennedy Toole created a literary hero—Ignatius J. Reilly—who deserves the adjective "literary" more than "hero." Reilly seems to defy one's ability to classify him. The minute that readers compare him to figures of the past, they will uncover all the ways his character is contrary. As Walker Percy introduces him in the foreword of the novel,

> Here at any rate is Ignatius J. Reilly, without progenitor in any literature I know of—slob extraordinary, a mad Oliver Hardy, a fat Don Quixote, a perverse Thomas Aquinas rolled into one—who is in violent revolt against the modern age.[1]

Ironically, Percy claims there is no literary forbearer for Reilly, and then names Quixote as an ancestor. When Percy connects Reilly to Aquinas, he chooses the modifier "perverse," which nullifies the very reference to this saint. In line with Percy's allusions, Reilly associates himself with Boethius, the philosopher who was unjustly executed by barbarian rulers of Rome, yet he misreads the foundational text *Consolation of Philosophy*. While Reilly despairs over society's sins and misconduct, he acts as foolishly, if not more viciously, than those around him. I will argue that the literary allusions embedded in *Confederacy* are the key for how to understand Reilly's disparate character. These allusions point to a relationship between reading and imitation that charges the reader with a responsibility to read rightly.

Toole was a student of medieval and Renaissance literature, first as an undergraduate at Tulane University, then as a graduate student at Columbia University. Also, he taught literature for several years before he penned *Confederacy*. So, it makes sense that the novel leads readers, as Richard

Simon writes, "through bits and pieces of literary history, repetitions of *Don Quixote, Gargantua, Henry IV, Gulliver's Travels, Joseph Andrews, Tristram Shandy, The Picture of Dorian Gray,* and *Gone with the Wind.*"[2] Not only do books appear throughout the novel, but characters were modeled on the literature faculty with whom Toole taught at the University of Louisiana-Lafayette (Robert Byrne inspired the creation of Ignatius Reilly and Patricia Rickels, Myrna Minkoff).[3] Combining his knowledge of literature with his knowledge of people formed by literature, Toole catalogues how literature affects a life. His hero is a literary anachronism, out of place in his own time and interacting more with dead writers than those who are living.

In addition to the novelist Toole's narrative, Reilly composes manuscripts in Big Chief tablets, including his own stories entitled "The Journal of a Working Boy, or, Up from Sloth" (a title reminiscent of Renaissance literature), sporadic paragraphs that will one day be comprised into a comparative history, and letters to his former girlfriend Myrna Minkoff who lives in New York. These works contribute to the literary nature of Reilly's character, reminding readers of canonical stories where characters themselves are authors: such as Augustine in his *Confessions,* where the elder author describes the journey of his younger self to Christianity; or Dante the poet creating Dante the pilgrim; or Chaucer's characters telling stories on the pilgrimage to Canterbury; or Cervantes who feigns the truth of Don Quixote's noble quest by calling his work an *historia.*[4] As readers, we must contend with not only Reilly the reader but also Reilly the writer.

Following the first chapter where Toole introduces the majority of his cast of characters, chapter two begins with Reilly in his room, surrounded by dozens of tablets of yellowed pages, lying in bed in a flannel nightshirt, "contemplating the unfortunate turn that events had taken since the Reformation."[5] Reilly concludes that the medieval period was one "in which the western world had enjoyed order, tranquility, unity, and oneness with its True God and Trinity," and readers wonder whether to read his claims about the divine genuinely or satirically.[6] Like Alonso Quixano, who becomes the self-fashioned Don Quixote, Reilly appears to the reader shut off from the rest of the world, poring over literature so much that it overtakes his mind. Cervantes writes of Quixano:

> He filled himself with the imagination of all that he read in the books. . . . And so assured was he of the truth of all that mass of fantastic invention of which he read that for him there was no other history in the world so certain.[7]

Not unlike the quarrels and battles of Quixano's knights-errant, Reilly's reading casts a particular lens over reality through which he sees the indulgences and consumerism of American culture.

After denouncing his society, Reilly follows this claim with an observation about his recent encounter with the law. Patrolman Manusco had attempted to arrest him while he waited outside the department store for his mother. Reilly interprets this moment as a signal of ill fortune approaching: "There appeared winds of change which spelled evil days ahead. An ill wind blows no one good. . . . Fortuna's wheel had turned on humanity."[8] Unwittingly, Reilly introduces here the major tensions of the novel: Are the events of the novel a result of society's rejection of the True God or the mishaps of the devious goddess Fortuna? Is Ignatius Reilly a holy fool amidst an unbelieving generation or a vicious hypocrite decrying the very evils in which he participates? And, how does the reader make sense of this farcical character who writes with such passion against the evils of his age but who is laughable, humiliating, and seemingly deplorable?

Reilly will return repeatedly to his reference to Fortuna, drawing his knowledge of the goddess from "a central concept in [Boethius'] *De Consolatione Philosophiae*."[9] Reilly worries that the attempt to arrest him indicates a turning downward of Fortune's wheel, and he begins to pray against this: "Oh, Fortuna, blind, heedless goddess, I am strapped to your wheel."[10] Humorously, not realizing that Reilly is praying to Fortuna (and not the Triune God of whom he just wrote), his mother asks him to say a prayer for her while he's at it. Problems arise in Reilly's interpretation of Boethius: he misreads the wheel of fortune episode apart from the whole text, dismissing the conclusions of Boethius. By doing so, Reilly's response to *Consolation of Philosophy* leads not to contemplation and virtue but to poor choices and ignoble actions.

Throughout medieval narratives, the imperative was placed upon readers to read rightly so that their reading may result in virtuous action. In Augustine's *Confessions*, for instance, the young Augustine bemoans his emotional response to Dido's suicide in *The Aeneid* because it led him to feel lovesick.[11] The older man scribbling his confessions denounces his younger self for misinterpreting the story and thus poorly imitating it. As an author, Augustine portrays for his readers a series of alternative positive imitations: Antony, who upon hearing the gospel account of a man being asked to give up all he owned, did so and became a hermit in the desert; Ponticianus, who heard Antony's story, became a Christian; and Augustine himself, having these accounts of conversion, then converts. The point of his story is that a listener must be able to encounter a text rightly in order to imitate it rightly. To further emphasize this lesson, Augustine juxtaposes a scene in which his younger self reads the Christian Scriptures and finds them bereft of beauty and sense, whereas his older self picks up the letter of Paul to the Romans (13:13–14), reads it, and follows the admonition to avoid sexual immorality from that day forward.[12] Augustine remarks that his pride blocked him from imitating the book, but upon the next reading, he submits to its meaning.

Medieval writers inherit Augustine's warning and continue the tradition. In Dante's *Inferno*, for instance, one of the damned, Francesca da Rimini, quotes from Augustine's *Confessions*—"that day we read no more."[13] However, in her imitation of Augustine, she perverts his meaning: the book Francesca refers to is not Scripture but the tales of Lancelot and Guinevere, and she closes the book, not to put away sexual immorality, but to commit adultery with her brother-in-law. She imitates in order to manipulate her listener, in this case, Dante the pilgrim, who faints like an overcome lover at the end of her story. He, too, misinterprets her story and responds poorly. These are examples of prideful readers—Dante admits as much throughout *The Divine Comedy*, confessing in *Purgatorio* that he will spend the most time repenting in the circle of pride.[14] Similarly, we see in Chaucer's *The Canterbury Tales*, pride obscures the meaning of texts. For example, the Wife of Bath portrays a strong reading of Scriptures, misinterpreting passages to fit her desire. As she says at the beginning of her prologue, "Experience, though no written authority in this world, is good enough for me."[15] She denounces the authority of the text for her own interpretation. Thus, Solomon, with his many wives becomes the ideal, not the pre-lapsarian couple Adam and Eve; and the Samaritan woman at the well needs no forgiveness from the Wife of Bath.[16] Like Dante—but with greater humor—Chaucer cautions against the prideful reader who will misinterpret texts and thus act in poor imitation of what she reads.

Reilly resembles more the Boethius at the start of *Consolation of Philosophy* where the condemned man, under the influence of muses who indulge his self-pity, is drafting poetry. In these opening sections of *Consolation*, Boethius laments his loss of fortune in similar terms to those that Reilly uses. Several scholars have noted that Toole may have only been familiar with the first part of *Consolation*.[17] In Vernon Leighton's article that traces influences on Toole, he records the novelist's knowledge of the wheel of fortune from an exam booklet on Shakespeare's tragedies and histories:

> The Wheel of Fortune is the old medieval device for explaining the rise and fall of illustrious men—*de Casibis Virorum Illustrium*. It is the Boethian notion of a blind goddess, Fortuna, spinning a wheel on which men's fortunes rise and fall.[18]

Reilly subscribes to this vision of the wheel of fortune, which Boethius the character in *Consolation of Philosophy* will subsequently relinquish.

Despite Reilly's protests that he cares little for worldly definitions of success, he visualizes himself—at the start of the novel—atop the wheel. The top of the wheel should be a place where one possesses all earthly goods: fame, money, reputation, power, and so forth. In medieval depictions, on the top of the wheel sits a happy king. However, Toole introduces Reilly to readers as living at home with his mother, gorging on jelly donuts, unable to pay bills, jobless, and criticized by everyone with whom he interacts. Much of the comedic effect stems from this dramatic dissonance between Reilly's self-perception and reality; more significantly, the misapplication of Boethius' text reveals Reilly's inability to read rightly.

Reilly also envisions himself as "strapped" to Fortune's wheel, which is a misreading of Boethius's philosophy that assumes a determined fate, whereas Boethius and Lady Philosophy argue about the place of free will in his understanding of fortune. When Lady Philosophy descends, she diagnoses Boethius as sick because he has "forgotten [his] true nature" as something "more" than a "rational and mortal animal."[19] Like Boethius, Reilly is lamenting his fate. He is scribbling poetic letters to leave to posterity and masturbating over the memory of his dead dog Rex—exemplifying a rational and mortal animal. In contrast to this vision of a determined world where "ups and downs of fortune happen haphazardly," Lady Philosophy counters with "the end and purpose of things" and the governor of that providence: Boethius should know that Fortune is not in control; the Triune God is.[20]

Any attentive reading of *Consolation of Philosophy* recognizes that Lady Philosophy rejects Fortuna and leads Boethius away from her seduction. She regards Fortuna as a "monster" who is unjust and deceptive.[21] When the wheel is described, the transcendent guide mocks Fortuna with negative adjectives:

With *domineering* hand she moves the turning wheel….
Her *ruthless* will has just deposed once fearful kings…
But *steely hearted* laughs at groans her deeds have wrung…. (*emphasis mine*).[22]

Now that Boethius finds himself thrown down by Fortune, he should see her random, changing nature.[23] However, Reilly does not view Fortuna in adversarial terms, but calls her "divinity."[24] By praising her as such, Reilly misses the point of *Consolation*.

What should strike readers is the dialogic nature of *Consolation of Philosophy*, which contrasts with Reilly's monologic response to reading, writing, and living. Like a female Socrates, Lady Philosophy asks Boethius questions and challenges his assumptions. She provides a second voice in conversation with Boethius that exposes his erroneous ways of thinking and leads to his transformation. At the start of *Consolation*, Boethius believes in Fortuna and her wheel. However, Lady Philosophy diagnoses him: "[Y]ou are suffering because of your misguided belief, and you can't blame events for that."[25] If only there was a Lady Philosophy to instruct Reilly, who blames Fortuna for everything. The day after his near-arrest, Reilly reclines in a movie theater and thinks:

> When Fortuna spins you downward, go out to a movie and get more out of life. Ignatius was about to say this to himself; then he remembered that he went to the movies almost every night, no matter which way Fortuna was spinning.[26]

This pause by Reilly is one of the few moments in the book where he stops himself from thinking poorly. Despite his hesitation to think fallaciously, Reilly does not change his behavior. He does not ponder the idea long enough to recognize how it should affect his life choices.

Moreover, Reilly consumes other voices—from the books he reads, the movies he watches, television shows he abhors, or Myrna's letters. As he sits in the dark theater, protruding into two other seats on each side, Reilly hurls insults at the film, to the annoyance of everyone around him. Reilly does not allow for other voices to register or engage his own. Everything becomes a product for him, an object to which he responds. In considering a tasteless television program, he assumes the vision of a tenth-century German canoness Hroswitha, conflating her eyes with his own: "the penetrating gaze of this legendary Sybil of a holy nun would exorcise the horrors which materialize before our eyes in the name of television."[27] Readers may enjoy the thought experiment: how would a medieval saint respond to modern reality shows? However, they should be careful not to imitate Reilly and suppose they know the answer.

Finally, in a similar manner to how Myrna misreads Reilly's letters—assuming much and reading between the lines—so too Reilly misinterprets her letters. They both talk past one another. Reilly writes of her correspondence, which tends "to urge me to participate in lie-ins and wade-ins and sit-ins and such . . . . I have ignored her advice."[28] He describes his neglect of her as "Miltonic isolation and meditation," associating himself with the contemplative stance of the seventeenth-century poet.[29] Yet, Milton produced epics for readers. Reilly only composes for himself. He refers to the "Myrna Minkoffs of the world," objectifying her rather than considering her as a unique person among persons.[30] Thus, Reilly cannot hear much difference between her letters and what he considers the noise of the world.

Reilly misreads—medieval culture especially—because of his lack of theology. He acts out a prayer to Fortuna: "oh!" he exclaims and calls her "divinity." Several times Reilly mentions prayer, but always with a sense of the dramatic. In one journal, for instance, he concludes, "I am going to pray to St. Martin de Porres, the patron saint of mulattoes, for our cause in the factory. Because he is also invoked against rats, he will perhaps aid us in the office, too."[31] Praying becomes a situation for comedy or insult. When he writes a note to his pretentious professor Dr. Talc, he advises him to pray to St. Cassian of Imola who "was stabbed to death by his student with their stlyli."[32] The admonition to pray is more of a death threat. In the medieval world, prayer was a response to God's calling, a kenotic imitation of the God who descended to become incarnate, and who thus allows penitent sinners to speak to Him. However much Reilly feigns a medieval Christian worldview, it is a humanistic one founded on pride rather than humility.

As Reilly notes, a change occurs after the Reformation, as more and more readers reject divine authority for personal experience; humility is no longer a necessary virtue for the reader. In Cervantes' seventeenth-century novel, for instance, Don Quixote exhibits traits of both the poor and the right reader. By fashioning himself as "Don Quixote" and setting out into the world an adventurer, the nobleman interprets all that he sees with this fantastical lens. Readers may observe some superficial similarities with Reilly, especially in the quixotic Spaniard's twofold goal: to achieve fame and to save the world from evil. Spanish literature scholar Ruth El Saffar notes, "The first goal suggests pride, the second, faith."[33] Reilly displays similar division—remember our first vision of Reilly with his large ears sticking out from his hat, "indicating two directions at once"?[34]—a hint, perhaps, at Reilly's twofold character. On the one hand, Reilly competes with Myrna for fame in his activist pursuits while he simultaneously devises a plan "to Save the World Through Degeneracy."[35] Reilly is our ambiguous hero, a "fat Don Quixote" as Percy called him, warring with his false vision of the world, unable to read rightly and thus unable to live rightly in reality.

Reilly writes because he wants to make a fortune and considers himself the savior of the degenerate generation. He quotes other authors as a way of placing himself in their company, misreading their claims for his own purposes. Each of his entries for "Journal of a Working Boy" begins with an epigram, a partial piece of a quote that removes it from context and misapplies it to the real situation. When pasted together, the quotes form a collage revealing Reilly's desires for fame from his writing. Quotes such as, "Books are immortal sons defying their sires," attributed to Plato.[36] Or, from Milton's *Aeropagetica*: "A good book is the precious lifeblood of a master-spirit, embalmed and treasured up on purpose for a life beyond."[37] Through these quotes, Reilly attempts to situate his own work in the pantheon of great authors.

Two of the epigrams are particularly telling in what Reilly omits. In the journal entry that retells of Reilly's failed labor union revolt, he begins with a quote from Lord Macaulay's essays: "A great writer is the friend and benefactor of his readers."[38] When Reilly borrows this line, he does not finish the sentence, which concludes "and they cannot but judge of him under the deluding influence of his friendship and gratitude."[39] Macaulay is highlighting the bias readers maintain on behalf of their beloved authors in spite of "disgraceful stories" we may hear about their lives. One may think of Reilly here hoping that his great work will live on, in spite of his ludicrous factory uprising. A second journal entry becomes further satirized when one finds the source material of its epigram. Reilly is plotting to save the world through degeneracy, so he chooses a Joseph Addison quote that refers to a "coxcomb": "Nature has sometimes made a fool; but a coxcomb is always of man's own making."[40] However, the original quote from the eighteenth-century magazine *The Spectator* indicts Reilly more than the young "dandy," Dorian Greene. Addison describes a coxcomb as "a contemptible example of talents misapplied."[41] Only Reilly would be too proud to recognize his own image in Addison's description. Instead, he reads coxcomb superficially and misconstrues how to apply his reading to his life.

Through his *via negativa* example, Reilly appears to show readers how *not* to read, unintentionally warning us against his methods of interpretation. The obstacles seem to be too much trust in fortune instead of reliance on providence and the corollary vice, trust in one's own merits or pride. Reilly would protest this reading of his character "since pride is a Deadly Sin which [he felt he] generally eschew[ed]."[42] Another explanation of Reilly's foolishness and destructive behavior, one that pushes the boundaries of plausibility as much as Reilly's bulge defies his buttons: what if Reilly is a holy fool? Toole was a Roman Catholic, and although not devout, his studies of medieval and Renaissance literature would have introduced him to the figure of the holy fool—both in history, such as St. Francis of Assisi and Brother Juniper, or in literature, Don Quixote having already been mentioned. While the "holy fool" held less sway in the Western imagination than in the East, its elements seem to fit Reilly all too well.

In a critique of Dostoevsky's holy fools, scholar Harriet Murav outlines its features. In opposition to the saint or the divine exemplar, the "'fool for Christ's sake' seems more to embody all that is carnal, fallen and demonic, mankind at its very worst."[43] Readers do not have read deeply to envision Reilly as carnal: he consumes unsanitary hot dogs from his traveling cart by the hour; he pockets a youth's pornography for his own use; and he abuses everyone he meets, including his mother. Moreover, holy fools are hermits, as is Reilly, intentionally outcast from society. Reilly admits, "[M]y exile is voluntary" and elsewhere, "[S]ince I have no peers, I mingle with no one."[44] Although no one would mistake Reilly for a saint, he could be a holy fool.

Whereas the saint conceals her good deeds and strives for anonymity, the holy fool performs "a kind of medieval street theater that plays itself out against two opposing backgrounds: the rigid hierarchical pageantry of the official world, composed of the state and the church, and the 'laughter culture' of the folk world."[45] In the theater of the holy fool, the spectators "become actors" in these scenes "abusing the saint."[46] The performances are not of holy acts. In fact, holy fools violate "notions about suitable bodily comportment."[47] Think of Reilly's disgusting belches and shows of gluttony. On a larger scale, Reilly performs his public foolishness with no possible outcome except for his humiliation. Despite Reilly's intentions to be a recluse scholar, when he joins the workforce, he discovers audiences. In attempt to correct what he perceives as social injustice at the Levy Pants factory, Reilly tries to "win the workers' confidence" by dancing to the jazz playing through the loudspeakers: "I shuffled about beneath one of the loud-speakers, twisting and shouting, mumbling insanely, 'Go! Go! Do it, baby, do it! Hear me talkin' to ya. Wow!'"[48] In response to this "insane" dancing, the workers begin laughing and pointing, which delights Reilly, who feels he has won them over. Reilly intentionally makes a fool of himself for the benefit of those watching. In a later episode, when Reilly tries to save the world by creating a queer mob, he decks himself with accessories from his pirate costume—the one he is compelled to wear to sell hot dogs in the French Quarter. To a party of dancers, Reilly shouts, "I am here tonight my friends, to show you how to save the world and bring peace."[49] The party-goers revile him: "He's truly mad."[50] Despite their "mewing and hissing," Reilly continues preaching, "The world today is in a state of grave unrest. [. . .] We must prevent the apocalypse."[51] Reilly is abused into silence, until he feels invisible, alone, and ignored. Murav points out, "The holy fool is beaten by mad people as if he himself were mad."[52] Or, as the epigram of the novel says, the confederacy of dunces deplores the "true genius" as though he is a dunce.

By permitting the option of viewing Reilly as a holy fool, readers confront a choice in how to respond to the novel. When one encounters a holy fool or reads a saints' *life*, the goal is active participation. The text demands that we think about *how* we are reading rather than merely enjoy the story for itself. Instead of consuming the novel then, the very suggestion that Reilly's comedy could be a holy narrative places responsibility on the reader to attend to the ways that she is reading. This level of intentionality becomes a protection against the reader imitating Reilly's poor reading, monologic responses, or Quixote-like performances. From this posture, one may read *Confederacy* for as much instruction as delight.

The last two chapters of the novel are as allegorical as a medieval narrative, giving readers a chance to practice right reading. Reilly is finally knocked down by the oncoming of Desire, a bus headed towards him as he stumbles in a daze into the middle of Bourbon Street. His position supine before the crowd of onlookers may remind readers of Don Quixote's fall after his first adventure with the windmills. When Don Quixote tries to fight the windmills, he proclaims that he is in the service of God, though readers see more clearly than the hero does. The windmills may represent the wheel of fortune, which repel Quixote's advances. Scholar Ziolkowski describes Quixote's fall as a "spectacle": "the image of the wretch sitting on a wayside in his misery, the laughing-stock of passersby."[53] He is associated with the Suffering Servant.

Could the same be said of Reilly—who appears "like a dead cow lying in the street"?[54] The holy fool who could not fight the whims of Fortune?

Scholars often read *Confederacy* in light of its medieval references. Leighton depicts the ending as an inversion of Chaucer's tales. Instead of Reilly playing the knight, Myrna Minkoff rides in with her white Renault and saves Ignatius. However, his escape, as Elizabeth Bell indicates, "is false salvation."[55] He is running from "Charity," the apropos name of the insane asylum which would show him *hospital*ity and perhaps correct his vision. Bell argues Reilly must reject "the allegorical interpretation of life he has held to throughout the novel, admitting that his own world view is false."[56] After all, Reilly is not a knight, a Quixote, or a Boethius, as he imagines. Not that he ever visualized himself as a holy fool, but he has been playing a part, one that seems to come to an end as he and Myrna flee the city.

Readers receive a few clues for how to read rightly this "new cycle" of fortune's wheel.[57] After reading the entire novel, we comprehend that Fortuna does not "save" or "crush" Reilly. He has been responsible for his falls. While Quixote renounced his fantasies before he died, claiming providence over fortune, Reilly still assumes the blind goddess's sovereignty. And, yet, two words in the final paragraphs introduce hope for the attentive reader. As the two outcasts drive, Reilly rolls down the window to take in air. Most of the narrative, he's been in the habit of emitting gas, but now he's taking in fresh air. Reilly reflects that this action is "purgative."[58] The word literally means cathartic, but has the root *purg*, as in *purgatory* or *purgation*. Reilly may be purging of his infernal past; there may be a more paradisal future ahead. As Reilly inhales, he observes Myrna's pigtail swinging before him. Considering her salvific arrival and intervention in his life, Reilly feels "grateful." He repeats "gratefully" to emphasize this new way of seeing: "He stared gratefully at the back of Myrna's head. . . . Gratefully."[59] For someone who previously considered himself un-obliged to the masses, this repeated word signals the potential for humility, a virtue we noticed strikingly absent from our hero.

NOTES

1. Walker Percy, "Foreword." *A Confederacy of Dunces* by John Kennedy Toole (New York: Grove Press, 1980), 8.

2. Richard Keller Simon, "John Kennedy Toole and Walker Percy: Fiction and Repetition in A Confederacy of Dunces," *Texas Studies in Literature and Language* 36, no. 1 (Spring 1994): 99.

3. Joel Fletcher, *Ken and Thelma: The Story of "A Confederacy of Dunces"* (Gretna, LA: Pelican, 2005), 20.

4. Bruce W. Wardropper, "Don Quixote: Story or History?" *Modern Philology* 57, no. 1 (1965): 1–11.

Cervantes calls his book "historia": "We know, of course, that he is fooling us. . . . We have to deal, then, with a story masquerading as a history, with a work claiming to be historically true within its external framework of fiction" (1).

5. *Confederacy*, 41.

6. *Confederacy*, 41.

7. Miguel De Cervantes, *Don Quixote*. Ed. and Trans. John Rutherford (Penguin Classics, 2003), 36–37.

8. *Confederacy*, 40.

9. *Confederacy*, 42.

10. *Confederacy*, 42.

11. Augustine, *Confessions*. Ed. and Trans. Henry Chadwick (Oxford: Oxford University Press, 2009), 15: "What is more pitiable than a wretch without pity for himself who weeps over the death of Dido dying for love of Aeneas, but not weeping over himself dying for his lack of love for you, my God?" (III.21).

12. Augustine, *Confessions*, 39, 153. Augustine writes of his first reading of Holy Scriptures:

> And this is what met me: something neither open to the proud nor laid bare to mere children; a text lowly to the beginning but, on further reading, of mountainous difficulty and enveloped in mysteries. I was not in any state to be able to enter into that (III.v.9).

Then, as an adult, he reads the scriptures again with humility: "I neither wished nor needed to read further. At once, with the last words of this sentence [in Romans], it was as if a light of relief from anxiety flooded my heart" (VIII.29).

13. Dante Alighieri, *Inferno*. Ed. and Trans. Anthony Esolen (Modern Library, 2005), I.v.138. The Italian reads, "Quel giorno piú non vi leggemmo avante," which literally translates: "That day no more did we read further" (52, *my translation*).

14. Dante Alighieri, *Purgatorio*. Ed. and Trans. Anthony Esolen (Modern Library, 2004), II.xiii.136–138. Dante confesses, "As for the torment on the lower track [meaning the circle of pride], far more's the fear that makes my spirit tense—already I feel the burden on my back." He refers to the *contra passo* experienced by the proud, carrying a boulder on their backs to keep their faces lowered.

15. Chaucer, *The Canterbury Tales*. Gen. ed. *The Riverside Chaucer*. Middle English text from Larry D. Benson (Houghton Miflin Company), https://sites.fas.harvard .edu/~chaucer/teachslf/wbt-par.htm. Accessed on February 12, 2019.

16. Santa is referred to by Ignatius as "Wife-of-Bath Battalgia" (*Confederacy*, 387).

17. Leighton cites William Bedford Clark (273) and Michael Kline (287), as well as Richard Simon (108).

18. On page 9 of his article, Leighton cites the source of this exam as archives Box 2, Folder 7 and remarks the similarity between Toole's answer and Reilly's exclamation in *Confederacy*: "*De Casibis Virorum Illustrium*! Of the Fall of Great Men! My downfall occurred. Literally" (*Confederacy*, 121). Leighton neglects to mention that the Latin allusion "de Casibis Virorum Illustrium" refers to Boccaccio's fourteenth-century work.

19. Ancius Boethius, *The Consolation of Philosophy*. Trans. Victor Watts (Penguin Classics, 1999), 20.

20. Boethius, *The Consolation of Philosophy.*

21. Boethius, *The Consolation of Philosophy,* 22.

22. Boethius, *The Consolation of Philosophy,* 24.

23. Boethius, *The Consolation of Philosophy,* 23.

24. *Confederacy,* 42.

25. *Consolation,* 29.

26. *Confederacy,* 67.

27. *Confederacy,* 58.

28. *Confederacy,* 138.

29. *Confederacy,* 139.

30. *Confederacy,* 139.

31. *Confederacy,* 139.

32. *Confederacy,* 140.

33. Ruth El Saffar, "Apropos of Don Quixote," *MLN* 85, no. 2 (March 1970): 269–273. Accessed on JSTOR January 27, 2019: 269.

34. *Confederacy,* 1.

35. *Confederacy,* 269.

36. *Confederacy,* 99.

37. *Confederacy,* 226.

38. *Confederacy,* 118.

39. Thomas Babington Macaulay, *Lord Macaulay's Essays and Lays of Ancient Rome* (London: George Routledge and Sons, 1892), 350.

40. *Confederacy,* 268.

41. Joseph Addison, *The Spectator* No. 404. Volume 6 (London, 1853), 39.

42. *Confederacy,* 135.

43. Harriet Murav, *Holy Foolishness: Dostoevsky's Novels & the Poetics of Cultural Critique* (Stanford, CA: Stanford University Press, 1992), 17.

44. *Confederacy,* 134.

45. Murav, *Holy Foolishness,* 23.

46. Murav, *Holy Foolishness,* 24.

47. Murav, *Holy Foolishness,* 24.

48. *Confederacy,* 133.

49. *Confederacy,* 332.

50. *Confederacy,* 332.

51. *Confederacy,* 332.

52. Murav, *Holy Foolishness,* 29.

53. Erick J. Ziolkowski, "Don Quijote's Windmill and Fortune's Wheel." *The Modern Language Review* 86, no. 4 (October 1991): 892–894. Accessed by JSTOR on January 25, 2019.

54. *Confederacy,* 348.

55. Elizabeth S. Bell, "The Clash of Worldviews in John Kennedy Toole's *Confederacy of Dunces.*" *The Southern Literary Journal* 21, no. 1 (Fall 1998): 20.

56. Bell, "The Clash of Worldviews in John Kennedy Toole's *Confederacy of Dunces.*"

57. *Confederacy,* 405.

58. *Confederacy*, 405.
59. *Confederacy*, 405.

BIBLIOGRAPHY

Addison, Joseph. *The Spectator* No. 404. Volume 6. London, 1853.

Alighieri, Dante. *Inferno*. Ed. and Trans. Anthony Esolen. Modern Library, 2005.

———. *Purgatorio*. Ed. and Trans. Anthony Esolen. Modern Library, 2004.

Augustine. *Confessions*. Ed. and Trans. Henry Chadwick. Oxford: Oxford University Press, 2009.

Bell, Elizabeth S. "The Clash of Worldviews in John Kennedy Toole's *Confederacy of Dunces*." *The Southern Literary Journal* 21, no. 1 (Fall 1998).

Cervantes, Miguel De. *Don Quixote*. Ed. and Trans. John Rutherford. Penguin Classics, 2003.

Chaucer, *The Canterbury Tales*. Gen. ed. *The Riverside Chaucer*. Middle English text from Larry D. Benson. Houghton Miflin Company. https://sites.fas.harvard.edu/~chaucer/teachslf/wbt-par.htm. Accessed on February 12, 2019.

El Saffar, Ruth. "Apropos of Don Quixote," *MLN* 85, no. 2 (March 1970): 269–273. Accessed on JSTOR January 27, 2019.

Fletcher, Joel. *Ken and Thelma: The Story of "A Confederacy of Dunces*," Gretna, LA: Pelican, 2005.

Leighton, Vernon H. "Evidence of Influences on John Kennedy Toole's *A Confederacy of Dunces*." Version 2.1 (June 2, 2014): 1–46.

Macaulay, Thomas Babington. *Lord Macaulay's Essays and Lays of Ancient Rome*. London: George Routledge and Sons, 1892.

Murav, Harriet. *Holy Foolishness: Dostoevsky's Novels & the Poetics of Cultural Critique*. Stanford, CA: Stanford University Press, 1992.

Percy, Walker. "Foreword." *A Confederacy of Dunces* by John Kennedy Toole. New York: Grove Press, 1980.

Simon, Richard Keller. "John Kennedy Toole and Walker Percy: Fiction and Repetition in A Confederacy of Dunces." *Texas Studies in Literature and Language* 36, no. 1 (Spring 1994).

Wardropper, Bruce W. "Don Quixote: Story or History?" *Modern Philology* 57, no. 1 (1965): 1–11.

Ziolkowski, Erick J. "Don Quijote's Windmill and Fortune's Wheel." *The Modern Language Review* 86, no. 4 (October 1991). Accessed by JSTOR on January 25, 2019.

Chapter 3

"Amusingness Forced to Figure Itself Out"

Ignatius J. Reilly, Aesthetic Individualism, and the Modernism of Anti-Modernism

Kenneth B. McIntyre

The character Ignatius J. Reilly in *A Confederacy of Dunces* has been famously described by Walker Percy as a perverse Thomas Aquinas, and Reilly's consistent invocations of Boethius, Hrosthwitha, and the Goddess Fortuna certainly suggest that his animadversions against the modern world are rooted in a comic neo-medievalism. Percy noted that Ignatius "is in a violent revolt against the entire modern age," and Percy's foreword to the novel has provided the conditions under which the novel and Ignatius have been judged since its publication.[1] However, in the same description, Percy suggests a more likely model in Don Quixote, whose rejection of his world is best understood as an expression of a kind of aesthetic individualism which is characteristic of modern, not medieval, civilization.[2] Others have also read the novel, at least in part, as a moral tale and have interpreted Ignatius as a moralist, albeit an extremely hypocritical one.[3] One of the great ironies of the consensus interpretation of the novel as a moral tale is that the novel was originally rejected largely because Robert Gottlieb, the editor at Simon and Schuster who reviewed it, did not believe that it had a moral purpose at all. He wrote to Toole that

> there must be a point to everything you have in the book, a real point, not just amusingness forced to figure itself out . . . [but] the book does not have a reason . . . it isn't really about anything.[4]

Of course, Toole could have written a moral treatise had he so desired, but instead he chose to engage in an act of aesthetic creation, and the main character in the novel, Ignatius J. Reilly, is one of Toole's most memorable aesthetic creations. However, Ignatius is not merely an aesthetic creation, he is also an aesthete, and, thus, a very modern kind of individualist. He lives in the aesthetic world (for the most part) and conceives of the world and himself in aesthetic terms. When he does find the world morally repugnant, he translates that repugnance into aesthetic creativity.

Thus, first, I will argue that *Confederacy* is a novel and not a moral or political treatise, and, thus, should be understood in terms of aesthetic categories and not in terms of "good" or "evil," or "truth" or "falsehood." In examining the character Ignatius J. Reilly, I will rely on the modal distinctions between the aesthetic world and the practical/moral world investigated and expounded by the English philosopher Michael Oakeshott to develop my claim that Ignatius is most appropriately considered in aesthetic and not practical terms. Second, I claim that Ignatius is not merely an aesthetic creation, but that he is also an aesthete in the Kierkegaardian sense of the term and that his aestheticism explains his careering career in the novel better than other attributes do. Kierkegaard believed that the aesthetic was an inadequate and ultimately unsatisfying stage of life superseded by ethical and religious stages. In contrast, Oakeshott has suggested that the aesthetic is one of several ways of conceiving the world (the others being the historical, scientific, and practico-religious), and that none of these are completely satisfactory nor is any one mode intrinsically superior the others. Thus, it is perfectly reasonable for a human being to approach the world, at least on some occasions, and consider it in terms of its capacity to delight, entertain, or surprise us. In addition, it is even more reasonable for an aesthetic creation, like Ignatius, to live and think in terms of the aesthetic character of the world.

Finally, I suggest that Ignatius's various creations, that is, his interactions with other characters, his reflections on his situations as related by both the omniscient narrator and his own statements, and his various writings, are expressions, not of some coherent neo-medieval moral critique of modernity, but of an aesthetic individualism which is thoroughly modern. Ignatius's critique of modernity, if it is to be referred to as such, has its intellectual roots and counterparts in thinkers like Jacob Burkhardt, José Ortega y Gassett, and Michael Oakeshott, not in the works of Pope Pius IX, Joseph de Maistre, or Carl Schmitt.[5] Reilly's Big Chief diaries, his "Journal of a Working Boy," and his running commentaries on contemporary life express an aesthetic critique of certain aspects of modernity and a defense of a radical kind of self-creative individualism which is characteristic of modernity itself. Whether Toole was intimately aware of the writers and thinkers mentioned above, and I am doubtful that he was, his creation Ignatius J. Reilly, like Quixote before him, is an expression of Toole's contemplation of the modern individual who inhabits multiple worlds and reveals a multiplicity of characters.[6]

IGNATIUS AS AN AESTHETIC CREATION

One of the central questions facing anyone attempting to offer an interpretation of a novel, or a poem, or a string quartet, or a painting is "what is it?" Is it a statement of protest against a corrupt world? Is it a claim about the direction of the march of history? Is it a critique of the previous generation of novelists, poets, composers, or painters? Is it an expression of the author's emotional state either when writing or at some other time? Is it an attempt to make some good old hard cash? Is it an expression of aesthetic wonder or delight? To answer "yes" to any one of these questions leads to a particular conception of art as either moral, political, personal, or artistic. Though the form of the novel offers greater temptations to read it as autobiography, cri de coeur, employment application, or political manifesto, insofar as the novel aspires to be art, then it should be considered under the categories appropriate to making judgments about art. Thus, the character of any theory of aesthetic experience must offer an account of the categories of consideration concerning art, or, in other words, provide the postulates that condition aesthetic experience.

Like other modern modes of human understanding such as history and science, the world of aesthetic experience has only slowly and intermittently emancipated itself from the world of social, moral, and practical considerations. The gravitational power of such moral considerations still holds much modern criticism in its orbit, and one does not have to look to Soviet realism to find examples of the malign effects of moralism on art.[7] In the United States, such moralists can be found at all points of the political and social compass, with Christian conservatives decrying the immoral and blasphemous nature of works like Andres Serrano's admittedly silly *Piss Christ* and the film version of *The Last Temptation of Christ* and self-described progressives banning *Huckleberry Finn* and the song *Baby Its Cold Outside* for manifesting improperly retrograde attitudes about racial minorities and women.[8] In the nineteenth century, artists and critics in Europe and America began to develop a defense of the autonomy of artistic expression. The Aesthetic Movement in Britain was one manifestation of this and the Formalist movement and the New Criticism in the twentieth century were more recent defenders of the distinctiveness of aesthetic experience and of the slogan "art for art's sake."[9]

In the early to middle years of the twentieth century, the English philosopher Michael Oakeshott engaged in a theoretical elaboration of the various strands of the "art for art's sake" critical movement of the late nineteenth and early twentieth century. He offered a pluralist account of human epistemology and experience which owed much to Hegel, but, instead of the various worlds of experience forming a pyramid in which each form superseded the form before it, Oakeshott's modes of experience are independent and irrelevant to each other and thus do not form any sort of hierarchical scale.[10] These modes of experience, which include the poetic/aesthetic, the historical, the scientific, and the practical are coequals, none having more philosophical validity than the others do. The world of practice is the one that we humans most commonly inhabit, and it is a world conceived under the postulate of its mutability. It is a world of good and evil, right and wrong, and success and failure. The world of history is conceived under the postulate of the unchanging pastness of the past, and it is a world of historical fact, truth, and falsehood. And the world of science is conceived in terms of the postulate of measurement, and it is also a world of fact, truth, and falsehood, but insulated from historical fact because of the differing postulates of the two.

Oakeshott distinguished the world of poetry/art/aesthetic experience from each of the other modes and, in so doing, offered his own defense of the autonomy of the aesthetic world. His philosophical aesthetics proposes that art or poetry forms its own realm of human experience having nothing to do with practical or moral concerns, historical questions, or scientific claims. The postulate of aesthetic experience is delightfulness, and the world of poetry or art is the world considered in terms of its capacity or possibility for delighting us. This delight is an intrinsic value and points to no other value outside of itself.[11] As Oakeshott notes, in art,

> there is no problem to be solved, no hypothesis to be explored, no restlessness to be overcome, no desire to be satisfied, or approval to be won. . . . At every turn what impels the activity and gives it whatever coherence it may possess, is the delight offered.[12]

Thus, Oakeshott's work serves the purposes of the literary/aesthetic critic as a negative aesthetics which, like a negative theology that tells us what God is not, provides a modal distinction which rules out the irrelevant concerns of the moralist, the politician, the hedge preacher, the historian, or the scientist.[13] In reading *Confederacy* as a work of art, therefore, it would be irrelevant to be concerned with Toole's biographical information, his personal politics, his possible mental illness, and so on. The novel manifests the author's keen eyes and ears for detail, but, considered aesthetically, these are not in service of some practical goal such as critiquing modern society or offering medieval-ism as an escape, but instead in the service of the aesthetic creation of objects of pleasure and delight. Further, Ignatius J. Reilly, considered aesthetically, is not a not mouthpiece for Toole, especially since the novel should not be read as an expression of some intention of Toole's. It is perfectly clear, of course, that an artist (e.g., a poet, a novelist, a painter, or a composer) often has mul-tiple purposes when creating his or her art. These often include non-aesthetic practical purposes like making money, becoming a famous artist, criticizing modern society, expressing latent homosexuality, being a spokesman for the working classes, expressing a distaste for Jews, expressing a belief in the inferiority of the lower classes, and so on, but these are all irrelevant to the character of the creation as an aesthetic expression (and they are usually not very interesting).[14]

In addition to ruling out certain kinds of questions and considerations as irrelevant to aesthetic experience, Oakeshott also offers an explanation of the distinctiveness of aesthetic experience which does not limit such experience to the creative artist. For Oakeshott, anything in our experience can become a subject of contemplation in terms of the delight that it is capable of producing. Anything can be conceived as art, including things that would normally be considered moral enormities. For example, incest (Sophocles' Theban plays), pedophilia (*Lolita*), hysteria (*Madame Bovary*), rape (*A Clockwork Orange*), and mental illness (*The Idiot*) have all provided artists with images which, though morally troublesome in various ways when considered in practical terms, continue to delight. Artists contemplate the aesthetic possibilities of seemingly mundane things like peasant boots (Van Gough), houses (Cezanne), goats (Rauschenberg), urinals (Duchamp), pipes (Magritte), colors (Rothko), shapes (Kandinsky), and lines (Mondrian), and composers consider the aesthetic qualities of sounds of all sorts like taxi horns (Gershwin), toy pianos (Cage), birdsong (Messiaen), and donkeys (Mendelssohn). Thus, an obese, boorish aesthete masturbating, farting, and wreaking havoc throughout New Orleans is a perfectly reasonable object of aesthetic consideration.[15]

The contemplation of anything from the morally reprehensible to the unremarkable and mundane in terms of its capacity to delight is possible because artistic expression is not propositional. As Oakeshott notes, "a poetic image can never 'lie' because it does not affirm anything."[16] Unlike the worlds of history, science, and, to a certain degree, practical morality, there are no "facts" in the world of aesthetic experience. Messiaen may strike a "false note," but it's not because his composition doesn't accurately reflect the sound of the black-eared wheatear, and Homer may nod, but it's not because he fudges on the body count in one of the battles in *The Iliad*. Thus, it is irrelevant whether "The sun-comprehending glass . . . shows Nothing, and is nowhere, and is endless," is an accurate description of the play between sunlight and windows, just as it makes no sense to ask Delmore Schwartz if he really has a "heavy bear who goes with me, A manifold honey to smear his face." The criteria of inclusion in art lie not in its correspondence to a factual world or in its capacity to ameliorate the human condition, but in its internal coherence as a work of art.[17] Thus, a poem of two lines might be too long and a novel of a thousand pages might be too short.

Oakeshott's elaboration of aesthetic experience offers a lens through which to view the world aesthetically, but also through which to examine certain objects which present themselves as works of art. These objects often stand out as aesthetic objects because they are "framed" as works of art.[18] However, Oakeshott's philosophical aesthetics does not offer a critical method, and, in fact, he rejects the notion that his work will be of much practical use to the artist or art critic. His primary concern was distinguishing between various ways of understanding or contemplating the world, and the aesthetic was just one of these ways.

IGNATIUS AS AN AESTHETE AND INDIVIDUALIST

A very different approach to the question of aesthetic experience was taken by the Danish philosopher Søren Kierkegaard. Like Oakeshott, he was influenced by Hegel, but his reaction to Hegel's work was starkly negative. Like Hegel (and Oakeshott), Kierkegaard posited the existence of a variety of forms of experience, but, for Kierkegaard, these forms or stages of life were primarily existential, not intellectual, and they were not lenses that one could put on and take off, but instead defined the worldview of those participating in them. The aesthetic stage was the first of these stages (the ethical and religious being the other two), and it was expounded most completely by Kierkegaard in his first work *Either/Or.*[19] Neither the ethical stage nor the religious stage are centrally relevant to Kierkegaard's discussion of the aesthetic stage, so they will not be dealt with here, other than to note that Kierkegaard insisted that the decision to adopt an aesthetic life was a premoral or amoral decision, and, thus, like Oakeshott, Kierkegaard deemed moral considerations irrelevant to aesthetic ones.[20] Further, for Kierkegaard, the aesthete is a modern individualist and could not be said to have existed before the advent of the modern world. In the voice of "A," he writes that "in the ancient world, subjectivity was not fully conscious and reflective.. . . Our age . . . has to leave the individual entirely to himself, so that in a stricter sense, he becomes his own creator."[21] Thus, for Kierkegaard, the aesthete is inevitably a modern individualist, which also involves a capacity for self-creation.

I suggest that the fictional character Ignatius J. Reilly is best understood as a Kierkegaardian aesthete in an Oakeshottian aesthetic creation.[22] The Kierkegaardian aesthete lives in a world of immediacy, and is concerned almost solely with the discovery and exploitation of pleasurable, interesting, and entertaining experiences. The aesthete's *summum malum* is boredom, and his experiences and experiments in living do not necessarily have to be successful in order to be pleasurable.[23] According to Kierkegaard, the aesthete is also destined to a life of ultimate despair. However, Ignatius is an aesthetic creation, not a human being, and the aesthete considered aesthetically is just as likely to have a comic destination as a tragic one. That is to say, the Kierkegaardian aesthete may be understood in terms of the practical possibilities available to him and the aesthetic life might be found wanting in those terms, but the aesthete (like the incestuous king, the pedophile intellectual, or the delusional Knight Errant) can also be conceived in terms of the aesthetic delight that he provides and, in this way, can be ultimately successful as an artistic creation.

So, what did Kierkegaard claim to be the exact character of the aesthete? Kierkegaard's works are notoriously difficult to interpret for a variety of reasons, the most notable being the pseudonymous character of many of his publications. He wrote *Either/Or* not only under a pseudonym but under several layers of them. The work is purported to have been discovered by the narrator in a locked secretary. It consists of a series of various types of commentaries by an aesthete called only "A" which include a further found manuscript titled "The Diary of a Seducer," and several letters to "A" from a Judge Vilhelm seemingly representing the ethical stage of life.[24] Thus, attributing to Kierkegaard particular judgments about the aesthetic and the ethical is somewhat difficult, and he does not actually compose a systematic theory of the aesthetic stage. Indeed, his narrator suggests that, though "A's papers contain a variety of attempts at an aesthetic view of life; to convey a unified aesthetic life-view is scarcely possible."[25] Like "A's" in *Either/Or*, the character Ignatius J. Reilly in *Confederacy* has a collection of Big Chief tablets containing his various attempts to construct a "view of life," and these are complimented in the novel by Ignatius's "Diary of a Working Boy." Like "A's" essays, Ignatius's various scribblings are connected not by an explicit theoretical commitment, but by an aesthetic sensibility. In Ignatius's Big Chief essays, he is offended as much by the vulgarity and banality of the contemporary world as by its abandonment of medieval philosophy. In his list of the ascendant Gods of the Modern world, the last and most important is "Bad Taste."[26] His bolded complaint about his fate is that "he was faced with the perversion of having to GO TO WORK."[27] It is the banausic reduction of life to the merely practical which Ignatius finds so offensive, not modernity itself.

Despite the inherent difficulties connected with creating a fully coherent picture of the aesthete, there are some characteristics that define the aesthetic stage for Kierkegaard and distinguish it quite clearly from other ways, notably the ethical, of relating oneself to the world. First, the aesthete is primarily concerned with the world in terms of its pleasantness, its capacity to entertain, and/or its capacity to excite wonder or awe, and not in terms of its moral goodness, his own success in the world, nor the justice or injustice of it. The aesthete lives in an aesthetic world and his judgments of that world are often made in terms of the Oakeshottian concept of delight, but Kierkegaard includes considerations of pleasure and entertainment which are more practical in Oakeshott's terms. The aesthete is not merely a hedonist, if the hedonist is defined as a person who wants to maximize his experience of pleasure but is indifferent to the type or quality of that pleasure. Instead, the aesthete often develops a particular sort of aesthetic action, like Don Giovanni's serial seductions or Don Quixote's sallies as a Knight Errant, but the aesthete cannot rest satisfied in the achievement of a conquest because the aesthete's entire life is a work of art and thus creation must continue.[28] Nevertheless, as Kierkegaard notes, for the aesthete, "boredom is the root of all evil."[29]

For Ignatius J. Reilly, in *Confederacy*, the external world exists to satisfy his curiosity, to entertain him (usually by provoking aesthetic disgust), to offer novel experiences, and so on. His habits consist of going to melodramatic movies, watching American Bandstand on television, consuming an odd assortment of food and drink (including, of course, hot dogs and Dr. Nutt), playing the lute (though he never actually plays it in the novel), writing his diaries, and berating his mother. His various Quixotic sallies into the real world in the novel are all characterized by his active participation in creating novel experiences, both for himself and for the other characters. As his mother Irene notes, "He makes trouble everywhere he goes."[30] His judgments about these various experiences are inevitably couched in aesthetic terms, not moral ones. There are "horrors" such as the "lasciviously gyrating children" of Bandstand; the "veneration of such things as 'Turkey in the Straw'"; "sub-human . . . folksingers"; and "rural rednecks" who hate progress.[31] There are delights such as his pirate outfit in which he "appeared rather fetching in a dramatic way"; Miss Trixie, "our Earth Mother of the world of commerce"; and his grandiose plans for the workers at Levy Pants and for the homosexuals in the French Quarter.[32] In terms of Ignatius's way of understanding the world around him, the character has a great deal more in common with the Don Giovanni of Mozart's opera or with Diderot's Rameau's nephew than with Savonarola or Alasdair MacIntyre.

The second characteristic of the aesthete according to Kierkegaard is that his life is marked by a continuous alternation between action and rest.[33] As Kierkegaard's "A" writes of the Seducer,

> enjoyment was what his whole life was organized around. In the first case, he savored the aesthetic element personally; in the second he savored his own person aesthetically. In the first the point was that he egoistically, personally, savored what in part reality gave him and what in part he himself had impregnated reality with; in the second case his personality was volatilized and he savored, then, the situation and himself in the situation. In the first case he was in constant need of reality as the occasion, as an element; in the second case reality was drowned in the poetic.[34]

Thus, in the active or objective stage, the aesthete goes forth into the world both experiencing it in terms of delight and attempting to manipulate the world so that it becomes even more delightful. This world consists of somewhat solid objects seemingly independent from the aesthete which he attempts to mold for his own purposes into an occasion from which he might derive diversion and entertainment. As suggested, this is the stage of frenetic or chaotic action, but it is aesthetic and not moral action. The aesthete sees the rest of the world, especially the other people who inhabit the world, as merely fodder for his own enjoyment. As Kierkegaard's "A" notes of the Seducer's actions, "individuals were merely his incitement; he cast them off as a tree sheds its leaves—he is refreshed, the leaf withers."[35] Thus, it is inherently reasonable that the aesthete's actions often lead other characters (or other actual human beings) to offer moral condemnation of him and, sometimes, to accuse him of madness.[36]

Ignatius's experiences with the external world are a series of démarches into an enemy territory which he attempts to mold to his own purposes. His job at Tulane ends with Ignatius dumping ungraded essays on the heads of students, and, of course, "the college was too small to accept this act of defiance against the abyss of contemporary academia."[37] His time at the New Orleans Library was also cut short because of Ignatius's self-confessed artistic compunctions. He informs his mother that "I had my own aesthetic about pasting those slips. On some days I could only paste in three or four slips and at the same time feel satisfied with the quality of my work."[38] The various misadventures described in more detail in the novel are each exemplary cases of the aesthete attempting to create a world of delight and being stifled by the intransigent and immutable stability of the material and human world. At Levy Pants, Ignatius initially succeeds in radically altering the working of the factory to satisfy his own aesthetic preferences. He gets people fired because they offend his sensibilities ("the awful sound of Gloria's stake-like heels . . . then, too, was all of that mascara and lipstick and other vulgarities,")[39]; he redecorates the office (a sign for Miss Trixie with a nosegay, a sign for Gonzalez with the crest of King Alfonso; a cross made from boxes of Libby's Tomato Juice and Kraft Jelly reading "God and Commerce"; beans growing on filing cabinets; monks cloth drapes; a statue of St. Anthony, patron saint of lost things); he "revolutionizes" the filing system by doing away with all of the files; and he organizes The Crusade for Moorish Dignity, which is an attempt to overthrow the manager of the company. He pays no attention to the reality of any of the other characters in the novel, admitting, for example, that "I really have little to do with [the black factory workers], for I mingle with my peers or no one, and since I have no peers, I mingle with no one."[40] His experience at Levy Pants is repeated at Paradise Vendors, and in the Save the World through Degeneracy campaign. At Paradise Vendors, Ignatius doesn't even pretend to work. Instead, his experiences consist of random encounters with the owner of the business, cats, tourists, and teenaged porn-mongers. In his last adventure with the homosexuals in the French Quarter, Ignatius proves once again that his primary concern is not actually changing the world in order to make it a better place but solely in order to satisfy his own imaginary wishes.

According to Kierkegaard, this external world, while offering the occasion for the aesthete's action also often severely limits the action. The outside world is often not as tractable as the aesthete supposes, and, thus, the aesthete's action often ends in failure, which he typically blames not on himself or his shortcomings but on circumstances, fate, or fortune. Ignatius repeatedly refers to the "blind, heedless goddess" Fortuna and her incessant foiling of his plans. He has also been "tricked by a conspiracy of sub-humans,"[41] as his plans have failed time and again, not through his own agency but through the malign interference of fate.

Kierkegaard refers to the experience with the outside world as the aesthete's extensive development. He describes this as a search for novel inter-actions, so if

> one is tired of living in the country, one moves to the city; [if] one is tired of one's native land, one travels abroad; . . . [finally] one burns half of Rome to get an idea of the conflagration at Troy.[42]

In any case, boredom is to be avoided at all costs. According to Kierkegaard, the problem with this objective or extensive stage is that repetition of any particular action leads to a diminution of pleasure, and "rotating" one's experiences in the objective world also rapidly leads to diminishing returns and disappointment.[43]

Thus, the aesthete turns inward to a subjective reflection on his various activities in the objective. This turning inward seems to those outside the aesthete's circle to be a kind of stagnant immobility or laziness, but, instead, the aesthete's subjective reflection presents a more complete opportunity for individualistic aesthetic expression. This intensive development is not nearly as limited by the actions of others and offers the aesthete the chance to enjoy his own enjoyment, often by allowing him the opportunity to create his own version of the objective world in which failure, as much as success, offers its delights. "A" writes, for example, that "unpleasantness is a piquant ingredient in the contrariety of life."[44] Just as for Oakeshott, anything is a potential object of aesthetic delight, and the Kierkegaardian aesthete, when reflecting upon his experience, can regard all of his experiences as material for his imagination to mold. This second phase of aesthetic life, thus, affords a renewed and distinctive occasion for the aesthete to create a world pleasing to himself. The delight in experiencing his old adventures through the prism of the subjective activity of remembering and forgetting provides a world of freedom from the restrictions of objectivity and results in the creation of a personal mythical aesthetic past. As Kierkegaard suggests, "in remembering poetically, what was experienced has already undergone a change in which it has lost all that was painful."[45] The aesthete in this subjective intensive world becomes much more clearly the artist who creates himself and his world. This sort of self-creation is, according to some, the apex of modernist individualism.[46]

For many readers of the novel, Ignatius's self-creating accounts of his experiences in the world are the most delightful sections of the novel. The character Ignatius acknowledges and manifests his aestheticism in a variety of ways throughout the novel. For example, from an early age, he had "developed [masturbation] into an art form, practicing the hobby with the skill and fervor of an artist and philosopher."[47] He compares himself to Proust, to Schiller, to Kurtz in *Heart of Darkness*, to a pirate, to Milton, and to Edison, Ford, and Rockefeller.[48] He becomes, in succession, a leader of The Crusade for Moorish Dignity, who "cannot abide those who would act cowardly in the face of social injustice;" someone who is "currently connected in a most vital manner with the food merchandising industry;" and "a mentor and guide" to his own self-created movement to Save the World through Degeneracy.[49] Throughout this period, Ignatius is writing his "Journal of a Working Boy, or Up from Sloth," but he is doing so under a succession of pseudonyms.

In both the reflections contained in the "Journal of a Working Boy" and in his comments and actions while actually engaged in his adventures, it is clear that Ignatius understands himself to be the creative artistic force defining his own authentic experience. He purchases a camera so that he can film the hoped-for riot in Levy Pants, and mentions in a letter to Myrna Minkoff, his sometime female companion, that it has "wonderful movie possibilities."[50] Indeed, he thinks of these adventures much like an auteur who writes, directs, and produces, and, even at the conclusion of the novel, Ignatius refers to the "Journal of a Working Boy," his last literary invention, as "a sociological fantasy on which I've been working. It is my most commercial effort. Wonderful film possibilities at the hands of a Walt Disney or a George Pal."[51] The fact that others are merely actors in Ignatius's movie comes out most clearly in the reflections collected in his Journal. The images of blacks and homosexuals that Ignatius brings to life are all based upon literary or cinematic experiences and not on practical ones. His thoughts about "Negroes" and "perverts" are among the most amusing in the novel, however, only when he is read as an aesthete. These are not real human beings with actual problems. Instead, they are the raw material out of which he constructs the world. His creative inventory is already loaded with images from the world of literature and the imagination, including images common to the time of cheerful black folks working happily in the cotton fields while singing spirituals, male homosexuals dressed up like female stars of Broadway musicals, and leather-clad Naziesque strippers. Only a philistine moralist (or a particularly contemporary type of vulgarian regressive progressive) could reduce Ignatius's descriptions of his encounters to the contemporary sins of racism, sexism, and other "isms." He describes the Levy Pants factory as:

> combin[ing] the worst of *Uncle Tom's Cabin* and Fritz Lang's *Metropolis*... It is mechanized Negro slavery; it represents the progress which the Negro has made from picking cotton to tailoring it. (Were they in the picking stage of their evolution, they would at least be in the healthy outdoors singing and eating watermelons [as they are, I believe, supposed to do when in groups alfresco].)[52]

He admits that he knows little to nothing about the actual lives of racial minorities in New Orleans, but still, he insists that watching "Les Africains . . . , I likened myself to Kurtz in Heart of Darkness. . . .I do remember imagining myself in a pith helmet and white linen jodhpurs, my face enigmatic behind a veil of mosquito netting."[53] He also imagines himself as a "rather huge and terrifying . . . Negro," an exile from American life, but his "exile is voluntary."[54] This particular flight of imagination, however, is not really an attempt to empathize with the plight of black Americans, but is another example of an aestheticized experience, as his primary wish in being black is that he not be pressured to have a job anymore.

His second great campaign, the campaign to "Save the World through Degeneracy," is also revealed in his "Journal" to be an aesthetic invention, and results in the same sort of comedic chaos as The Crusade for Moorish Dignity. In this sally, Ignatius attempts to encourage the homosexual population of the French Quarter to begin an infiltration of the world's military institutions in order to end the prospect of war. Unlike his dalliance with the black factory workers, Ignatius's dealings with homosexuals in the novel reveal that he finds them morally objectionable, but, as the aesthete does, he transforms his own moral distaste into aesthetic delight. Once again, the images that he conjures are all clichés. His discussion with Dorian Greene leads him to conclude that, were the militaries of the world taken over by homosexuals, then:

> As soldiers, they will all be so busy in fraternizing with one another, tailoring their uniforms to fit like sausage skins, inventing new and varied battle dress, giving cocktail parties, etc., that they will never have time for battle. . . . Perverts around the world . . . will enjoy not war but global orgies conducted with the utmost protocol . . . .The Chief of Staff, the President, and so on, dressed in sequins and feathers, will entertain the leaders, i.e., the perverts, of all other

countries at balls and parties . . . .Ballets and Broadway musicals . . . will flour-
ish everywhere.[55]

As with his reflections on his experience at Levy Pants, what Ignatius has
created here is a monument to aesthetic remembering and aesthetic forgetting. What remains are a series of brilliantly hilarious *mises en scène* in which
conventions and norms are held up for imaginative destruction.

The final characteristic of the aesthete, according to Kierkegaard, is that
the alternation between activity (feverish or no) and passivity mentioned
above never ceases. The aesthete constantly moves back and forth between
the objective aesthetic and the subjective one. For the aesthete, the choice is
always a temporary one, and, thus, the subjective aesthetic can be abandoned
for the objective and vice versa, depending upon which of the two worlds
happens to hold the most interest.[56] As Kierkegaard has Judge Vilhelm write,
the aesthete's

> mind draws up a hundred plans, everything is prepared for the assault. Should
> it fail in one direction, instantly your well-nigh diabolical dialectic is ready to
> explain that away as a necessary part of the new plan of operation . . . you are
> the epitome of all possibility.[57]

The necessary mutability of the aesthete's interests severely limits the
capacity of the aesthete to maintain the commitments that normal human
beings find natural. Kierkegaard's "A" claims that "what one must watch out
for is never to stick fast, and for that one must have one's forgetting up one's
sleeve."[58] This refusal to commit oneself completely to anything is closely
connected with the aesthete's disdain for the workaday world of getting and
spending, feeding and breeding. The aesthete:

> never accepts any vocational responsibility. If one does so, one simply becomes
> Mr. Anybody, a tiny little pivot in the machinery of the corporate state; you
> cease to direct your own affairs. . . .Though one abstains from vocational
> responsibility, one should not be inactive but stress all occupation that is identi-
> cal with idleness; one must engage in all kinds of breadless skills.[59]

Ignatius's most consistent complaint throughout the novel is that he is being
forced to get a job, to make a commitment, to become "a little pivot in the
machinery of the corporate state." He refuses to reduce the world to practical
considerations, and, thus, maintains the independence of the aesthete from
worldly concerns. He notes that "employers sense in me a denial of their
values."[60] When asked if he has a job, Ignatius replies caustically "I dust a
bit . . . . In addition, I am at the moment writing a lengthy indictment of our

century. When my brain begins to reel from my literary labors, I make an occasional cheese dip."[61] Indeed, Ignatius's individualism is most obviously manifested in his refusal to conform to the expectations of contemporary mass consumerism, and his usual complaints about the modern world are connected to its uniformity and mediocrity, not to its abandonment of natural law theory.

As noted, Kierkegaard insisted that the aesthete was an inherently modern character because of his individualistic self-consciousness. Further, Michael Oakeshott noted that modernity is characterized both by the emancipation of modally distinct ways of understanding or conceiving the world, like science, art, and history, from their practical/religious origins and by the emergence of self-conscious individualism. This sort of individualism is not connected to any economic system, but it does place a primary value on individual choice.[62] Thus, if what I have suggested is true and Ignatius is understood as an aesthete, then claiming that Ignatius is a representative of a neo-medieval critique of modernity or modern America is inherently anachronistic.[63] Indeed, the act of choosing to be a medievalist is very much the act of a modern individualist, and Ignatius's various jeremiads share a great deal more in common with various individualist critiques of modern mass society than they do with neo-medieval critiques of modern individualism.

In this way, Ignatius's selective and self-chosen medieval notions and heroes are evidence not of a Boethius resurrected in the French Quarter, but of a highly eccentric and individualistic caste of mind. This caste of mind is neither communal nor collectivist, and it is not even very Catholic. Indeed, Ignatius abandons Catholicism, not because of doctrinal laxity (Vatican II had not yet occurred), but because the Church would not acquiesce in his eccentric desire to have a funeral mass said for his dog.[64] For Ignatius, Boethius is a piece of furniture in a large aesthetic house, much like Boethius' book serving as a prop in Lana Lee's pornographic photograph. As Anthony Powell suggested, books do furnish a room. Ignatius's medievalism isn't historical at all, but is instead an aspect of his own aesthetic imagination. For example, his invocations of Boethius and the goddess Fortuna necessarily avoid mention that Boethius' book was written, in part, as a critique of the centrality of Fortuna in human affairs.[65] Though it is true that Ignatius rails against the modern age, he just as often directs his ire at "the insipid philosophy of the middle class."[66] He also rejects modern psychiatry, not because it is modern, but because it involves an attack on his individuality. He responds to his mother when she suggests that he see someone in that field not by invoking Boethius, but by proclaiming that "psychiatry is worse than communism. I refuse to be brainwashed. I won't be a robot! . . . They would try to make me into a moron who liked television and new cars and frozen food."[67] It is not modernity, but mass consumerism that is the object, and, of course, his distaste for communism is connected to its soul-killing conformity and uniformity. Ignatius announces, "Do you think that I want to live in a communal society with people like that Battaglia acquaintance of yours, sweeping streets and breaking up rocks or whatever it is people are always doing in those blighted countries."[68] He is also critical of the impersonality of highly bureaucratized government, noting that "you can always tell employees of the government by the total vacancy which occupies the space where most other people have faces."[69] None of these criticisms have anything to do with medieval communalism, and, instead, reinforce the notion that Ignatius is very much a modern individualists, albeit an elitist and aesthetic one.[70] Even Ignatius's mantra-like invocation of the lack of theology and geometry in the worldview of others is taken, not from some medieval theologian but from a modern horror story by H. P. Lovecraft.[71]

CONCLUSION ON DESPAIR

It may very well be true, as Kierkegaard claimed, that any actual human being attempting to live life completely in the aesthetic mode is bound to end in despair. Indeed, one might accept that notion without necessarily accepting his paradoxical claim that the aesthete who claims that he does not despair is actually in a deeper state than the one who admits that he does. Walker Percy, one of those responsible for the eventual publication of Toole's novel and an extraordinary novelist and thinker in his own right, was a self-acknowledged student of Kierkegaard's work.[72] He used a phrase from Kierkegaard as an epigram for his first novel, *The Moviegoer*, which Toole almost certainly read. The phrase was "the specific character of despair is precisely this: it is unaware of being despair," and it was taken from Kierkegaard's *The Sickness unto Death*. The protagonist of that novel, Binx Bolling, is certainly a Kierkegaardian aesthete who is suffering from despair. I would suggest that one way of connecting the two novels is by noting that Toole in his novel rejects the necessary connection between the aesthetic life and despair, and that Ignatius J. Reilly is a successful version of the comic aesthete.[73] Oakeshott also noted that a completely aesthetic life was a human impossibility, noting that "to listen to the voice of poetry is to enjoy, not a victory, but a momentary release, a brief enchantment."[74] However, Ignatius J. Reilly is not a human being, but an aesthetic creation, so the expectation that he end up in a state of despair is inappropriate. Nonetheless, he is a very modern character and his animadversions against the inadequacies of the modern world are not best understood as an expression of a neo-medieval worldview, but as the expression of a modern aesthetic individualist.[75] Ignatius's individualism is manifested not in any significant case of character development, but instead in the proliferation of himself through his various creations. To borrow a characterization from Oakeshott, he is like "Proteus—a character distinguished from all others on account of his multiplicity and of his endless power of self-transformation."[76]

NOTES

1. John Kennedy Toole, *Confederacy*, foreword by Walker Percy (New York: Grove Press, 1980), viii.

2. Percy described Ignatius as "a mad Oliver Hardy, a fat Don Quixote, a perverse Thomas Aquinas rolled into one," and the novel as "a farce of Falstaffian proportions." Toole, *Confederacy*, viii, ix.

3. See, among others, Cory MacLauchlin, who claims that "the underlying tension in the novel, which plagues the mind of Ignatius, is a conflict between Boethian philosophy and pragmatism;" Peter McCluskey, who writes that "'The love of money is the root of all evil' encapsulates the serious message underlying Toole's comic novel;" Elizabeth Bell, who asserts that the novel presents "the clash of two mutually-exclusive world views . . . : Ignatius's chosen and believed medieval world view and the reader's inherited and fondly-held contemporary world view;" and Peter Freese, who suggests that "the novel's constitutive tension [lies] between medievalism and modernity." Cory MacLauchlin, *Butterfly in the Typewriter: The Tragic Life of John Kennedy Toole and the Remarkable Story of Confederacy* (Boston, MA: Da Capo Press, 2012), 51; Peter McCluskey, "Selling Souls and Vending Paradise: God and Commerce in *Confederacy*," *Southern Quarterly* 47 (2009): 9; Elizabeth S. Bell, "The Clash of Worldviews in John Kennedy Toole's 'Confederacy,'" *The Southern Literary Journal* 21 (1988): 16; and Peter Freese, "A Medieval Crusader in Twentieth-Century New Orleans: John Kennedy Toole's 'Confederacy,'" *Amerikastudien/American Studies* 59 (2014): 365–366.

4. MacLauchlin, *Butterfly in the Typewriter*, 172, 175. Gottlieb's great error in rejecting the manuscript was not that he missed a great novel; that happens to every editor. It was that he rejected it because of his philistine notion that a novel ought to have a moral at all. Gottlieb had early published *Catch-22*, whose moral was "war is unpleasant"? For a compelling critique of Gottlieb's actions concerning the publication of *Confederacy* , see Leslie Marsh, "Review of *Butterfly in the Typewriter*," *The Journal of Mind and Behavior* 34 (2013): 290–296.

5. See Jacob Burckhardt, *The Civilization of the Renaissance in Italy*, trans. S. G. C. Middlemore (London: Penguin Books, 1990); José Ortega y Gasset, *The Revolt of the Masses* (New York: Norton & Co., 1932); Michael Oakeshott, "The Masses in Representative Democracy," in *Rationalism in Politics and Other Essays*, rev. ed. (Indianapolis: Liberty Fund, 1991), 363–383; Pope Pius IX, *The Syllabus of Errors* (*Syllabus Errorum*), 1864 http://www.ewtn.com/library/PAPALDOC/P9SYLL.H TM; Joseph de Maistre, *Considerations on France*, trans. Richard LeBrun (Cambridge: Cambridge University Press, 1974); and Carl Schmitt, *The Crisis of Parliamentary Democracy*, trans. Ellen Kennedy (Cambridge, MA: MIT Press, 1985). Both de Maistre's and Schmitt's critiques of modernity are also quite modern in their own

way, especially in the centrality of unified and centralized power to both of their conceptions of community life. Conversely, the two most influential neo-medievalist philosophers of the twentieth century, Ètienne Gilson and Jacques Maritain, were committed to adapting medieval Thomism to the modern world, especially the modern liberal democratic world. See Ètienne Gilson, *The Spirit of Medieval Philosophy*, trans. A. H. C. Downes (New York: Charles Scribner's Sons, 1936); and Jacques Maritain, *The Person and the Common Good*, trans. John J. Fitzgerald (Notre Dame: University of Notre Dame Press, 1966).

6. For an examination of John Kennedy Toole's intellectual world, see H. Vernon Leighton, "Evidence of Influences on John Kennedy Toole's Confederacy, Including Geoffrey Chaucer," Version 2.1 (June 2, 2014), http://course1.winona.edu/vleighton/toole/Leighton_Toole_Chaucer.pdf.

7. What actually counted as the "the Art of the Revolutionary Proletariat" was never completely clear, of course. For a perfect example of the fluctuating fortunes of an artist operating in a situation in which art is subordinate to political, moral, and economic concerns, see Laurel E. Fay, *Shostakovich: A Life* (Oxford: Oxford University Press, 2005). For an engrossing fictional account, see Julian Barnes, *The Noise of Time* (New York: Vintage International, 2016).

8. In a more amusing example that cannot be totally reduced to moralism, a person in Toronto requested that the Toronto library ban both Ian McEwan's *Atonement* and Dave Eggers' *A Heartbreaking Work of Staggering Genius* for poor grammar and sentence structure. Hank Reichman, "Censorship Dateline," *Journal of Intellectual Freedom and Privacy* 4 (2017): 42–43.

9. Oscar Wilde observed that "there is no such thing as a moral or an immoral book. Books are well written or badly written," while James Whistler insisted that "art should be independent of all claptrap—should stand alone [. . .] and appeal to the artistic sense of eye or ear, without confounding this with emotions entirely foreign to it, in devotion, pity, love, patriotism and the like." Oscar Wilde, "Preface," *The Picture of Dorian Gray* in *The Complete Works of Oscar Wilde* (New York: HarperCollins, 2008), 17 and James Whistler, *The Gentle Art of Making Enemies* (New York: Dover, 1967), 134. Also see, Lionel Lambourne, *The Aesthetic Movement* (London: Phaidon Press, 1996) and Michalle Gal, *Aestheticism: Deep Formalism and the Emergence of Modernist Aesthetics* (Bern: Peter Lang AG International Academic Publishers, 2015). In the twentieth century, the foremost proponent and one of the foremost practitioners of this approach to art was Vladimir Nabokov, who wrote "I have no social purpose, no moral message; I've no general ideas to exploit . . . . A work of art has no importance whatever to society. It is only important to the individual, and only the individual reader is important to me. I don't give a damn for the group, the community, the masses, and so forth." Vladimir Nabokov, *Strong Opinions* (London: Penguin Books, 2011), 26, 48.

10. See Michael Oakeshott, *Experience and Its Modes* (Cambridge: Cambridge University Press, 1933) and Michael Oakeshott, "The Voice of Poetry in the Conversation of Mankind," in *Rationalism in Politics and Other Essays, rev. ed.* (Indianapolis: Liberty Fund, 1991), 488–541.

11. Leslie Marsh calls it "autotelic" in that it has itself as the end of its own activity. It is, he writes, "the idea that art should not answer to any extrinsic consideration, political, economic, or scientific." Marsh, "Review of *Butterfly in the Typewriter*," 286.

12. Oakeshott, "The Voice of Poetry," 513.

13. This claim does not deny that a person might consider a work of art under different categories than the aesthetic. For example, one might consider Fernand Léger's *Contraste de Formes* in a purely practical way, noting that it sold for $70 million last year. Or one might consider it in scientific terms, asking questions about the chemical composition of the paint used, the type of wood used for the frame, and so on. And one might consider it historically, observing that it was completed in 1913 at the height of Cubism and was influenced by the Italian Futurists. None of these, however, contributes to an aesthetic understanding of the painting, which is concerned with the brushwork, color, and contrast, the novel use of chiaroscuro, the return to two-dimensionality, and so on. The art historian is the closest to the art critic, and a knowledge of the artistic character of Cubism and Futurism would add something to the aesthetic understanding of the painting, but merely connecting the terms Cubism, Futurism, and Léger would not so contribute.

14. Pearl-clutching critics who worry about Ignatius's (or the author's) supposedly retrograde attitude toward blacks and/or homosexuals confuse the aesthetic with the practical mode, and their comments are completely irrelevant to the aesthetic character of the novel. In similar fashion, the attempt to read the novel as some sort of cry for help from a latent homosexual offers nothing in the way of aesthetic criticism but does tell us a great deal about the critic's obsessions. Finally, the notion that Toole is writing "an affirmation of a decidedly conservative view of . . . society" involves a similarly confused reading of the novel. All three approaches offer excellent examples of the *ignoratio elenchi* as it relates to literary criticism. For examples of each respectively, see Freese, "A Medieval Crusader in Twentieth-Century New Orleans," 365–366, Michael Hardin, "Between Queer Performances," *Southern Literary Journal* 39 (2007): 58–77, and K. D. Miller, "The Conservative Vision of John Kennedy Toole," *Proceedings: Conference of College English Teachers of Texas* 48 (1983): 30. For a relevant response to such critics, one can do no better than to offer Nabokov's comments in his Foreword to the English translation of *Despair*. He wrote that "*Despair*, in kinship with the rest of my books, has no social comment to bring in its teeth. It does not uplift the spiritual organ of man, nor does it show humanity the right exit. It contains far fewer 'ideas' than do those rich vulgar novels that are acclaimed hysterically in the short echo-walk between the ballyhoo and the hoot. The attractively shaped object or Wiener-schnitzel dream that the eager Freudian may think he distinguishes in the remoteness of my wastes will turn out to be on closer inspection a derisive mirage organized by my agents." Vladimir Nabokov, "Foreword," *Despair* (New York: Vintage International, 1989), xii.

15. It is odd that the so-called likeability of Ignatius plays such a central role in much of the negative criticism of the novel. See, for example, Freese, "A Medieval Crusader in Twentieth-Century New Orleans," 357–386. From the evidence provided in MacLauchlin's biography, it seems likely that Robert Gottlieb's dislike of some

of the characters, including Ignatius, was central to his rejection of the novel. See MacLaughlin, *Butterfly in the Typewriter*, 171–190.

16. Oakeshott, "The Voice of Poetry," 519.

17. Oakeshott suggests that an artist's aesthetic purposes are "like the Spanish painter Orbaneja, of whom Cervantes tells us: when a bystander asked what he was painting, he answered, 'Whatever it turns out to be.'" Oakeshott, "The Voice of Poetry," 527. Corey Abel makes Oakeshott's comments on Orbaneja the center of his excellent essay on Oakeshott's aesthetics. Corey Abel, "Whatever It Turns Out to Be: Oakeshott on Aesthetic Experience," in *A Companion to Michael Oakeshott*, eds. Paul Franco and Leslie Marsh (University Park: Penn State University Press, 2012), 151–172.

18. For example, a urinal in a junkyard usually evokes little more than a cursory glance at a discarded piece of refuse, but a urinal in an art museum titled "Fountain" and marked by the unusual signature "R. Mutt" screams to be considered as a work of art of some sort.

19. For an examination of the aesthete that directly influenced the overall direction of this essay, see Alasdair MacIntyre, *After Virtue*, 2nd ed. (Notre Dame: Notre Dame Press, 1984), 20–50. The secondary literature on Kierkegaard is immense, but each of the following works offer reasonable accounts of Kierkegaard's conception of the aesthetic stage of life. Stephen N. Dunning, *Kierkegaard's Dialectic of Inwardness* (Princeton: Princeton University Press, 1985); Regis Jolivet, *Introduction to Kierkegaard*, trans. W. H. Barber (New York: E. P. Dutton, 1946); George Connell, *To Be One Thing: Personal Unity in Kierkegaard's Thought* (Macon: Mercer University Press, 1985); and Patrick Gardiner, *Kierkegaard* (Oxford: Oxford University Press, 1988).

20. In the voice of the ethical Judge Vilhem, Kierkegaard writes that "my either/ or does not denote in the first instance the choice between good and evil, it denotes the choice whereby one chooses good and evil or excludes them. The question here is, under what categories one wants to contemplate the entire world and would oneself live." Soren Kierkegaard, *Either/Or: A Fragment of Life*, trans. Alastair Hannay (London: Penguin, 1992), 486. It is not completely clear whether Kierkegaard believed that the choice between the aesthetic, the ethical, and the religious was a rational one or merely a leap of faith. For a discussion of this question, see John Davenport and Anthony Rudd, eds., *Kierkegaard After MacIntyre: Essays on Freedom, Narrative, and Virtue* (Chicago: Open Court, 2001).

21. Kierkegaard, *Either/Or*, 142, 148.

22. The only other examination of Toole's novel in Kierkegaardian terms is found in Richard Keller Simon's essay comparing *Confederacy* with Walker Percy's novel, *The Moviegoer*. However, Simon is more concerned with the influence of Percy's novel on Toole's than with the significance of Kierkegaard's conception of the aesthete for an interpretation of the character Ignatius J. Reilly. See Richard Keller Simon, "John Kennedy Toole and Walker Percy: Fiction and Repetition in *Confederacy*," *Texas Studies in Language and Literature* 36 (1994): 99–116.

23. I use the personal pronoun "he" in this paper when referring to the aesthete not because there are no female aesthetes (after all, one of the most fascinating aesthetes

ever created was Emma Bovary), but because the fictional character who is the focus of this essay, Ignatius J. Reilly, is undoubtedly a male. I am also following Kierkegaard's usage in *Either/Or* in which all of the aesthetes and examples of aesthetes are male (e.g., Don Giovanni, "A," the Seducer). Finally, since it is characteristic of the Kierkegaardian aesthete to be something of an individualist, using the plural "aesthetes" instead of the singular "aesthete" to address the pronoun question is conceptually misleading.

24. One irony of considering Ignatius as a Kierkegaardian aesthete is that it involves dealing with a work of fiction which was, though not completely "discovered in a secretary," published initially with a framing preface by Walker Percy detailing the "losing" of the manuscript. *Either/Or*, on the other hand, is a work of philosophy which appropriates the traditional fictional device of the frame to distance the actual author from the opinions of his literary/philosophical creations, suggesting that it can be read either as a moral treatise or as an aesthetic one.

25. Kierkegaard, *Either/Or*, 36. The following exegesis of Kierkegaard's conception of the aesthetic stage is taken largely from the chapter titled "Crop Rotation: An Attempt at a Theory of Social Prudence." Kierkegaard, *Either/Or*, 222–241.

26. *Confederacy*, 28

27. *Confederacy*, 29

28. For a compelling argument that Mozart's *Don Giovanni* is the supreme aesthetic achievement of the modern world, see Kierkegaard, *Either/Or*, 61–161.

29. Kierkegaard, *Either/Or*, 227. Kierkegaard writes that Don Giovanni "savors the satisfaction of desire; as soon as he has savored it he seeks a new object; and so on endlessly." Kierkegaard, *Either/Or*, 104

30. *Confederacy*, 205

31. *Confederacy*, 46, 155, 182, 11

32. *Confederacy*, 228, 74.

33. Or, as Kierkegaard's spokesman for the ethical life Judge Vilhelm phrases it, the aesthete's "life lies between two huge antitheses; sometimes [he is] intemperately energetic, at others just as immoderately indolent." Kierkegaard, *Either/Or*, 503.

34. Kierkegaard, *Either/Or*, 249.

35. Kierkegaard, *Either/Or*, 251.

36. For example, Don Quixote, Emma Bovary, Binx Bolling, Rameau's Nephew, et al. were all accused of immorality, madness, or both by other characters in their respective novels.

37. *Confederacy*, 52. These days, Ignatius would not be fired for his actions at Tulane, but would, instead, be forced to undergo diversity and harassment reeducation training at the hands of the Tulane Human Resources Department.

38. *Confederacy*, 51. This brings to mind another modern aesthete. Melville's *Bartleby the Scrivener* had a similar attitude about his work.

39. *Confederacy*, 75

40. *Confederacy*, 122.

41. *Confederacy*, 340

42. Kierkegaard, *Either/Or*, 233.

43. As the female protagonist in Hemingway's "Hills Like White Elephants" observes, "I wanted to try this new drink. That's all we do, isn't it—look at things and try new drinks?" Ernest Hemingway, "Hills Like White Elephants," in *The Collected Stories*, ed. James Fenton (London: Everyman's Library, 1995), 200.

44. Kierkegaard, *Either/Or*, 236.

45. Kierkegaard, *Either/Or*, 234.

46. The most convincing interpretation of the work of Friedrich Nietzsche is that he considers aesthetic self-creation as the highest achievement available to modern human beings. See Alexander Nehamas, *Nietzsche: Life as Literature* (Cambridge, MA: Harvard University Press, 1985).

47. *Confederacy*, 31

48. *Confederacy*, 47, 47, 120, 100, 227.

49. *Confederacy*, 101, 183, 270

50. *Confederacy*, 115

51. *Confederacy*, 391. It is perhaps not surprising that Ignatius is not interested in possible competitors. He only attends popular American movies, and avoids the theater when a film by Ingmar Bergman comes to town.

52. *Confederacy*, 119.

53. *Confederacy*, 120

54. *Confederacy*, 122.

55. *Confederacy*, 269–270. In a case of farce becoming reality, Ignatius also asks, "can you name one good, practicing transvestite in the Senate? No! These people have been without representation long enough."

56. In the world of children's literature, Mr. Toad in *The Wind in the Willows* is an exemplary aesthete, discarding old manias for new every other chapter.

57. Kierkegaard, *Either/Or*, 387, 391.

58. Kierkegaard, *Either/Or*, 236.

59. Kierkegaard, *Either/Or*, 238, 239.

60. *Confederacy*, 51

61. *Confederacy*, 6. I would like to think that the Coen brothers had this line in mind when writing *The Big Lebowski*, especially the scene in which the following dialogue occurs:

> The Big Lebowski: Are you employed, sir?
> The Dude: Employed?
> The Big Lebowski: You don't go out looking for a job dressed like that? On a weekday?
> The Dude: Is this a . . . what day is this?
> The Big Lebowski: Well, I do work sir, so if you don't mind...
> The Dude: I do mind, the Dude minds. This will not stand, ya know, this aggression will not stand, man.

62. Oakeshott describes the birth of the modern individualist as occurring when "the *uomo singulare*, whose conduct was marked by a high degree of self-determination and a large number of whose activities expressed personal preferences, gradually detached himself from his fellows." Michael Oakeshott, "The Masses in

Representative Democracy," in *Rationalism in Politics and Other Essays, rev. ed.* (Indianapolis: Liberty Fund, 1991), 366. See also, Jacob Burckhardt, *The Civilization of the Renaissance in Italy*, trans. S. G. C. Middlemore (London: Penguin Books, 1990), 98–119.

63. See, for example, Peter Freese, "A Medieval Crusader in Twentieth-Century New Orleans," and Elizabeth S. Bell, "The Clash of Worldviews in John Kennedy Toole's 'Confederacy.'"

64. Jacob Burkhardt notes in his discussion of the rise of individualism in Renaissance Italy that the prototypical individual, Leon Battista Alberti, noted for his aesthetic theory and his architecture, also "wrote . . . a funeral oration on his dog." Burckhardt, *The Civilization of the Renaissance in Italy*, 103.

65. Boethius claims, in the voice of Philosophy, that "if God imposes order upon all things, there is no opportunity for random events." Boethius, *The Consolation of Philosophy*, trans. V. E. Watts (London: Penguin, 1969), 147.

66. *Confederacy*, 270

67. *Confederacy*, 306

68. *Confederacy*, 213

69. *Confederacy*, 207.

70. These sorts of comments share much in common with the work of Ortega y Gassett who wrote that "a characteristic of our times is the predominance . . . of the mass and the vulgar. . . . [T]he mass crushes beneath it everything that is different, everything that is excellent, individual, qualified and select." José Ortega y Gasset, *The Revolt of the Masses* (New York: Norton & Co., 1932), 16, 18.

71. Lovecraft actually never mentions theology, but one of the characters in his short story "The Call of Cthulhu" says on three different occasions about Cthulhu's fortress of R'lyeh that "the geometry of the place was all wrong." H. P. Lovecraft, "The Call of Cthulhu," in *The Call of Cthulhu and Other Weird Stories*, ed. S. T. Joshi (New York: Penguin Books, 1999), 158, 166.

72. Bradley R. Dewey, "Walker Percy Talks about Kierkegaard: An Annotated Interview," *The Journal of Religion* 3 (1974): 273–298.

73. Walker Percy, *The Moviegoer* (New York: Alfred Knopf, 1961). For a comparison of *The Moviegoer* and *Confederacy*, see Simon, "John Kennedy Toole and Walker Percy," 99–116.

74. Oakeshott, "The Voice of Poetry in the Conversation of Mankind," 540.

75. Ignatius claims to be a monarchist in the novel, but his monarchism would not conflict with what Ortega defines as liberalism. He writes, that "liberalism is that principle of political rights, according to which the public, in spite of being all-powerful, limits itself and attempts, even at its own expense, to leave room in the State over which it rules for those to live who neither think nor feel as it does, that is to say as do the stronger, the majority. Liberalism . . . is the supreme form of generosity; it is the right which the majority concedes to minorities and hence it is the noblest cry that has ever resounded in this planet. It announces the determination to share existence with the enemy; more than that, with an enemy which is weak . . . . [I]t is not be wondered at that this same humanity should soon appear anxious to get rid of it. It is a discipline

too difficult and complex to take firm root on earth." Ortega y Gasset, *The Revolt of the Masses*, 77.

76. Michael Oakeshott, "The Masses in Representative Democracy," 366.

BIBLIOGRAPHY

Abel, Corey. "Whatever It Turns Out to Be: Oakeshott on Aesthetic Experience." In *A Companion to Michael Oakeshott*, edited by Paul Franco and Leslie Marsh. University Park, PA: Penn St. University Press, 2012.

Barnes, Julian. *The Noise of Time.* New York: Vintage International, 2016.

Bell, Elizabeth S. "The Clash of Worldviews in John Kennedy Toole's 'A Confederacy of Dunces.'" *The Southern Literary Journal* 21 (1988).

Boethius. *The Consolation of Philosophy.* Trans. V.E. Watts. London: Penguin, 1969.

Burckhardt, Jacob. *The Civilization of the Renaissance in Italy.* Trans. S.G.C. Middlemore. London: Penguin Books, 1990.

Connell, George. *To Be One Thing: Personal Unity in Kierkegaard's Thought.* Macon, GA: Mercer University Press, 1985.

Davenport, John and Anthony Rudd (eds.) *Kierkegaard After MacIntyre: Essays on Freedom, Narrative, and Virtue.* Chicago: Open Court, 2001.

Dewey, Bradley R. "Walker Percy Talks about Kierkegaard: An Annotated Interview." *The Journal of Religion* 3 (1974)

Dunning, Stephen N. *Kierkegaard's Dialectic of Inwardness.* Princeton: Princeton University Press, 1985.

Fay, Laurel E. *Shostakovich: A Life.* Oxford: Oxford University Press, 2005.

Freese, Peter. "A Medieval Crusader in Twentieth-Century New Orleans: John Kennedy Toole's 'Confederacy.'" *Amerikastudien/American Studies* 59 (2014).

Gal, Michalle. *Aestheticism: Deep Formalism and the Emergence of Modernist Aesthetics.* Bern: Peter Lang AG International Academic Publishers, 2015.

Gardiner, Patrick. *Kierkegaard.* Oxford: Oxford University Press, 1988.

Gilson, Ètienne. *The Spirit of Medieval Philosophy.* Trans. A. H. C. Downes. New York: Charles Scribner's Sons, 1936.

Hardin, Michael. "Between Queer Performances." *Southern Literary Journal* 39 (2007).

Hemingway, Ernest. "Hills Like White Elephants." In *The Collected Stories*, edited by James Fenton. London: Everyman's Library, 1995.

Jolivet, Regis. *Introduction to Kierkegaard.* Trans. W.H. Barber. New York: E.P. Dutton, 1946.

Kierkegaard, Soren. *Either/Or: A Fragment of Life.* Trans. Alastair Hannay. London: Penguin, 1992.

Lambourne, Lionel. *The Aesthetic Movement.* London: Phaidon Press, 1996.

Leighton, H. Vernon. "Evidence of Influences on John Kennedy Toole's Confederacy, Including Geoffrey Chaucer," Version 2.1. 2014. http://course1.winona.edu/vleighton/toole/Leighton_Toole_Chaucer.pdf.

Lovecraft, H.P. "The Call of Cthulhu." In *The Call of Cthulhu and Other Weird Stories*, edited by S.T. Joshi. New York: Penguin Books, 1999.

MacIntyre, Alasdair. *After Virtue*, 2nd ed. Notre Dame, IN: Notre Dame Press, 1984.

MacLauchlin, Cory. *Butterfly in the Typewriter: The Tragic Life of John Kennedy Toole and the Remarkable Story of Confederacy* . Boston, MA: Da Capo Press, 2012.

Maistre, Joseph de. *Considerations on France*. Trans. Richard LeBrun. Cambridge: Cambridge University Press, 1974.

Maritain, Jacques. *The Person and the Common Good*. Trans. John J. Fitzgerald. Notre Dame: University of Notre Dame Press, 1966.

Marsh, Leslie. "Review of *Butterfly in the Typewriter*." *The Journal of Mind and Behavior* 34, no. 3 and 4 (2013): 285–298.

McCluskey, Peter. "Selling Souls and Vending Paradise: God and Commerce in *A Confederacy of Dunces*." *Southern Quarterly* 47 (2009).

Miller, K.D. "The Conservative Vision of John Kennedy Toole." *Proceedings: Conference of College English Teachers of Texas* 48 (1983).

Nabokov, Vladimir. "Foreword." *Despair*. New York: Vintage International, 1989.

———. *Strong Opinions*. London, Penguin Books, 2011.

Nehamas, Alexander. *Nietzsche: Life as Literature*. Cambridge, MA: Harvard University Press, 1985.

Oakeshott, Michael. "The Masses in Representative Democracy." In *Rationalism in Politics and Other Essays, rev. ed*. Indianapolis: Liberty Fund, 1991.

———. "The Voice of Poetry in the Conversation of Mankind." In *Rationalism in Politics and Other Essays, rev. ed*. Indianapolis: Liberty Fund, 1991.

Oakeshott, Michael. *Experience and Its Modes*. Cambridge: Cambridge University Press, 1933.

Ortega y Gasset, José. *The Revolt of the Masses*. New York: Norton & Co., 1932.

Percy, Walker. *The Moviegoer*. New York: Alfred Knopf, 1961.

Pope Pius IX, *The Syllabus of Errors* (*Syllabus Errorum*) 1864, http://www.ewtn.com/library/PAPALDOC/P9SYLL.HTM.

Reichman, Hank. "Censorship Dateline." *Journal of Intellectual Freedom and Privacy* 4 (2017).

Schmitt, Carl. *The Crisis of Parliamentary Democracy*. Trans. Ellen Kennedy. Cambridge, MA: MIT Press, 1985.

Simon, Richard Keller. "John Kennedy Toole and Walker Percy: Fiction and Repetition in *A Confederacy of Dunces*." *Texas Studies in Language and Literature* 36 (1994).

Toole, John Kennedy. *Confederacy* . New York: Grove Press, 1980.

Whistler, James. *The Gentle Art of Making Enemies*. New York: Dover, 1967.

Wilde, Oscar. "Preface." *The Picture of Dorian Gray* in *The Complete Works of Oscar Wilde*. New York: Harper Collins, 2008.

Chapter 4

Theology and Geometry
and Taste and Decency

Leslie Marsh

In *A Confederacy of Dunces* the two leitmotifs "theology and geometry" and "taste and decency" converge, refracted via John Kennedy Toole's channeling of Boëthius. Boëthius' linking of the structure of the soul and mathematics ("theology and geometry") connotes the sacred, while "taste and decency" connotes the profane.[1]

The sloganized "theology and geometry" apparently entered Toole's consciousness via his friend Robert Byrne's oft repeated invocation of an H. P. Lovecraft phrase.[2] Though the concept of the sacred has religious connotations, its use here is intended as more of a *nooúmenos* sense of awe or worthy of respect. Boëthius stands at the providential transition from the dominance of the Greeks' rational speculation and search for truth to the dominance of Roman law and the respect for authority. Boëthius' *The Consolation of Philosophy* is a leading, albeit an inanimate "character" in *Confederacy*. The work has substantive though *suggestive* import, and as a mere object, is deployed as a narrative thread. *Consolation* connotes the sacred. The Sodom and Gomorrah that is New Orleans' Vieux Carré, another "character," is emblematic of the profane.

The character counterparts to the sacred and the profane are embodied in Ignatius, an anti-modern, and his foil Myrna, the countervailing modern.[3] Whereas Myrna sees the lamp of man's reason encrusted by dogma and superstition, distrusting order and authority, Ignatius's theological-metaphysical dissent understands impious curiosity, free from divine constraint, to have unleashed moral and social corrosion. Just as Boëthius' great fear was the erasure of the classical Greek cultural inheritance, so was Ignatius concerned, albeit in a love-hate manner, with the ubiquitous vulgarity and relentless corrosiveness of standards by the kitschification of culture—kitsch being a prominent symptom of an unbridled monomaniacal commitment to the market as the sole determinant of moral and aesthetic value. This is what Michael Oakeshott termed "a dense macabre of wants and satisfactions."[4] Toole himself experienced an ever-creeping marketocracy, whereby a fool could rise to the top of the economic pile while genius could languish in the precariat.[5]

Toole's *Confederacy* mounts a scathing critique of the more philistine manifestations of (an acquisitive) American culture and the smorgasbord of secular religions that vainly try to fill the void of a long-lost sanctity. The widespread sense of instability and discontinuity makes instant gratification a "reasonable" thing to strive for; temperance and restraint are deemed musty, anachronous relics. The religious impulse is temporarily assuaged by what Eric Voegelin termed "the secularization of the soul."[6] This "fix" of low-grade happiness (material and ideological) can be purchased, consumed, and wasted at the expense of the examined life.[7] Unparalleled economic growth and attendant mass communication and transportation add a poignant tenor to Southern alienation and its faded traditions of behavior: the writings of Richard Weaver, Walker Percy, Endora Welty, Flannery O'Connor, and Robert Penn Warren were all drenched in this. This alienation was, of course, earlier expressed by Coleridge and continued through John Ruskin and Matthew Arnold down to T. S. Eliot, F. R. Leavis, and the contemporaneous American "Southern Agrarians"; its most prominent representative being John Crowe Ransom.[8]

Confederacy is a satirical meditation on an uncritical doctrine of progress. The speeding up of life, and as a consequence, the very commodification of time, points to a dialectical complexity among modernity, time, progress, and decadence.

Just as St. Augustine judged Rome's decline and fall just recompense for her pride and many sins, all of which can be traced to man's original Fall, the United States in Ignatius's view, must surely be following a generalized cyclical telos.[9] With the decline of civic virtue, the atomization[10] of social life and attendant moral relativism, Ignatius's New Orleans shares many of the elements of Donne's London and Juvenal's Rome.[11] Ignatius's French Quarter is an area which houses every vice that man has ever conceived in his "wildest aberrations"[12] populated by degenerates, wrecks and drifters, grifters, gamblers, prostitutes, exhibitionists, anti-Christs, alcoholics, sodomites, drug addicts, fetishists, onanists, pornographers, frauds, jades, litterbugs, and lesbians, B-girls, floozies, harlots, sluts, strumpets, and trollops, a litany of decadent types not dissimilar to Juvenal's Rome "filled with foreigners, homosexuals, adulterers, nymphomaniacs, blackmailers, flatterers, skinflint landlords, corrupt politicians, and bad poets" and many more permutations thereof. While New Orleans had decadence deeply woven into its cultural fabric from the beginning,[13] it wasn't until the onset of post-War material prosperity that it became a byword to the out-of-towner (middle-class tourists[14] and conventioneers) for indulgences that wouldn't be tolerated across suburban USA, or at least in the South. This was the New Orleans in which Toole came of age.

New Orleans operates as the wider circle of orientation for Ignatius,[15] the main backdrop to the action being the French Quarter, that small area the world at large often mistakes as being coextensive with the City. The only other city besides Baton Rouge (for Ignatius, an inner circle of Dante's inferno) in his mind's eye is New York City. Myrna's stomping ground and the font of the "liberal doxy"[16] is a hive of "communis" activity, the ghettos of Gotham and of that handmaiden to consumerism, the propaganda or "manufacturing of consent"[17] industry that is Madison Avenue and the media.[18]

New Orleans itself has a dualistic quality woven into its DNA. Its raucous frontier "improvisational style" raised to an *organizational* principle belies the fact that when it came to planning, early New Orleans may well have been one of the most deliberately planned towns in all of colonial North America. As Lawrence Powell points out: "Its designation came at the acme of enlightened absolutism, when crown and court were experimenting with visionary projects for reorganizing the 'social' problem."[19] The social problem was that New Orleans had come to epitomize "disorder and debauchery," manifested by the shared proclivities of the French and the Canadians to "drown their regional differences" in ways functionaries[20] could not comprehend—that is, through drink, gastronomy, and other forms of carousing. The hyper-rationalistic and ultimately doomed attempt to do away with this raucousness reflected "a wider and deeper illicitness intrinsic to the colony at large" that harked back to efforts by Enlightenment planners to reform the dregs of France and keep the underlying population in its place by "etching a new and better hierarchy into the town's original grid."[21]

The Quarter, of course, is a byword for decadence. Decadence, a term of amorphous meaning, has been of philosophical interest since Plato.[22] Decadence connotes a state of change, *typically* for the worse, though not exclusively so. As with all "grand narrative" notions, on closer scrutiny it is subject to philosophical weaknesses since there is no Archimedean point from which decadence can be definitely assessed.[23] Every change alters some state of affairs, destroying or modifying it, and this is especially true when it comes to technological development. Cyril Joad provides three typical features marking decadence, no single item being a necessary and sufficient condition: (1) scepticism in belief; (2) epicureanism and hedonism in conduct; and (3) subjectivism in thought, art, and morals.[24]

Our industrialized age reflects Nietzsche's idea that decadence's seduction technique is through its instrisic presentism.[25] This broadly corresponds to Joad's second condition. Since our time-conscious age values the "saving" and the "killing" of time, modernity's radical presentism is a negation of aesthetic transcendence and of the ideal of permanence, its most conspicuous manifestation being that of kitsch[26] (Joad's third condition). Jacques Barzun conceives of decadence as a *loss of possibility* brought on by boredom.[27] Boredom goes some way to account for the ever more exotic and bizarre stimulations characteristic of late modernity's enfeebled will.[28] Technology and consumerism,[29] being a Goneril and Regan to the hierarchy of settled traditions,[30] has disposability built into it.

What then is meant by the transcendental in *Confederacy*? To answer this one has to turn to Boëthius, but briefly before that one has to address a standard criticism of Toole.[31] Critics, including Bobby Byrne, Toole's scholarly friend, deemed Toole's knowledge of Boëthius dilettantish, the thrust of his claim being that Toole's knowledge of Boëthius was primarily refracted through Chaucer.[32] This criticism completely misses the mark. If one overlooks the fictive status of *Confederacy* (it is after all a novel), then one is bound to misattribute Toole's intention. The favorable assessment of Toole by Robert Lumiansky (tutor to both Byrne and Toole), later to become president of the American Council of Learned Societies, offsets Byrne's analysis.[33] A scathing review by Mary Margaret McCabe of Alain de Bottom's *The Consolations of Philosophy* (2000) that could well have been uttered by Ignatius is salient here:

> It is deeply dispiriting, then, that the latest attempt to popularize philosophy— that is to say, to make philosophy into televisual fodder—does so precisely on the basis that philosophers can provide us with useful tips, convenient attitudes to strike in the muddle of our practical lives. . . . Nothing in this travesty deserves its title; Boëthius must be turning in his grave.[34]

On these terms one cannot plausibly accuse Toole of vulgarizing Boëthius— if one grasps the nature of his project. Perhaps the most controversial aspect to Toole's Boëthius congeals around that old philosophical chestnut, determinism versus free will. As Vernon Leighton explains:

> As we have seen in the context of Chaucer, the view that blind fortune dominates the human condition does not entail either determinism—in the sense of no free will—or meaninglessness. . . . Toole may have shared Ignatius Reilly's rejection of the idea that one can improve the human condition through enlightened social progress. That possible concession does not mean that Toole was a determinist or a nihilist in the sense of rejecting the possibility of freely chosen action in the teeth of blind, worldly fortune. *Confederacy*, then, is not a repetition of Boethius directly . . . but a repetition of Chaucer's technique for handling Boëthian fate and free will.[35]

I can't speak to Chaucer's assimilation of Boëthius but Leighton's view that several of the characters "will have to take their good fortune and make something of it" is compatible with so-called "soft" determinism whereby moral responsibility is consistent with, or even requires, the truth of determinism, most famously argued for by David Hume.[36]

The conjoining of theology and geometry has a long provenance. For Thomas Aquinas, Albertus Magnus, and William of Auxerre, geometry was propaedeutic to studying theological questions. Very much within the neo-Platonic tradition, Boëthius continued this link between the structure of the soul and mathematics. Contemporary mathematician John Conway explicitly imbues mathematics with an aesthetic sensibility: "Mathematics is actually an aesthetic subject almost entirely."[37] It was Vico who wrote that "just as he who occupies himself with geometry, is in his world of figures, a god (so to speak), so God Almighty is, in his world of spirits and bodies, a geometer (so to speak)."[38] Eminent Boëthius scholar Henry Chadwick says that Boëthius "writes as one whose skill lies in dialectic and who sees some untidiness in the ecclesiastical garden."[39] Via Toole's channeling of Boëthius, we begin to intuit the aesthetic dimension to Ignatius's obsession (though not in practice) with order, balance, harmony, proportion and "taste and decency". In Plato's *Republic*, for the well-ordered city, there are specific moral characteristics that are in some way aligned to the virtuous soul; in Aristotle ethical activity *is* beauty.[40] The neo-Platonist view was that "people not only believed that mathematics *could* be applied to philosophy and theology, but that it *had* to be applied".[41]

Marc Champagne poses the following question: What could a religious issue like belief or disbelief in God possibly have to do with the stark topic of geometry? He goes on:

> For René Descartes, the two matters are intimately connected. In fact, Descartes thinks that, if you do not believe in God, you cannot really carry out geometrical proofs . . . believing in God is not only salutary from a spiritual standpoint, it actually serves a crucial epistemological function, since it allows the human mind to spread beyond its temporal finitude and secure ownership of whatever was previously achieved by deductive reasoning. . . . He also makes a negative claim, namely that an atheist is prevented from attaining a full hold on the truths of geometry. Descartes does not deny that "an atheist is clearly and distinctly aware that the three angles of a triangle are equal to two right angles." But, since truths like these only guarantee their veracity while they are being contemplated, Descartes insists that the geometrical demonstrations of an atheist "will never be free of this doubt [of possible deception] until he [the atheist] acknowledges that God exists."[42]

Champagne doesn't accept Descartes' negative claim. What I think motivates Descartes' negative claim is that the atheist has even heavier lifting to do than the theist. As it is, those who posit the existence of God are on very tricky territory: that is, outside of the mystical, theology cannot be considered a proper object of epistemological study since the concept of God does not achieve enough clarity and distinctness to be discussable. When we cite the divine attributes—omniscience, omnipotence, and so on—one doesn't have the least purchase on these ideas. Those who posit the negation (¬P), themselves, make an even stronger claim, incomprehensibly made in that most opaque of epistemic domains. The theist claims that one can posit the existence of God on a certain understanding of the various relevant attributes, say a1, a2, and so on. But the anti-theist (atheist) would have to show that there is no God: that is, that there is no understanding of these attributes a1, a2, and so on under which the existence of a being possessing them could be true. So it would seem that the atheist has more work to do and thus is in no position to disparage theistic coherence.[43]

To reiterate: it's worth bearing in mind that Boëthius thinks that it does not follow that one must choose between divine omniscience and human freedom and contingency. God is eternal, he is sempiternal: that is, there is no time in which God did not exist nor will there be any time in which God does not exist.[44] On one influential view, Boëthius' *Consolation* is not distinctively Christian,[45] though it is consistent with Judeo-Christian humility that understands that world had a beginning and will have an end. The question of whether Boëthius was a Church Father or an ancient philosopher is neither—and both.[46]

Nietzsche's proclamation of the "death of God," marked the onset of modernity's nihilism: that is, society being inadequately equipped for coping with the terrors of existence and the existential need for meaning, ushered in a new age of idolatry.[47] By modernity one means the rise of skeptical philosophy, philosophy that rejects that any single consistent set of values could be ordained by God.[48] The proliferation of revolutionary-utopian doctrines including a smorgasbord of nationalisms, for all intents and purposes operated as secular mythologies. As Michael Frederici puts it: "Because modern ideologies are the consequence of varying degrees of existential and intellectual closure to divine reality, they are apt to identify the source of order in man's revolt from God."[49] Ideologues are the monomaniacal bores crashing the conversation of mankind, tone-deaf to the notion that "reality is as conservative in its means as it is prodigal in its effects," as Norman Kemp Smith once wrote.[50] Ideologies, sociopolitical or aesthetic, are what Michael Oakeshott termed "cribs," off-the-peg principles that supplant practical activity and experience. And as cribs they necessarily traffic in the "politics of the felt need," generating spurious remedies to misdiagnosed problems. This style of politics bears the hallmarks of and coincides with the rise of kitsch. Thorsten Botz-Bornstein explains the continuities:

There are certain rules to follow and kitsch skips some of those necessary aesthetic stances, for example those of adequacy, appropriateness, sophistication, and thenecessity of effort and seriousness in art. Most typically, kitsch does so in order to obtain cheap effects of intense emotion. This is similar to how bullshit works in politics, where claims or ideologies often move too quickly toward desired political aims without being backed by critical thought.[51]

Political and aesthetic cribs are kitsch in that they express counterfeit emotion, whose sole purpose is to draw the *consumer* through shallow (unearned) effort.[52] The politician's or the celebrity's display of public emotion is just that, a staging in the hope of "certification," (as Walker Percy put it) or, in current parlance, virtue-signaling.[53] Ignatius's Crusade for Moorish Dignity,[54] Dadaist in its absurdity,[55] satirizes this tendency, replete with the tacit fiction that human behavior is not stochastic and the explicit fiction that successful implementation would, *ceteris paribus*, really work *this* time round. Ideologies that posit stages of development through which all human societies must pass, as projected by Marx and Comte, are merely secularized versions of a providential pattern or redemptive schemes. The confluence of the aesthetic and the political have paradigmatic instantiations in Nazism and Sovietism, the Nuremberg rallies and social realism. A substantial factor in the "kitschification" of culture is the role of mass media. We live in a culture of a general "dumbing down," politically, educationally, and more besides.[56] Ignatius is, of course, a voracious consumer of films.[57] In his mind, any deviance, nonconformism, or radicalism can be digested by the market and normalized and regurgitated as a studied counterculture *lifestyle*.[58] Matei Calinescu articulates this as follows:

> Seen as a lie, a kitsch work implies a close relationship and even a collaboration of sorts between the kitsch-artist and the kitsch-man. The latter wants to be "beautifully" lied to and the former is willing to play the game in exchange for financial gain. The responsibility is clearly shared by both. In this game of illusions and spurious impressions, the liar may end up believing that what he says is the truth.[59]

In this sense, much like Botz-Bornstein, kitsch has been thought of as being an ethical defect,[60] a defect of mediocrity, mental passivity, spiritual laziness, and sentimentality.[61] Karsten Harries proclaimed that "to isolate aesthetics from ethics is to misunderstand what art is all about."[62] Kitsch, it should be noted, is not the sole preserve of the masses—having the financial wherewithal does not inoculate one against its seduction. Religion, too, has not been immune from kitschification. In some denominations, the drive towards social justice activism on the one hand, and on the other hand, churches competing for one's dollar in a crowded market reveals just how impious religion has become. Kitsch disguises a loss of faith and reveals a spiritual malaise.[63]

"Bullshit" can be understood as a rhetorical analog to kitsch:

> As a matter of fact, bureaucracies produce a lot of "efficiency bullshit" that can very well be opposed by producing . . . bullshit. Political correctness, though initially designed to prevent discrimination, can easily go over the top and become a dictatorial sort of bullshit in its own right.[64]

This "water-cooler Taylorism" (or Taylorism "lite") bullshit is what Toole was driving at when Ignatius utters: "Employers sense in me a denial of their values";[65] "Apparently I lack some particular perversion which today's employer is seeking";[66] and "'Clean, hardworking, dependable, quiet type.' Good God! What kind of monster is this that they want. I am afraid that I could never work for a concern with a worldview like that."[67] Daniel Bell pointed out a paradox of climbing the corporate ladder. Despite wanting an organization man, this very same person is bombarded with advertisements promoting relaxation and letting go: one is to be "straight" by day and a "swinger" by night.[68]

In the preface to Thomas Bradwardine's *De Geometria speculative* (quoting Boëthius) Bradwardine writes "whoever omits mathematical studies has destroyed the whole of philosophic knowledge."[69] For Boëthius the Liberal Arts comprised of grammar, rhetoric, and logic, the *trivium*, and served as the bedrock for all other disciplines, religious or secular. Ignatius, as we all know, is "over-educated," though unlike his revered Boëthius, he has an inflated sense of superiority, tenuously aligning himself with Schiller, Proust, and Milton. While Ignatius is educated and grandiloquent in speech, one cannot infer that his education was Boëthian in the sense of a Victorian gentleman's education,[70] wherein "[t]heology is the Mistress-science, without which the whole educational structure will necessarily lack its final synthesis."[71]

The *quadrivium* (a term coined by Boëthius) had arithmetic, music, geometry, and astronomy, united under the aspect *sub specie quantitates*.[72] The inclusion of music might seem odd, but if one understands music as patterned structure, then it comfortably fits with the idea of relations and proportionality. Boëthius' Pythagorean and Platonic infused interest in musical theory was part and parcel of understanding the cosmos. Since cosmology requires a knowledge of all the other elements of the *quadrivium* "it lifts music to the highest level of its meaning in the metaphor of the harmony of the spheres."[73] Indeed as Chadwick notes, in his tract on *Christian Instruction*, Augustine "is certain that 'music and number' are keys to unlock the exegesis of scripture": numbers are governed by immutable rules and are a signpost to the unchanging Creator.[74] Arithmetic directs the mind towards immutable truths unaffected by the contingencies of time and space. It is only in the bodiless activity of geometry that we participate in the divine activity of pure creation or providential genius. But music advances even further towards that "summit of perfection" (heaven) for which the *quadrivium* is a prerequisite. In the pursuit of truth, the good student needs to have competence across all four components, though for some, Boëthius wavers between requiring competence across all four disciplines or ascending to the highest learning via any one single one of them.[75] Music, at the very heart of Providence's ordering of things, is not a matter of cheerful entertainment or superficial consolation, but it is a central clue to the interpretation of the hidden harmony of God and nature, in which the only discordant element is evil in the heart of man.[76] Ignatius shares in Boëthius' (aristocratic) snobbery in looking down on scantily-clad girls or theatrical harlots, as frivolous and meretricious entertainers of the *commedia dell'arte*.[77]

The significance of Boëthius to Toole, who was clearly working through his own philosophical and existential problems, was that the Romans provided a perpetual example of the successful search, not for metaphysical truth, but for the authority and certainty that are attainable only through stable institutions and inherited traditions of law and serious citizenship. Civil society requires the certainties and reassurances of well-established customs and habits of thought, and it is only undermined by the restless and arrogant inquiries of philosophers and marketocracts. An unlikely (current) ally to this view can be found in Nassim Nicholas Taleb. For Taleb, one of the follies of modernity, under the guise of Reason, has been the deliberate and arrogant repression of disruption in both natural and nonnatural systems. For Taleb the medieval European was "robust" and "antifragile" in his or her fine-tuned situated or orientated traditions of authority.[78] Only in a phase of final decadence, towards the end of a civilization's cycle, does a restless probing into the philosophical basis of obedience shake individuals free of their ties. Then we can be sure that a regression to barbarism is not far away, "the barbarism of reflection," to use Vico's striking phrase. Eric Voegelin also expresses a similar outlook:

> When the critical standards of civilizational values which stem from the *bios theoretikos* and the life of the spirit are abandoned, when the empirical process itself has to furnish the standards, then a special doctrine is needed to bestow grace on the present and to heighten an otherwise irrelevant situation of fact into a standard by which the past and the future can be measured, This act of grace, bestowed by the intellectual leaders of Enlightenment on themselves and on their age, is the source of the genuine revolutionary pathos that animates the idea of progress, as well as of its plight when the by no means negligible values

of utilitarian scientism have run their course. This end seems to have come in our time, when the revolutions are becoming "reactions" and spiritual regeneration is the burning problem of the age.[79]

Toole shares Ruskin and Voegelin's concern with the utilitarian dimension to action.[80] A generic understanding of utilitarianism is that actions are good or bad, right or wrong, according as they promote or hinder the maximization of intrinsically valuable states of affairs. In other words, it's a teleological theory that links morality with interest or advantage through assumptions about rational choice. Expressed thus, we can see why Toole would find it an anathema in light of, in his view, the marketocratic appeal to the lowest common denominator. On this understanding utilitarianism interferes with—or corrodes—an individual's "integrity":[81] a powerful criticism famously leveled by Bernard Williams. For Williams integrity is a matter of commitment to principles from which one should not feel obliged to deviate under pressure of coercion or of inducement.

If one is familiar with the writings of Walker Percy, it is quite evident the appeal *Confederacy* would have had for him. Percy too recognized that the pursuit of happiness is an elusive quarry if it is prosecuted solely through material acquisition. Percy wrote that even "places are consumed nowadays. The more delectable the place, the quicker it is ingested, digested, and turned into feces"[82] creating what Jonathan Haidt calls "lifestyle enclaves."[83] On a deeper level, pointing to Toole's medievalist cross weave, Percy identified and articulated the South's distinctive moral manners, a remnant of an honor culture he terms "Southern Stoicism"; this residual stoic outlook, distantly echoing an agrarian society and a traditional social hierarchy. Percy, though, does not take Christianity and Stoicism to be antithetical.

Toole and Ruskin recognized a spiritual wholeness and social cohesion that was vanishing from the world of industrial capitalism. All that was most valuable in life depended upon transcending the motive of profit and the spirit of calculation. Toole's device of appealing to a medieval sensibility reinforces the point that work and the pursuit of excellence, where ends and means coincide, is as an act of piety. This is conspicuously missing in an age of radical time compression and mass consumption. This view should not be taken as nostalgic—it's merely an epochal observation.

Whatever Toole's religious or sociopolitical commitments might or might not have been, it would be a distortion to attribute to him a vindication of the separation humanities from theology at its foundation, and specifically from the metaphor or myth of the Fall. Theology and geometry and taste and decency are Janus-like in simultaneously looking to the eternal and the profane.

NOTES

1. *Confederacy*, 25. "With the breakdown of the Medieval system, the gods of Chaos, Lunacy, and Bad Taste gained ascendance. . . . After a period in which the western world had enjoyed order, tranquility, unity, and oneness with its True God and Trinity, there appeared winds of change which spelled evil days ahead. . . . Having once been so high, humanity fell so low. What had once been dedicated to the soul was now dedicated to the sale. . . . Merchants and charlatans gained control of Europe, calling their insidious gospel 'The Enlightenment.'"

2. "The Call of Cthulhu," https://repository.library.brown.edu/studio/item/bdr:42 5219/. See Leighton, "Dialectic," note 4.

3. Bell, "Clash," 18 takes the view that for Ignatius, the cast of characters he comes across, are one-dimensional representatives of allegorical issues he must confront.

4. Oakeshott, *Voice*, 93.

5. MacLauchlin, *Butterfly*, 47–48, 34–35.

6. Cited in Federici, "Voegelin," 6.

7. Peter McCluskey perceptively notes Toole's choice of "Paradise Vendors" for the mobile hotdog company that features in the novel. See McCluskey, "Selling Souls." That all values had been lost to the shallowness of bourgeois materialism was anticipated by Dostoyevsky in *The Brothers Karamazov* (see D'Auria, "Progress," 691).

Confederacy, 263: "Every asylum in this nation is filled with poor souls who simply cannot stand lanolin, cellophane, plastic, television, and subdivisions."

8. See Ruppersburg, "The South." This cultural turmoil is also echoed in Ransom's near contemporary Robert Musil's great modernist novel *Der Mann ohne Eigenschaften* (*The Man Without Qualities*) which takes place against the dissolution of the Austro-Hungarian Empire.

9. *Confederacy*, 37: "The United States needs some theology and geometry, some taste and decency. I suspect that we are teetering on the edge of the abyss."

Confederacy, 103: "Any connection between American art and American nature is purely coincidental, but this is only because the nation as a whole has no contact with reality."

10. Richard Weaver looked to the European Middle Ages as the civilizational zenith, only to be brought down by nominalism, which broadly speaking is the rejection of universals and/or abstract objects.

11. *Confederacy*, 232: "Degeneracy, rather than signaling the downfall of a society, as it once did, will now signal peace for a troubled world. We must have new solutions to new problems. I shall act as a sort of mentor and guide for the movement, my not inconsiderable knowledge of world history, economics, religion, and political strategy acting as a reservoir, as it were, from which these people can draw rules of operational procedure." Boëthius himself played a somewhat similar role in degenerate Rome. As Chesterton has said of Boëthius, "Thus he truly served as a guide, philosopher, and friend to many Christians; precisely because, while his own times were corrupt, his own culture was complete." See Greenberg on Juvenal's Rome, *Satire*, 66.

12. *Confederacy*, 195.

13. Powell, *Accidental*, 35.

14. *Confederacy*, 182.

15. *Confederacy*, 182, 103.

16. *Confederacy*, 185.

17. "That the manufacture of consent is capable of great refinements no one, I think, denies. The process by which public opinions arise is certainly no less intricate than it has appeared in these pages, and the opportunities for manipulation open to anyone who understands the process are plain enough . . . . Under the impact of propaganda, not necessarily in the sinister meaning of the word alone, the old constants of our thinking have become variables" Lippmann, *Public Opinion*, Chapter XV, 248. See McCluskey's discussion of Burma Jones' aspirations 15.

18. *Confederacy*, 37.

19. Powell, *Accidental*, 60.

20. *Confederacy*, 179: "You can always tell employees of the government by the total vacancy which occupies the space where most other people have faces."

21. Powell, *Accidental*, 39.

22. "The men of early times were better than we and nearer to the Gods"—Plato cited in Trigg, *Aesthetics*, 98. Montesquieu's *Considérations sur les causes de la grandeur des romains et de leur decadence* (1734) and Voltaire's *Essai sur les moeurs et l'esprit des nations* (1756) are the modern prominent philosophical progenitors.

23. Barzun, *Dawn*.

24. Joad, *Decadence*, 100.

25. "Presentism" contends that everything that exists, exists now. By contrast "eternalists" hold that past and future things not only exist but are equally real (see Merricks, "Goodbye," 103–110).

26. *Confederacy*, 209–210.

27. Barzun, *Dawn*, xvi.

28. Conway, "Decadence," 25.

29. *Confederacy*, 1–2, 140.

30. *Confederacy*, 45, 46, 183–184, See Leighton, "Dialectic," and Miller, *Conservative*.

31. See Leighton, "Refutation."

32. To my knowledge there is only one bona fide medievalist aware of *Confederacy*—see Shanzer, "Interpreting," 245.

33. MacLauchlin, 50–51. See also Leighton, "Refutation."

34. McCabe, Review, 14.

35. *Confederacy*, 66, 280. See Leighton, "Evidence," 35–36.

36. Discussion of *fortunà* deserves closer-grained attention which cannot be undertaken here, namely Polybius's *tyche* and Boëthius' and Machiavelli's *fortunà*. See Thornton, *Polybius*.

37. Sinclair and Higginson, *Mathematics*, 58.

38. "Unde geometra in illo suo figurarum mundo est quidam deus, uti Deau optimus maximus in hoc mundo animorum et corporum est quidam geometra." *Vico vindicate* XVI.

39. Chadwick, *Boëthius*, xiv.

40. Kraut, *Aristotle*, 231–250.

41. Tummers, *Geometry*, 112. My emphasis.

42. Champagne, "Descartes," 299–300.

43. Swinburne, *Coherence*.

44. Stump and Kretzmann offer a fascinating rational reconstruction of Boëthius idea of eternity.

45. Chadwick, *Boëthius*, 251.

46. Marenbon, "Boëthius," 137. This very question is asked of Philo of Alexandria: Was he a Greek or a Jew? The same answer applies.

47. Conway, "Decadence."

48. Lilla, *Vico*.

49. Frederici, "Voegelin," 6.

50. Kemp Smith, *Credibility*, 337.

51. Botz-Bornstein, "Kitsch," 313.

52. *Confederacy*, 110, 108, 232. See Scruton, *Culture* and *Beauty*.

53. *Confederacy*, 220: "Politicians always seem to want to shake hands with mongoloids in ethnic and native costumes."

54. *Confederacy*, 232.

55. Dadaism made play of extremes of buffoonery and provocative behavior ostensibly to shock people out of corruption and complacency. It is one of Ignatius's many inconsistencies that Dadaism deliberately flouted accepted standards of beauty that Ignatius himself subscribed to.

56. Mosley, *Dumbing*.

Many of Ignatius's sentiments finds voice in a more recent satirical publication called *The Chap Magazine*. "Chappism" takes an "anarcho-dandyist" stand against the vulgarity of the contemporary world, a good-mannered and well-dressed revolution against a world of bland, homogenized consumerism, sportswear and branded clothing, poor diction, and "art" that has "become a kind of corporate furniture, specifically created to fill empty spaces which businessmen want to fill with something 'meaningful.'" Perhaps Chappism's strongest and most subversive commitment is to the "shirk ethic," as per Ignatius's time at Levy Pants and Paradise Vendors, Incorporated.

57. *Confederacy*, 87.

58. *Confederacy*, 271.

59. Calinescu, *Five Faces*, 259.

60. Solomon, "Kitsch," 342.

61. See Anderson and Mullen, *Faking it*.

62. Harries, *Meaning*, 75.

63. *Confederacy*, 52: "I refuse to 'look up.' Optimism nauseates me. It is perverse. Since man's fall, his proper position in the universe has been one of misery."

64. Botz-Bornstein, "Kitsch," 318. For more on workplace bullshit I refer the reader to David Nobbs' series of novels featuring the subversive middle-class, middle-aged, middle manager, Reginald Perrin.

65. *Confederacy*, 44.

66. *Confederacy*, 134.

67. *Confederacy*, 54.

68. Bell, *Capitalism*, 71–72. *Confederacy*, 269.

69. Olson, "Measuring," 414–427.

70. Rosenthal-Pubul, *Theoretic*. "All well-educated southern gentlemen knew their Cicero and their Horace, their Virgil and their Seneca, as well as their Marcus Aurelius"—Walker Percy cited in Gretlund, 78.

71. Sayers, "Learning," 251.

Confederacy, 219: "Then you must begin a reading program immediately so that you may understand the crises of our age. . . . "Begin with the late Romans, including Boethius, of course. Then you should dip rather extensively into early Medieval. You may skip the Renaissance and the Enlightenment. That is mostly dangerous propaganda. Now that I think of it, you had better skip the Romantics and the Victorians, too. For the contemporary period, you should study some selected comic books."

72. Boëthius does not use this phrase.

73. Masi, *Liberal Arts*, 29.

74. Chadwick, *Boëthius*, 80.

75. Masi, *Liberal Arts*, 30, note 11.

76. Chadwick, *Boëthius*, 101.

77. See Chadwick, *Boëthius*, 86. Toole's choice of a Cockatoo as Darlene, the aspiring stripper's novelty double act, renders her masquerade of innocence (see McCuskey's *Selling Souls*) improbable since word Cockatoo carries the bawdy innuendo "A cock or two."

78. Taleb, *Antifragile*.

79. Voegelin, *Enlightenment*, 84–85.

80. MacLauchlin, *Butterfly*, 49. "The Development of the Babbitt-American" Box 2 Folder 2 in the Toole Papers, kindly provided to me by MacLauchlin.

81. Smart and Williams, *Utilitarianism*.

82. Percy, *Signposts*, 5.

83. Haidt, *Righteous*, 364.

BIBLIOGRAPHY

Anderson, Digby C. and Peter Mullen, eds. *Faking It: The Sentimentalisation of Modern Society*. London: Social Affairs Unit, 1998.

Barzun, Jacques. *From Dawn to Decadence: 500 Years of Western Cultural Life*. New York: Harper Collins, 2001.

Bell, Daniel. *The Cultural Contradictions of Capitalism*. New York: Basic Books, 1976.

Bell, Elizabeth S. "The Clash of World Views in John Kennedy Toole's *A Confederacy of Dunces*." *The Southern Literary Journal* 21, no. 1 (Fall, 1988): 15–22.

Botz-Bornstein, Thorsten. "Kitsch and Bullshit." *Philosophy and Literature* 39, no. 2 (October 2015): 305–321.

Calinescu, Matei. *Five Faces of Modernity: Modernism Avant-Garde Decadence Kitsch*. Durham, NC: Duke University Press, 1987.

Chadwick, Henry. *Boëthius: The Consolations of Music, Logic, Theology, and Philosophy*, Oxford: Clarendon Press, 1981.

Champagne, Marc. "God, Human Memory, and the Certainty of Geometry: An Argument Against Descartes." *Philosophy & Theology* 28, no. 2 (2016): 299–310.

Conway, Daniel W. "The Politics of Decadence." *The Southern Journal of Philosophy* XXXVII (Supplement, 1999): 19–33.

D'Auria, Matthew. "Progress, Decline and Redemption: Understanding War and Imagining Europe, 1870s–1890s." *European Review of History: Revue européenne d'histoire* 25, no. 5 (2018): 686–704.

Federici, Michael P. "Eric Voegelin and Enlightenment Rationalism." In *Critics of Enlightenment Rationalism,* edited by Gene Callahan and Kenneth McIntyre. Cham: Palgrave, forthcoming.

Goldblatt and Lee B. Brown, eds. *Aesthetics: A Reader in Philosophy of the Arts*. Oxford and New York: Routledge, 2016.

Greenberg, Jonathan. 2019. *The Cambridge Introduction to Satire*. Cambridge: Cambridge University Press.

Gretlund, Jan Nordby. "On the Porch with Marcus Aurelius: Walker Percy Stoicism." In *Walker Percy: Novelist and Philosopher*, edited by Jan Nordby Gretlun and Karl-Heinz Westarp. Jackson: University Press of Mississippi, 1991.

Haidt, Jonathan. *The Righteous Mind: The Righteous Mind: Why Good People Are Divided by Politics and Religion*. New York: Vintage, 2012.

Harries, Kartsten. *Meaning of Modern Art*. Evanston: Northwestern University Press, 1979.

Joad, Cyril. *Decadence—A Philosophical Inquiry*. London: Faber & Faber, 1948.

Kemp Smith, Norman. *The Credibility of Divine Existence: The Collected Papers of Norman Kemp Smith*. Ed. A. J. D. Porteous, R. D. MacLennan and G. E. Davie. New York: St. Martin's Press.

Kraut, Richard H. "An Aesthetic Reading of Aristotle's Ethics." In *Politeia in Greek and Roman Philosophy*, edited by Verity Harte and Melissa Lane. Cambridge University Press, 2011.

Leighton, H. Vernon. "A Refutation of Robert Byrne: John Kennedy Toole's *A Confederacy of Dunces*, Chaucer, and Boethius." *Notes on Contemporary Literature* 42, no. 1 (January 2012).

———. "The Dialectic of American Humanism: John Kennedy Toole's *A Confederacy of Dunces*, Marsilio Ficino, and Paul Oskar Kristeller." *Renascence* 64, no. 2 (2012): 201–215.

———. "Evidence of Influences on John Kennedy Toole's *A Confederacy of Dunces*, Including Geoffrey Chaucer," Version 2.1 (2014). http://course1.winona.edu/vleighton/toole/Leighton_Toole_Chaucer.html.

Lilla, Mark. *G. B. Vico: The Making of an Anti-Modern*. Cambridge, MA: Harvard University Press, 1993.

Lippmann, Walter. *Public Opinion*. New York: Harcourt, Brace, 1922.

MacLauchlin, Cory. *Butterfly in the Typewriter: The Tragic Life of John Kennedy Toole and the Remarkable Story of a Confederacy of Dunces.* Boston: Da Capo Press, 2012.

Marenbon, John. "Boethius's Unparadigmatic Originality and Its Implications for Medieval Philosophy." In *Boethius as a Paradigm of Late Ancient Thought*, edited by Herausgegeben von Thomas Böhm, Thomas Jürgasch und Andreas Kirchner, 137–148. Berlin and Boston: De Gruyter 2014.

Masi, Michael. "The Liberal Arts and Gerardus Ruffus' Commentary on the Boethian De Arithmetica." *The Sixteenth Century Journal* 10, no. 2 (Summer, 1979): 23–41.

McCabe, Mary Margaret. Review of Alain de Bottom *The Consolations of Philosophy*. *The Times Literary Supplement* Issue 5073 (June 23, 2000): 14.

McCluskey, Peter M. "Selling Souls and Vending Paradise: God and Commerce in *A Confederacy of Dunces*." *Southern Quarterly* 47, no. 1 (Fall 2009): 7–22.

Merricks, Trenton. "Goodbye Growing Block." In *Oxford Studies in Metaphysics. Vol. 2*, edited by Dean Zimmerman, 103–110. Oxford: Oxford University Press, 2006.

Miller, Keith D. "The Conservative Vision of John Kennedy Toole." In *Proceedings of Conference College Teachers of English Texas* 48 (1983): 30–34. Lubbock.

Mosley, Ivo, ed. *Dumbing Down: Culture, Politics and the Mass Media*. Thorverton: Imprint Academic.

Oakeshott, Michael. *The Voice of Liberal Learning: Michael Oakeshott on Education*. Ed. Timothy Fuller. New Haven: Yale University Press, 1989.

Olson, Glending. "Measuring the Immeasurable: Farting, Geometry, and Theology in the Sumner's Tale." *The Chaucer Review* 43, no. 4 (2009).

Percy, Walker. *Signposts in a Strange Land*. New York: Picador, 1991.

Powell, Lawrence. *The Accidental City: Improvising New Orleans*. Cambridge, MA: Harvard University Press, 2013.

Rosenthal-Pubul, Alexander. *The Theoretic Life A Classical Ideal and its Modern Fate Reflections on the Liberal Arts*. Cham: Springer, 2018.

Rudnicki, Robert. "Euphues and the Anatomy of Influence: John Lyly, Harold Bloom, James Olney, and the Construction of John Kennedy Toole's Ignatius." *The Mississippi Quarterly* 62, no 1/2.

Ruppersburg, Hugh. "The South and John Kennedy Toole's 'A Confederacy of Dunces.'" *Studies in American Humor*, New Series 2, 5, no. 2/3 (Summer, Fall 1986): 118–126.

Sayers, Dorothy. "The Lost Tools of Learning." In *Education in a Free Society*, edited by Anne Husted Burleigh, 229–263. Indianapolis: Liberty Fund, 1973.

Scruton, Roger. *Beauty*. Oxford: Oxford University Press, 2009.

———. *Modern Culture*. London: Continuum, 2012.

Shanzer, Danuta. "Interpreting the *Consolation*." In *The Cambridge Companion to Boethius*, edited by John Merenbon. Cambridge: Cambridge University Press, 2009.

Simon, Richard Keller. "John Kennedy Toole and Walker Percy: Fiction and Repetition in A Confederacy of Dunces." *Texas Studies in Literature and Language* 36, no. 1 (1994).

Sinclair, Nathalie and Higginson, William, eds. *Mathematics and the Aesthetic: New Approaches to an Ancient Affinity.* New York: Springer, 2007.

Smart, J. J. C. and Williams, Bernard. *Utilitarianism: For and Against.* Cambridge: Cambridge University Press, 1973.

Solomon, Robert. "Kitsch." In *Aesthetics: A Reader in Philosophy of the Arts*, edited by David Goldblatt and Lee B. Brown. New York: Routledge, 2016.

Stump, Eleonore and Kretzmann, Norman. "Eternity." *The Journal of Philosophy* 78, no. 8 (August 1981): 429–458.

Swinburne, Richard. *The Coherence of Theism.* Oxford: Oxford University Press, 1993.

Taleb, Nassim Nicholas. *Antifragile: Things That Gain from Disorder.* New York: Random House, 2014.

Thornton, John. "Polybius in Context: The Political Dimension of the Histories." In *Polybius and His World: Essays in Memory of F. W. Walbank*, edited by Bruce Gibson and Thomas Harrison. Oxford: Oxford University Press, 2013.

Toole, John Kennedy. *A Confederacy of Dunces.* Harmondsworth: Penguin, 1981.

Trigg, Dylan. *The Aesthetics of Decay: Nothingness, Nostalgia, and the Absence of Reason.* Pieterlen and Bern: Peter Lang, 2006.

Tummers, Paul M. J. E. "Geometry and Theology in the XIIIth Century: An Example of their Interrelation as Found in the Ms Admont 442 The Influence of William of Auxerre?" *Vivarium* 18, no. 2 (1980).

Voegelin, Eric. *From Enlightenment to Revolution*, 84–85. Durham, NC: Duke University Press 1975.

Chapter 5

The *Consolation* of *Dunces*

Stephen Utz

In slight gestures and thickly woven plot elements, John Kennedy Toole's novel *A Confederacy of Dunces* is comedic and profound. It is also dramatically hectic, stylistically arch, and enigmatic in purpose. Can it then have philosophical content as well? Walker Percy's admiration for and promotion of the novel does tell us that he considered Toole a soulmate[1], and Percy certainly strove in his own novels to explore deep conceptual issues.[2] Perhaps he and Toole both do this. The ingenious combination of humor and moral theory in *Confederacy* is the main theme of this essay. I believe the surface entertainment of Toole's novel overlies a background commentary on the problem of moral luck that Boethius grasped and attempted to solve. Not only does the novel ingeniously interpret the earlier thinker's work, but it also clarifies and attempts to improve his philosophical thesis. I will argue that Toole tested and tried to make a new, though facetious, contribution to philosophical ethics. He chose to do this in a literary work of which the reflective component was not superfluous or superficial.

There is a difference between merely repeating and independently shaping philosophical views in an artistic medium. Most literary attempts of this kind at best paraphrase the work of others. In *On the Consolation of Philosophy*, the goddess Philosophy's first words to Boethius, to whom Reilly as protagonist of *Confederacy* is devoted, are a bold warning that the muses of poetry can only get in the way of his philosophical efforts. "Get out of here, you Sirens, even to your own destruction, and leave this dear one to my curative and healthy muses." [Bk 1, § 1 (prose) lines 39–41]. For example, Pope's *Essay on Man*[3] only versifies a list of apothegms from nonliterary philosophical sources. Several recent novels make philosophical themes part of the furniture of their characters' lives without delving into them substantively. But *Confederacy* is different, more akin to Basho's *Narrow Road to the Deep North*[4] in the reciprocal engagement of its narrative with metaethical reasoning.

New Orleans is beautifully captured in the novel and pervades everything in it. This is the city in the days before Katrina destroyed much of it, causing ethnographic changes that altered its atmosphere. It is still the city in which the struggle to get by segregated but also unified the black, Irish, Italian, Jewish, and other minorities. Quaintly urban idiosyncrasy defines the novel's characters—surprising and almost unrelated episodes bring them into focus—not only as interesting in themselves but also as unifying the narrative without strain.

It is useful at the outset to note one of *Confederacy's* quirks, that the author's somewhat stiff prose style is indistinguishable from the protagonist Ignatius Reilly's own. Yet the shared voice of narrator and hero reinforces our sense of their alienation from life's goals, as is completely natural. And this, while it makes the book's vocabulary humorous from the outset also subtly raises the question why alienation is so strong an element. Reilly is an eccentric in conversation and dress, unable to find work as an academic, scarcely tolerant of or tolerated by his mother, with rough indifference on both sides. His isolation and the slow pace of his prolonged search for a university position lead to the awkward stream of episodes in which the protagonist takes refuge from failure in spoofs and perverse counter measures, not all of which he understands himself, but all of which do magnify his separation from the people around them. The prose style, like the flow of episodes, stress his refuge in awkward life pursuits, not all of which he fully understands.

As the novel begins, random events propel Reilly into a steep decline he does not resist but also does not acknowledge to himself. On the busiest corner of the city, he is almost arrested for standing out among an army of bizarre locals. Mancuso, the police officer, to prove his mettle to his superiors, quickly shifts from Reilly to another man. This figure, Claude Robichaux, later meets another of the novel's characters, Burma Jones, a modest but facetious black man, at the police station. Reilly and his mother leave the crowded street so that she can have a strong drink in a sleazy bar, where she and a B-drinker schmooze, until the Lana the bar's owner shoos them out of the place. Unflustered by this rudeness, Reilly's mother turns her tough side on Reilly, pressuring him to get a life, which he eventually thinks he has done by taking a job as filing clerk to a very minor trouser manufacturer, Levy's Pants, typical of the city's low-key capitalism. In this compromised setting, he encounters others of the city's strange and comic characters.

Reilly and Levy the owner interact amicably, as Levy fails to grasp that Reilly has concocted a variety of whimsical innovations in the factory's shop rules and odd benefits for employees. Later chapters of the novel, leaving Reilly aside, dwell on the slight but emotional discord between Levy and his wife. The only person Reilly takes seriously is his girlfriend Myrna Mynhoff, with whom he has broken up before the novel begins. She does not appear until the novel closes, but letters pass between them, and at the end we learn that she has suddenly let him know she will rescue him from his mother's threat to commit him to a mental institution.

The oddity of Reilly's relation to the world around him lies mainly in his impracticality and scorn for normal life concerns. Indeed, his incomprehension leaves him no choice but to parody the practical assumptions of ordinary people. He is by implication a skeptic about the material world's reality. Early on he displays this, doubting that anything of supposed practical importance works, especially the know-how we all take for granted concerning everyday life. His skepticism extends to the basics of getting things done, and he is not only skeptical but also scornful. So he sets himself indignantly apart, paying attention and cooperating with others only to the extent necessary for playing tricks on them, perhaps also on himself. Given the juxtaposition of Reilly's thoughts on the world with his bitter regrets at not having found an academic job, it is natural to link the two, as if the worldly failure he took so seriously had fouled his beliefs in everything. Reilly's journal seems also to connect these compartments of his thought.

His admiration for Boethius, bluntly described as the hero of his philosophical views, becomes the recurrent, yet tantalizingly vague, touchstone of the novel. "As a medievalist, [Reilly] believed in the *rota Fortunae*, or wheel of fortune, a central concept in *De Consolatione Philosophiae*, the philosophical work which had laid the foundation for medieval thought".[5] In the same passage, Boethius's theory of fortune is tersely given: "[W]hile unjustly imprisoned by the emperor [Theodoric], [Boethius] had said that a blind goddess spins us on a wheel, that our luck comes in cycles".[6] Thereafter, Reilly invokes or complains about Fortuna repeatedly,[7] but he never discusses the core of the *Consolation*, an elaborate argument that unpredictable luck makes the consequences of virtue and principled conduct so unreliable that goals of a worldly sort are irrelevant to moral deliberation. An aspiring academic, Reilly had written an article about Boethius.[8] Much further along, in an utterly farcical eruption, Reilly is floored with reverence on seeing a "pornographic photograph" in a friend's possession.

A nude woman was sitting on the edge of a desk next to a globe of the world. The suggested onanism with the piece of chalk intrigued Ignatius. Her face was hidden behind a large book. . . . Ignatius scrutinized the title on the cover of the book: . . . *The Consolation of Philosophy.* "Do I believe what I am seeing? What brilliance. What taste. Good grief."[9]

These serious and jocular references put beyond doubt that the conspicuous recurrence of Fortuna in the narrative all refer to the *Consolation*. In fact, the woman in the photograph, with her academic setting, may be Philosophy.

In this connection, it is vital to note the focus on this central problem of modern moral theory. Bernard Williams, the influential Anglo-American ethical theorist, coined that phrase in an early essay and explored its significance extensively in later works.[10] His starting point was that ex post facto valuations of a person's moral worth often differ from valuations made earlier in the person's life, even when they focus on the same moral decisions made by that person. Using Paul Gauguin's transition from unfaithful husband and abandoning parent to great painter, Williams comments that the "justification, if there is to be one, will be essentially retrospective," hence "a matter of luck."[11] Moral judgments of individuals' lives also assume that it makes sense to ignore life's abrupt end. As Samuel Scheffler has recently observed, we all think as if there were an afterlife. We decide what to do, valuing consequences and avoiding threats that death will prevent us from experiencing.[12] Indeed, we value consequences that would be valueless only if all other human beings were extinguished.

> [T]here are many projects and activities whose importance to us is not diminished by the prospect of our own deaths. . . . So if by the afterlife we mean the continuation of human life on earth after our own deaths, then it seems difficult to avoid the conclusion that, in some significant respects, the existence of the afterlife matters more to us than our own continued existence . . . because it is a condition of other things mattering to us.[13]

The most effective theoretical achievement of the *Consolation* is its drawn-out and crushing disproof of the worldly rewards of virtuous conduct. Both Philosophy and Fortuna blast the weakness of "doing well" in life. As the goddess Philosophy tells Boethius, the state of human good fortune is always partly defective. A person never has it all, nor does any possession of good things last forever. One man has a good deal of property, but regrets his low birth. Another conceals a distinguished birth because he is shut in by personal poverty. A third man is rich in both birth and property, but has no partner to share it with. A married person without children holds onto wealth for some else's children to inherit. And the married parent is brought down by the children's faults (*Consolation* II 64–72). These devastating patterns of mixed good and ill fortune occupy at least half of the work (*Consolation* II–V). Rebutting the goddess of Fortune, Boethius argues that there is *some* consistency in the way all things behave, a sort of ordered realm (*arx*) along which the variations fall (*haec in sua simplicitatis arce composita multiplicem rebus egendis modum statuit*) (*Consolation* IV 25–27). This he calls "divine providence," but his God is the Platonic idea of the good and not an anthropomorphic person. The gap between the God of Christianity and this impersonal God is taken up elsewhere in Boethius's writings. The sciences, he believed, are concerned with the ideal content of things (*forma*), not with matter (*materia*), and it is a form that is the essence of what is (De Trinitate II 1–23).

This content of the *Consolation* appears in *Confederacy* without being cited to that source. At a critical stage in his story, Reilly's diary concludes that "when Fortuna spins us downward, the wheel sometimes halts for a moment and we find ourselves in a good, small cycle within the larger bad cycle".[14] This closely paraphrases Boethius's analysis of providence, "[f]or as of orbs which turn about the same centre, the inmost draweth nigh to the simplicity of the midst, and is as it were the hinge of the rest" (*Consolation* Bk 4, prose VI). But given Reilly's eccentric and chaotic life choices, the calm rationalism and enhanced Stoicism of Boethius seem foreign to him. The philosophical exploration is never more explicitly unpacked. Kant made drastic structural restrictions on moral goodness to limit the relevance of uncontrollable factual circumstances to the "goodness" of the will. Reilly might well have brought Kant into his musings, if he were interested in this aspect of Boethius's argument. That, however, would go beyond Reilly's enthusiasm for the medieval approach.

As whimsical as these allusions to the *Consolation* may appear, the narrative subtly reveals his grasp of its core puzzle and argument. Despite jibes against Stoicism (*Consolation* I 22–27), Boethius' clear purpose was to perfect the Roman variant of Stoicism familiar to Vergil, Cicero, and Horace. We must recall how this passionate though pessimistic worldview dominated the Hellenistic and Roman era. The Epicureans, chosen by the first Stoics as their philosophical foils, accepted a materialist view of reality that denied the afterlife of the soul. For them a happy life in this world brings the best kind of pleasure because it is the only kind. While agreeing that this world's pleasures are forfeited at death, the earliest Stoics argued for something more like traditional morality—"a good flow of life" (Zeno of Citium) or "living in agreement with nature" (Zeno's follower Cleanthes) (*Arius Didymus*, 63A–B). Later Stoics offered variations on this theme, relating the good life to the adaptation of habitual modes of conduct through intelligent reflection on experience. These were the sketchy framework of Stoic ethics in the Roman continuation of that tradition. Notably, Horace memorably commented that Fortune places a crown first on this person and then on that (*Odes* 1.34), although he also endorsed the "golden mean" (*Odes* 2.10). Cicero's *De Officiis* advances the familiar virtue-based method of deciding how to live one's life, acknowledging a modest form of despair concerning luck. Boethius strongly echoes these prominent, much earlier Stoics (Cicero xviii–xix). The affect of Stoicism in Cicero and Horace contrasts with the harsh reality to which Lucretius pointed. Based on his atomistic physics and metaphysics, the author of *De Rerum Natura* was as radical as Dostoevsky in his rejection of the existence of any God. So drastic was this departure from the Greek and Roman belief in many unruly Gods that Lucretius's own contemporaries found it difficult not to condemn him. His message is so clear that, when the manuscripts of his atheistic epic were found again in Western medieval times, its impact on elite readers caused a permanent shift in theologians' openness to other aspects of secular philosophy.[15]

The correspondence of Reilly's worldview with that of sophisticated Romans is limited to his detachment from the type of goal-centered life most of us take seriously. (Does he ever reject the afterlife? We are not told.) Superficially, he is detached from the usual life concerns of others. He neither plans nor considers courses of action that will improve his own well-being. He does carry out schemes, which are courses of action that have no valuable goals other than to reveal weaknesses in what others believe or to induce others to reveal the weakness or wrongness of the plans they take seriously. Stoicism was in essence a practical approach to an unsolvable problem, while the latter tries to solve the problem. The problem is how norms of conduct can be defended against the objection that bad luck destroys their purpose. To the extent that *Confederacy* reflects or even only bounces off Stoicism, this distinction is vital to our understanding the novel.

Philosophy appears as a goddess to Boethius in prison and challenges his understanding of moral purpose, which his death sentence undermines. She insists that the order of the universe rests on a *summum bonum* ("highest good") that "strongly and sweetly" pervades both practical and moral issues (*Consolation* Bk 3, prose II, 103). Having posed the problem, she retreats to allow Fortuna, a second goddess, to challenge the prisoner's belief that some rational and moral overview can exist. Rising to rebut the goddess Fortuna's absolute dismissal of moral purpose, Boethius theorizes that despite her maiming of what most people believe to be the justification of good action, another existential force that he calls Providence makes it possible for the human agent to find at least limited scope for rational ethical decisions. The consolation of the book's title is that Providence allows chaos and poor quality of material forms nevertheless to point to a greater "simplicity" and higher quality in life.

> For just as, of a number of [orbs] turning about the same centre, the innermost one approaches the simplicity of middleness and is a sort of pivot for the rest, . . . in a similar manner, that which is furthest separated from the first mind is entangled in the tighter meshes of fate, and a thing is the more free from fate the more closely it moves towards the centre of things. (*Consolation* IV ll. 65–76)

The geometry of existence consists of these orbs and makes virtue intelligible as a goal, thus at least partly rewarding human effort despite Fortuna's interference. Hence, Reilly's interest in "theology and geometry." "Possession of anything new or expensive only reflected a person's lack of theology and geometry; it could even cast doubts upon one's soul".[16] In explaining his views on the nature of being, Boethius had given primacy to physics, mathematics, and theology. He distinguished these fields of thought by how separable or inseparable they are from the subject matter of motion and change, theology being separable from both. In his view, "nothing is said to be because of its matter but because of its distinctive form" (Boethius, *De Trinitate* 2, ll. 28–29). This, of course, is an expression of belief in Plato's Theory of Forms, according to which existence is also a matter of form. As Socrates in the *Republic* hypothesized, in proposing an analysis of being, the visible and intelligible realms of things that exist are separate and may be envisioned as falling along a divided line. The first type of visible existence belongs to shadows, then reflections in bodies of water, solid, smooth, and shiny materials. The second type includes "animals around us, every plant, and the whole class of man-made things." Next are two intelligible categories that are not in themselves visible. The first of these categories consists of abstract geometric shapes of visible things, that is, figures that may be used in geometric proofs. The most intelligible consists of "what reason itself grasps by the power of dialectical discussion . . . moving through forms to forms, and ending in forms" (Plato 511b). Despite the importance of reason and the restriction of true knowledge to the intelligible sections of the line, all visible and intelligible items exist. The greater importance of the intelligible portions lies in their serving alone as the subject matter and content of what is knowable, while the merely visible things are only the matter of fallible belief.

Boethius was certainly a Christian, though with a Platonic twist, as both *Consolation* and his theological tracts make plain. Despite his use of the term Providence, his understanding of what God is and of how God influences the content of the world's and human souls' existence stands apart from the tradition in which God has thoughts and a will. As for Plato, the highest being is not a God with a personality but the form of the Good, which Socrates hypothesized as the highest in the hierarchy of existence. The borrowing from Plato will be traced more fully later in this essay.

Toole obviously brought Boethius into the novel to signal that his project is both literary and, in some sense, philosophical just as *Consolation* was, with its alternating brief verse and prose dialogue sections that recount the author's introspective thoughts in a dialectic with divine female figures. Certainly, Toole wanted this to be obvious. Boethius comments indirectly on his hope of bringing the muses and philosophy together before giving the reader even an overview of the work. He tells us he is mourning some horrible fate in the first verse segment of the book, then falls asleep and the goddess Philosophy appears to him, beginning a dialogue that continues through the first third of the book. But while *Consolation* was also literary in form, including poetry and dialogue between its author and divine beings, the content of the work is otherwise straightforwardly argumentative.

Reilly's allusion to Boethius's partially consistent "orbs" as "cycles" within which virtue can be practiced is clearly meant to explain why Reilly commits himself to the job of administrative assistant in the firm of Levy's Pants. In the course of Chapters 3 through 12, Reilly, for the first time in his life apparently, pursues goals related to matters in the external world. Mr. Levy pays little attention to the business of his firm, and Reilly takes advantage of this lack of supervision to thrust himself into a primary role of planner and innovator of firm tactics. None of them concerns the firm's manufacture of trousers. Instead he rearranges the filing cabinets, makes cardboard signs to direct employees' behavior, alters the format and content of office form letters, begins to write about his life as a leading employee, and influences Mrs. Levy's judgment of her husband's management style.

With all Reilly's resolve and energy as a worker, this orb of his life has no practical benefit for him or others, apart from everyone's smiling endorsement of his efforts. Indeed, this dimension of the novel is also one of the most humorous. It is ambiguous whether Reilly understands the humor of what he is doing: how can he not understand it, given his relentless invention of silly office projects, but how can he take those projects as seriously as he does, if he knows how silly they are? These unanswered questions, of course, reinforce the reader's enjoyment of the entire charade. What is less obvious is their relationship to the problem of Fortuna, with which Reilly has made clear that his commitment to Levy Pants began.

To see how, we must dwell further on the merit of Boethius's solution to the problem of moral luck. If Fortuna can deprive the most ardent moral agent of the worldly outcomes of good conduct, there cannot be reliable knowledge that good conduct will produce any valuable result. It is true that virtue in itself can be rewarding. Aristotle had argued that happiness, not pleasure, is the reward of virtue, and that this kind of happiness is entirely within the agent's mind. Virtue is a habit, or family of habits, gradually shaped by good deeds. It is something worth having, no matter what the purpose of the individual deeds may be. Yet Aristotle had to admit that if an agent's life is cut short, before the full development of all the habits needed for virtue, the agent is a failed member of the virtuous species, that is, not a member of the species after all. The same applies to an agent who inhabits and thrives within an orb that Fortuna rarely visits; no such orb can immunize its inhabitants against the random disappointment of bad luck. Put differently, Boethius does not solve the problem of luck's interference with moral conduct's purpose. He merely observes that *some* of us may not experience that interference, because there are continuous spheres of action within which—again by chance—the bad consequences of chance are absent.

The problem of Fortuna receives significant further development in Toole's novel. Above all, Reilly's humorous endurance of setbacks contrasts with Boethius's solemn bravery. Boethius withstood long imprisonment by Christian Vandals and had little else to think about except his ultimate execution at their hands. He was an emotional surveyor of the challenge that unequal fortune raised against the value of virtue, suggesting the pointlessness of virtue, and argues for the opposite view throughout *Consolation*. In fact, by writing the *Consolation*, Boethius exercised and perfected a sort of virtue, despite his impending doom, and despite the foreseeable interference of Fortuna. This indeed is what *Consolation* achieved for him: it was both consoling to him to fulfill the goal of writing this book as death awaited him and consoling to his readers to be given a Platonic solution to the ravages of bad Fortuna. For Reilly, on the other hand, the wheel of fortune, as he sometimes calls it, offers only opportunities to avoid responsibility by feigning it. His career at Levy's Pants and his escape from commitment to a mental institution at the end of the novel are both dodges aided by fate, rather than made worse by it. Thus, Toole's take on what Boethius called providence is to represent the irrationality of life as more like a playground's rides. One can fall off them and then get back on.

Along with Boethius, Reilly also invokes Plato in his journal,[17] not surprisingly, because Boethius and some of those he imitates had challenged pre-Stoic Greek classical tradition in ethics. Toole presumably understood Boethius's extraordinary and explicit reliance (*Consolation*, Bk 3, prose IX, 9–104) on Plato's Theory of Forms (Plato 2004, 51d–53c) and his mythic hypothesis concerning the Spindle of Necessity (*Id.* 614b–621c; Plato 1962, 47e–49b). Pre-Hellenistic Greek thought had uniformly made virtue and not goodness the focal concept of moral reasoning. Aristotle, following Plato's own articulation of Greek tradition, had made virtue a more central concept than the Good as a guide to value in human endeavor. The problem for this emphasis on virtue was that Fortuna casts extreme doubt on its reward. Although the highly accomplished warrior or athlete usually received not only society's approval but also the concrete benefits of their achievements, this was not inevitable. Boethius struggled with the fact that virtue's reward was not always accessible, and that Fortuna often conferred rewards randomly, without regard to virtue.

In Homer and the Greek tragedians, judgment of the value of conduct or character always stresses what is "seemly" and the alternative courses of conduct exemplified by one's fellows, usually only those in the same community. The earliest discussion we have of this view is in the *Republic*. Throughout this work, the primary subject is justice (*dikaiosune*), spoken of as a characteristic of both the state and the individual. Socrates's idea of individual justice is not a purely normative quality like moral goodness, but *excellence* (*arête*, also translated as "virtue"), a factual but also a normative trait—what modern philosophers have called a "thick concept."[18] Since social justice must be about rules of organization that protect the interests of individuals or groups within society, the individual counterpart is about something like choices of how to act so as to optimize the *soul*'s "management, rule, deliberation and the like" in order to be able to accomplish one's ends in the world (Plato 2004, 353d). Reilly's reference to Plato is best understood as referring to the Myth of Er in the *Republic*, where he postulates a process of metempsychosis in which those who had not been adequately virtuous in earlier lives were given another chance, until eventually metempsychosis came to an end and they escaped Hades to inhabit a nontraditional Greek heaven as reward for the quality of their accomplishment, even if the world had not rewarded them appropriately. Virtue had to have its reward. Plato, however, recounted Er's myth not as truth but as a dramatization of the problem.

The problem emerged soon after Plato's death as the groundwork of more than one movement with philosophical roots but no very serious philosophical aspirations. Plato's student Aristotle, his most important successor in advancing most fields of philosophy, took a labored approach to the details of virtue ethics. He also thought that happiness or flourishing (*eudaimonia*) depends on and follows from *arête*. There is a parallel with assumptions, or perhaps hints, contained in *Republic* Book II, where Socrates frames the question about justice that he will try to answer as: whether justice is desirable in itself or only for its consequences. He later indicates that justice in itself makes a person happy, although pleasure separately follows from or accompanies that happiness. Aristotle had also famously said that pleasure is to happiness as the bloom of youth is to youth. This of course suggests that virtue is its own reward, even if pleasure does not flow from it.

As should now be evident, the problem moral luck poses for modern subjectivist ethical theory also vexed the ancient view of virtue's, and its opposite shame's, supremacy in determining the goodness or badness of individual action. It is useful to note that modern morality and ancient virtue-based ethics do not judge human conduct in the same way. So different are they that it can be misleading to speak of both as rival schemes of morality or ethics. I will use both these terms here in order to stress their common subject matter, because they have the same goal in the valuation of conduct, despite approaching that task very differently.

Many interpreters of the *Republic* have thought that Plato's main quarry is the soul and not the city or state. If this is correct, then Plato must be using the terms *arête* and *dikaios* in ways that are not central or even common within our contemporary moral tradition. But at the *Republic*'s conclusion, Socrates recounts a fantasy about life after death for which he cautiously takes no personal responsibility. In an invented oracular tale, the Myth of Er, Plato obviously felt the need to give an account of free will (of humans and animals as well) that would reconcile this with "necessity," that is, causal determination of events in the world. No one had previously attempted anything of the sort, although Heraclitus, among others, ironically called attention to the problem with the surviving dictum, "Even the sun stays (must stay) within its boundaries" (Heraclitus). To explain how this works, Socrates recounts a fable told by the apparently imaginary sovereign Er. In it, souls (*psychai*) in Hades have their futures determined by a "spindle" of fate. The spindle gives those who have lived a life of virtue the immediate reward of an afterlife of happiness and satisfaction. Other souls are given indefinitely many "second" chances to achieve the same goal. The three fates Klotho, Lachesis, and Atropos turn the spindle, which assigns souls that are to be reincarnated to a place in a queue for choosing freely what characteristics they will have in their next lifetimes. (There is a close parallel between Plato's spindle of fate, which incorporates the moon and the planets' motions, and Anaximander's and Parmenides' similar spindles in similar myths.)[19] Plato was unable to decide whether reincarnation and "heaven or hell" rewards should take priority. His account awkwardly makes *post mortem* rewards permanent and punishments impermanent, though long lasting. Souls that do fail to get to heaven are given a completely unconditional new chance to choose their fates, apparently limited only in the order they are allowed to make their choices and in the number of predestined highs and lows available to be chosen. Odysseus chooses the humblest future lot, when he chooses his next life, just as Achilles in Hades had advised him that he himself would if he could only come back to life (Homer, Bk 12, ll. 484–491).[20]

Plato concocted the myth of Er to stress how damaging the problem of chance is for the Greek conception of individual justice (*dikaiosune*), the concept analogous in that era to modern morality. Ethical systems, and theorists of ethics, have tried hard to eliminate the element of *chance* from the individual's ethical success or failure. Plato does this in the myth of Er by giving the soul that is about to be reincarnated complete freedom to choose the character and life circumstances he or she will have. To show how impartial he was, Plato also gives animals the choice of becoming human and humans the choice of becoming animals. Consistent with his view of existence as including living beings of all kinds, this may be taken as a suggestion that animals can, like humans, be good or bad in a moral sense (Plato, 509d–511e).[21]

Necessity appears a second time in Plato's *Timaeus*, where the myth teller describes the world's mind as combining with necessity to determine the relationship between the Being of the Forms and the Becoming of worldly objects that participate in the Forms (Plato, 48a).[22] The account is too long to be summarized in detail, but it is notable that geometric sequences (*Id.* 42e–44a) play a more conspicuous role this time than they did in the Myth of Er and identifies the four elements (earth, air, fire, and water) with solid geometrical figures the cube, the octahedron, the tetrahedron, and the icosahedron. A "nurse" (*trophos*) mediates between mind and necessity to effect a world with sufficient reliability for purposive action despite its chaotic orbs (*Id.* 48e–49b). Although the *Timaeus* does not explain how these elements embody the Forms beyond giving them ideal geometrical shapes, the implication is that the realm to which the Forms belong, called "Sameness" here, determines the content of the realm of "difference" or motion and change (Plato 53c).[23] For our purposes, it is crucial that Boethius focused closely on this dialogue and its vision of how the levels of existence differ from and relate to each other. Indeed, the goddess Philosophy tells him that the Timaean cycles provide the best insight into the relationship between the *summum bonum* and imperfect worldly experience (*Consolation* III 99–104). Here in the *Consolation*, the association of "theology and geometry" is clearly made. What it implies, however, is that existence must have chaotic fringes in which the forms, including that of Goodness, are not faithfully and fully realized. If this is the nature of existence, then the purpose of moral effort cannot be worldly success but something more like "good form." Yet Boethius and Plato postulate that in the "orbs" where simplicity is stronger, so also is the likelihood that moral effort will yield approximate worldly success as well.

Reilly's belief that he was within an orb of life that made him safe from Fortuna's havoc[24] requires us to consider whether his reading of Boethius was satiric. Certainly, Reilly's vigorously teasing approach to his job at Levy's Pants makes this likely. In the novel, extremes of all sorts are the counterparts of the calmer Boethian slices of life. This, however, may be taken as a Toole's test of the role Boethius assigned to the safer and simpler orbs of reality, for there can be no reason to believe that the simplicity of the highest forms is found only in the most civilized circumstances. Indeed, Boethius's own circumstances—prison, the prospect of execution—cast doubt on the providential role of civilization.

Toole's selection of providential orbs of course included the interaction of Reilly with Myra Mynhoff. At the beginning of the novel, their relationship had been declared to be over. Reilly meditates on her, with uncritical admiration, and she writes letters to him in which she is harshly critical of almost everything about society and politics in the United States which the 1960s represented. A hippie with New York–based cynicism about where the country is going, she travels to take part in rough demonstrations for what she considers higher values, behaving as eccentrically and loosely as she can. She jibes at Reilly's failure to leave New Orleans and get a life. But at the end of the novel, she returns to save him from his mother's planned commitment of him to a mental institution. The chaotic content of Myra's personal views and her role as Reilly's redemptress place her in Fortuna's camp. She is unpredictable but in some cases exercises an upward pull. She is not the overwhelmingly negative and impersonal Fortuna of Boethius, who all the same technically did good as well as harm. The cycles of the wheel of fortune could be benevolent. Myra represents this. The novel leaves us to speculate whether Reilly and Myra will stay with each other, protecting him from his own foibles as an intellectual and her from the frustrations of too free a spirit.

In conclusion, Toole and Reilly both view the wheel of fortune as conferring benefits regardless of virtue or moral excellence. As "providential" as Boethius thought the resolution of moral luck might be, *Confederacy* demonstrates that it can simply provide an escape route for the eccentric. It may also be worthwhile to speculate that Toole believed this to be providential in a more traditional sense, given that some of the eccentrics who benefit from it deserve our sympathy. Their talents, though no fault on their part, are ill-suited to the world in which they live.

NOTES

1. *Confederacy*, 1–2.
2. Utz, 151–152.
3. Pope, 501–547.
4. Basho, 1994.
5. *Confederacy*, 30.
6. *Confederacy*, 30.
7. *Confederacy*, 72, 229, 268–271, 285, 386.
8. *Confederacy*, 99.
9. *Confederacy*, 288.
10. Williams, 20–39.
11. Williams, 24–25.
12. Scheffler, 2012.
13. Scheffler, 2013, 26.
14. *Confederacy*, 76
15. Greenblatt, *The Swerve: How the World Became Modern*, 2012.
16. *Confederacy*, 1.
17. *Confederacy*, 99.
18. Foot, 1958.
19. Morrison, 1955.
20. *The Odyssey*, 1974.
21. *Republic*.
22. *Collected Dialogues*.

23. *Collected Dialogues.*
24. *Confederacy*, 30, 76.

BIBLIOGRAPHY

Basho, Matsuo. *Narrow Road to the Deep North.* Trans. Nobuyuki Yuasa. New York: Penguin, 1967.

Boethius, Anicius Manlius Severinus. *Philosophical Tractates/The Consolation of Philosophy.* Ed. H.F. Stewart, E.K. Rand, and S.J. Tester. Loeb Classical Library, Harvard University Press, 2d ed., 1973 [524 CE].

Cicero, Marcus Tullius. *De Officiis* [*On Obligations*]. Trans. P.G. Walsh. Oxford: Oxford University Press, 2000 [44–46 BCE].

Foot, Philippa. "Moral Arguments." *Mind* 67 (1958).

Greenblatt, Stephen. *The Swerve: How the World Became Modern.* New York: W. W. Norton & Co., 2012.

Homer. *The Odyssey.* Trans. Robert Fitzgerald. New York: Doubleday Publishers, 1974.

Horace, Quintus. *Horati Flacci Opera.* Ed. Edward C. Wickham. Oxford: Oxford University Press, 1901.

Heraclitus. *Fragments of Heraclitus.* Ed. John Burnet, 1912.

Kirk, G. S., J. E. Raven and M. Schofield. *The Presocratic Philosophers. A Critical History with a Selection of Texts*, 2nd ed. Cambridge: Cambridge University Press, 1983.

Morrison, J. S. "Parmenides and Er." *Journal of Hellenic Studies* 75 (1955).

Percy, Walker. *The Moviegoer.* New York: Alfred A. Knopf, 1960 (Vintage ed. 1998).

Plato. *The Collected Dialogues of Plato.* Ed. Edith Hamilton and Huntingdon Cairns. Princeton: Princeton University Press, 1962.

———. *The Republic.* Trans. C. D. C. Reeve. Cambridge, MA: Hackett Publishing Co., 2004.

Pope, Alexander. "An Essay on Man." In *The Poems of Alexander Pope*, edited by John Butt. London: Methuen Press, 1963.

Scheffler, Samuel. *The Afterlife—The Tanner Lectures on Human Values.* Berkeley: University of California Press, 2012.

———. "The Importance of the Afterlife. Seriously." *New York Times.* September 21, 2013.

Toole, John Kennedy. *A Confederacy of Confederacy.* New York: Grove Press, 1980.

Utz, Stephen. "The Itch for Omniscience: Walker Percy and the Examined Life." *Explorations XXI Century* 13 (2016).

Väyrynen, Pekka. "Thick Ethical Concepts." In *The Stanford Encyclopedia of Philosophy*, edited by Edward N. Zalta, Summer 2019 Edition 2012, https://plato.stanford.edu/archives/sum2019/entries/thick-ethical-concepts/.

Williams, Bernard. *Moral Luck: Philosophical Papers 1971–1980.* Cambridge: Cambridge University Press, 1981.

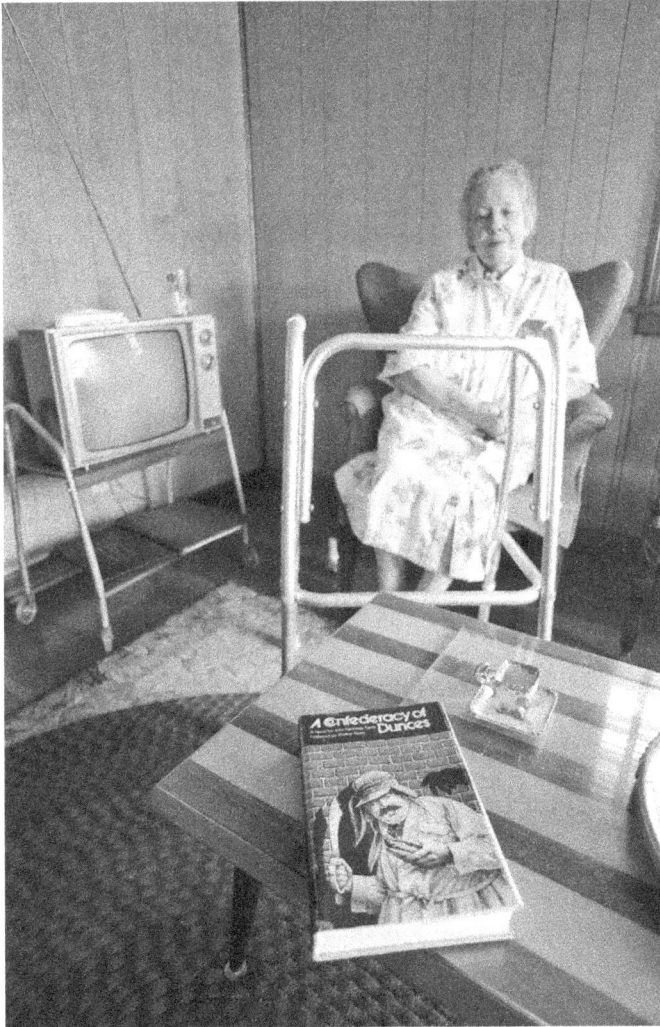

Figure 1 *Source*: Courtesy of Christopher R. Harris.

Figure 2 *Source*: Courtesy of Christopher R. Harris.

Figure 3 *Source*: Courtesy of Christopher R. Harris.

Figure 4 *Source*: Courtesy of Christopher R. Harris.

Chapter 6

Ignatius Reilly as the Knight of Faith

W. Kenneth Holditch

Despite the broad and outrageous humor of *Confederacy of Dunces*, readers should be aware that this novel is a philosophical and even a religious one. Certainly, readers may be amused at Ignatius Reilly's antics or may marvel at the collection of bizarre characters, the flamboyant language, the unique dialects, and the improbable events, but ultimately its primary significance lies on the level of Ignatius's worldview. Ignatius considers himself a medievalist trapped in an age devoid of "proper geometry and theology,"[1] lost in a time he does not understand and of which he does not approve, "a seer and philosopher cast into a hostile century."[2] His radical friend from New York, Myrna Minkoff, aptly envisions him as a monk, who has chosen to shut himself off from the modern world and live without love in his own medieval worldview.

Ignatius writes in one of his many Big Chief school tablets that "with the breakdown of the Medieval system, the gods of Chaos, Lunacy, and Bad Taste gained ascendancy."[3] He proclaimed the Middle Ages to be a time during which the Western world had enjoyed "order, tranquility, unity, and oneness with its True God and Trinity."[4] Then, he says, Fortuna's wheel—alluding to Boethius, a favorite philosopher of his—took a spin, "the luminous years of Abelard, Thomas à Becket, and Everyman dimmed,"[5] and an age of mercantilism followed, an age in which "what had once been dedicated to the soul was now dedicated to the sale."[6] Ignatius holds the age of Enlightenment in contempt, because it put the Western world on "the disaster course that history has taken for the past four centuries."[7] Ignatius's philosophy could very well have been articulated by Henry Adams, author and historian, who argued in his two major works, *Mont St-Michel and Chartres* (1904) and *The Education of Henry Adams* (1907, 1918), that in Western Europe, the Middle Ages produced an abundance of original thought and art, including the great soaring cathedrals. This age was characterized by unity—unity of religious belief, unity of philosophy, and unity of life styles. Adams believed that solidarity emanated from devotion to the Virgin Mary. The nineteenth and twentieth centuries, in contrast, were eras of multiplicity during which power had been dissipated in all directions. Religions and philosophies of life had proliferated, and people were no longer certain of anything. A cathedral, Adams argued, would not, could not be constructed in such an age, lacking as it did devotion to such a common unifying and power-generating factor as the Virgin. In his notebooks, Nathaniel Hawthorne remarks on a similar inclination, noting that Herman Melville appeared hungry to believe, but was unable to do so. The marked distinction between Henry Adams and Ignatius Reilly is, however, the fact that while Ignatius is a believer—Adams remained unconvinced. Despite his intense devotion to the Middle Ages and what it had accomplished, Adams seemed to passionately yearn for faith while Ignatius nourished his belief.

Seeing himself as a total anachronism in his unfriendly and heathen century, Ignatius continually berates the world around him. He deplores what has happened to the Catholic Church as well as to the pope. Although not named in the novel, Ignatius is probably referring to Pope John XXIII, who instigated major liberal changes in the Church. When his dog Rex died, his mother recalls, Ignatius "goes over to the priest and ax him to come say something over the dog."[8] When the priest refused, Ignatius conducted the ceremony himself and subsequently abandoned the Church.

The character of Ignatius certainly contains elements, albeit usually of an ironic and oblique nature, of what we know of several historical, religious icons, such as St. Thomas Aquinas, Martin Luther, Hroswitha, the German nun-poetess, Ignatius Loyola, and, from a later period, poet and polemicist John Milton. Like Aquinas and Luther, Ignatius is a pioneer and innovator—although in his case in a perverse way—rebelling against the status quo. Those two medieval thinkers and religious philosophers, on opposite sides of the great theological debate, were not afraid to bring new ideas to the forefront in the face of widespread rejection. Similarly Ignatius, almost in a parody of Aquinas and Luther, launches his attack on those institutions—the Church, popular culture, and the political establishment—that he deems to be inappropriate to the faith. Although Ignatius would seem to be at odds with Aquinas's piety and devotion to Roman Catholicism, Walker Percy perceives a relationship between the two when he refers to Ignatius as "a perverse Thomas Aquinas . . . an Aquinas gone to pot."[9] Toole's protagonist's connection to Martin Luther is even more ironic and "perverse," and Ignatius is something of a reverse image of his namesake, Loyola, the founder of the Jesuit order, who advocated an austere ascetic life. Finally, both Ignatius and Luther publicly displayed their printed protests against the current state of religion and both suffered from bowel complaints.

Hroswitha was a tenth-century German nun, abbess, and poet—the first known German female poet—who wrote using various poetic forms, including epics. Ignatius identifies her as "a sybil of a medieval nun," whom he views as a guide.[10] He tells Dorian Green that Hroswitha "could have predicted" that Green and his gay friends would take over the world. Hroswitha was also a playwright, who reputedly started writing dramas in order to combat the popularity of the Latin author Terence, whose comedies, sensual and erotic, were offensive to her and, she felt, too popular with other nuns. Thus Ignatius invokes her as one who would, because she represents for him the best and most spiritual elements of the medieval world, be opposed to the popular entertainments of his day—movies and television. Ignatius's protest, of course, takes a very strange, even bizarre direction. He watches television shows featuring teenaged dancers that offend his sensibilities almost as if deliberately to drive himself into a rage. He relishes contemporary movies such as *Jumbo* with Doris Day and Jimmy Durante, and romantic comedies, starring Doris Day and Rock Hudson while at the same time railing against them. Ironically, he decides not to go to the Prytania Theatre where a "Swedish drama of a man who is losing his soul" is playing, an allusion to the Ingmar Bergman film, *The Seventh Seal*, set in the Middle Ages. This movie is the artistic sort that Ignatius might be expected to relish, given his propensity for the medieval, but he is always, if anything, unpredictable, and therein lies a facet of his uniqueness as a character.[11]

Another medieval element in *Confederacy* and influence on the character of Ignatius is Dante's *Divine Comedy*. As Walker Percy observes, the novel itself is "a commedia"[12] surely in the same sense as Dante's epic. *The Readers' Companion to World Literature* defines commedia as "progress from grief to joy," from "damnation to heavenly bliss," an apt definition of the *Divine Comedy*. Although the conclusion of the novel finds Ignatius Reilly in a state of bliss, it hardly seems heavenly; the narrative does move from the grief of the tumult in front of D. H. Holmes Department Store and the subsequent automobile wreck and its uproarious, slapstick aftermath to the joy Ignatius experiences as he sucks on Myrna's pigtail while she drives the two of them out of the city of New Orleans.

New Orleans, or at least the French Quarter, comes to represent hell for Ignatius, as it does for characters in other novels, notably John Rechy's *City of Night*, and *Confederacy* frequently alludes to *The Divine Comedy*. While Ignatius pushes a Paradise Vendors hotdog wagon through the French Quarter, Toole often refers to infernos and purgatories throughout the book. Ignatius views the French Quarter both as Sodom and Gomorrah and as "an allegorical forest of evil"[13] in which a bus named almost hits him.[14] Ignatius, speaking of the "degenerates and wrecks and drifters"[15] in the Quarter that buy his hotdogs, sees himself as "trapped in a limbo of lost souls," although he sympathizes with them to a degree, he says, because "I have always been forced to exist on the fringes of its society, consigned to the Limbo reserved for those who do know reality when they see it."[16] These derelicts are "resounding failures in our century" imparts to "them a certain spiritual quality,"[17] since for him, the twentieth century is an abomination. "For all we know," he writes, "they may be—these crushed wretches—the saints of our age." However, this remark is undercut by a humorous aside: "whatever spiritual qualities it might possess, skid row is definitely sub-standard in the matter of physical comfort." In the spirit of the medieval era that he so admires, Ignatius sees New Orleans as one continuous allusion to hell.

Moving to the other end of the Christian spectrum, Ignatius has a medieval devotion to saints that verges on hagiology, though in an ironic, even comic sense. During his campaign to organize the factory workers at Levy Pants, he prays to "St. Martin de Porres, the patron saint of mulattoes," who "is also invoked against rats."[18] He envisions Batman as a modern media saint "who tends to transcend the abysmal society in which he's found himself" through his "rather rigid."[19] Ignatius writes in his "Journal of a Working Boy" that as he pushes his hotdog cart through the French Quarter, "Many a loud prayer rose from my chaste pink lips, some of thanks, some of supplication."[20] For Mr. Clyde, his employer, he prays to St. Mathurin, who was the patron of lepers and clowns, and because of his own digestive complaints, he invokes "St. Medericus, the Hermit, who is invoked against intestinal disorders." He prays as well to St. Zita of Lucca, who was devoted to household chores, to aid his mother "in fighting her alcoholism and nighttime roistering."[21] This "interlude of worship," he imagines, has strengthened him, and he feels "like a Crusader" as he proceeds into "the allegorical forest of evil" that the French Quarter is for him.

Ignatius is likewise devoted to the work of the Roman philosopher Boethius, whose ideas influenced Dante and other medieval authors and thinkers. The most famous work of Boethius, *The Consolation of Philosophy*, provides the major image and symbol of *Confederacy*, the Wheel of Fortuna. Ignatius insists that "a blind goddess spins us on a wheel," the *rota fortuna*, and that "our luck comes in cycles."[22] In the *Consolation*, the power of Fortuna upon human destiny is described by Boethius:

So with imperious hand she turns the wheel of change
This way and that like the ebb and flow of the tide,
And pitiless tramples down those once dread kings,
Raising the lowly face of the conquered–
Only to mock him in his turn.[23]

His obsession for "geometry" leads Ignatius to write of "small" cycles "within the larger bad cycle" for the "universe," which is "based upon the principle of the circle within the circle."[24] Boethius was a Christian convert whose worldview was founded on a combination of faith and reason, and from the latter he derived a method of thought that paved the way for St. Thomas Aquinas. Ignatius quotes Christian apologist and author G. K. Chesterton as saying that Boethius "truly served as a guide, philosopher, and friend to many Christians; precisely because while his own times were corrupt, his own culture was complete."[25] Ignatius surely sees himself in a similar role, guiding Dorian Green and his degenerate friends in the development of a new political "movement." His self-image is, after all, that of "a seer and philosopher cast into a hostile century."[26] On the other hand, he also states that "Boethius will show you that striving is ultimately meaningless, that we must learn to accept,"[27] an axiom that certainly does not govern Ignatius's actions.

The religious strain in Ignatius's character is conveyed in many oblique ways. In the opening scene of the novel, Ignatius judges his clothing to be "acceptable by any theological and geometrical standards,"[28] a passage that sets the tone for his view of himself as a spiritual person throughout the novel. Myrna reminds him that on one occasion he launched a project "to nominate a candidate for president by divine right,"[29] drawing on a decidedly medieval notion. Throughout the novel, he judges the world around him and its inhabitants, including himself, in theological terms. He creates a cross to use for his planned revolt of the workers against the management of Levy Pants but ironically uses gold leaf to inscribe "God and Commerce" on the symbol.[30] After the factory rebellion fails, he notes that he did not complain "since Pride is a Deadly Sin which I feel I generally eschew," a statement in which his doubts about his own infallibility are embedded. Surprisingly, given the havoc he wreaks at the plant, Mr. Levy retrospectively comments on Ignatius's idealism, stating that he believes his bizarre ex-employee really loved the plant and wanted to improve it.

Like the Catholic Church, Ignatius, despite "his absurdities and tics and postures and excesses,"[31] struggles over and over again to become a "spiritual instrument" for the other characters—and indeed, strange as it seems, does sometimes succeed. In his lecture on Toole and *Confederacy*, Robert Coles conceives of Ignatius as "a representation of the Catholic Church itself, struggling in the midst of a crooked and unjust and often enough quite crazy world."[32] Toole saw that, Church in the 1950s, Coles asserts, as still lacking and yet desiring "theology and geometry," a comment from the novelist that conveys, according to Coles, a message of "order, hierarchy, structure, interdependence—all under Heaven's exceedingly alert eyes!" Coles draws a parallel between Toole's creation and the ideas of Simone Weil, whose idea of "gravity and grace"[33] is similar to the "geometry and theology" about which Ignatius rails. Coles interprets Weil's use of "gravity" as "the ever-present 'weight' of our minds, our bodies," while grace is exhibited in "moments . . . of transcendence, strange moments, even unexpected ones." He is intrigued by analogies between Weil's "love for the Greek mathematicians," as well as love for the medieval church and an "adamant theology" with Ignatius's insistence on the need for geometry and theology. Coles concludes his analysis by insisting that we must remember "the wonderfully astute" Toole was "a dialectician in the Augustinian tradition, able to envision the Devil as a prodding if not provocative ally,"[34] thus authoritatively categorizing *Confederacy* as a novel in the Judeo-Christian tradition.

Despite the obvious connections between Ignatius and religion, his relationship to the church itself is ambivalent. When Irene Reilly "forced him to accompany her to mass on Sunday he had collapsed twice on the way to the church and had collapsed once again during the sermon about sloth."[35] Ignatius broke with what he called "the modern church" when the parish priest refused to bury his dog, Rex, and he observes on one occasion, "I have learned to expect little from today's clergyman."[36] The reason that he "cannot support the Church"[37] is the fact that the priest does not require more penance of his mother for what Ignatius sees as her egregious offenses. When Mr. Robichaux advises Irene to consult a priest about her obstreperous son, she replies that "Ignatius won't listen to no priest. He calls the priest in our parish a heretic,"[38] and she states on another occasion that "Ignatius don't like novenas either."[39] He is outraged that his mother buys beads supposedly containing water from Lourdes from the Jewish Lenny's store on Magazine Street, which Ignatius views with a jaundiced eye: "Never in my life have I seen a shop filled with so much religious hexerei. I suspect that that jewelry shop is going to be the scene of a miracle before long. Lenny himself may ascend."[40] On Santa Battaglia's television sits a statue of the Virgin Mary purchased from Lenny, which she names "Our Lady of the Television."[41]

Toole was fascinated and amused by the New Orleans version of Catholicism, which included veneration of saints, including St. Expedite, St. Zita, and St. Odo of Cluny. Like his mother and father, Toole grew up in the church, but by the time he went to college, both he and his parents seem to have abandoned regular attendance. Like many modern Catholics, they seem to have been devout in their own ways, while eschewing close association with the church or clergy. Thelma Toole once remarked to Joel Fletcher, a family friend, "that whenever she had to deal with a nun or a priest she always got a headache."[42] However, rejecting childhood faith is not an easy task, and Toole's fiction shows the strong influence of his upbringing. These attitudes again suggest the parallels between Ignatius and the views of Martin Luther and John Milton. Ignatius's catalog of the offenses of modern-day religion is a sort of ironic version of Martin Luther's theses, extending beyond the local priests to include the "current Pope" who is not his idea of "a good authoritarian Pope."[43] All the broad satire of religion in the novel serves finally as a serious comment on faith and theology in a world filled with dunces, as Ignatius and perhaps his author believe.

If Ignatius disparaged Catholicism, however, he reserved his most vehement attacks for Protestantism. When Myrna brands Protestants as "a class of humans who as a group specialized in ignorance, cruelty, and torture," he replies, "I am not too fond of them myself."[44] Although he says on more than one occasion that he emulates John Milton, the English poet and Protestant apologist, "spending my youth in seclusion, meditation, and study to perfect my writing skill," just as Milton had done,[45] he holds the Protestant faith of those like Milton in contempt. "White Protestants" he refers to as "a class of humans who as a group specialized in ignorance, cruelty, and torture,"[46] and he abhors "spirituals and those deadly nineteenth-century Calvinist hymns," preferring, of course, the medieval music of the lute. The black factory workers he organizes at Levy Pants sing

Oh, Jesus, walk by my side,
Then I always, always be satisfied
You take my hand
And I feel grand
Knowing you walking
Hearing me talking.[47]

Ignatius is offended by what he considers their "egregious blasphemy," even though he is not above using it for his own purposes.

Medieval thought is not the only Christian influence on Ignatius, for two contemporary authors—Walker Percy and Flannery O'Connor—had a marked effect on his worldview. What may have attracted Walker Percy to the novel, among other elements, was the fact that he recognized in it the same Christian Existentialist strain that was an integral part of his own fiction. Fittingly, Percy rescued *Confederacy* from oblivion, since John Kennedy Toole counted Percy, along with Flannery O'Connor, among his favorite writers. What must have drawn Toole to the works of these two seemingly disparate but philosophically similar authors is the fact that both are Christian writers. O'Connor, indeed, has been characterized by Jacques Barzun as a "Medieval Christian,"[48] whose work can only be understood if the reader puts her in the context of religion before St. Thomas Aquinas brought reason to bear upon it. Ignatius perceives of himself as a philosopher, and like the original thinkers in any age, he is an outsider, looked upon by many of those around him as a freak. Similarly, Flannery O'Connor's true believers, Francis Marion Tarwater in *The Violent Bear It Away*, for example, and Hazel Motes in *Wise Blood*—two unlikely "knights of faith," to use Soren Kierkegaard's phrase (*Fear and Trembling*)—are perceived as fanatics, whose behavior seems bizarre, even lunatic to the well-adjusted social types. These characters are reminiscent of some of the Old Testament prophets and of St. John the Baptist, outcasts from society but bearing the truth to those who will accept it. Perhaps viewing Ignatius in the same terms is a stretch, but Toole appears to have been impressed by those outcasts in O'Connor's fiction, as their religious faith is ultimately what matters. On the desperate trip across the country and back that preceded his suicide, he apparently made a pilgrimage to Milledgeville, Georgia, where O'Connor lived and is buried.

All three of these writers were strongly influenced by Soren Kierkegaard, who is generally acknowledged as the father of Christian Existentialism. The Danish philosopher argued that the modern human being who was a true believer, who has taken the leap of faith from the physical to the spiritual, to belief in God, becomes a Knight of Faith. As such, his actions might seem absurd to those not committed to belief, but he must persevere, much as T. S. Eliot at the end of "The Waste Land" suggests that to be a believer in the modern world is to be considered a fool and absurd. In the conclusion of the poem, Eliot uses a line from sixteenth-century English dramatist Thomas Kyd's drama, *The Spanish Tragedy*—"Why then Ill fit you. Hieronymo's mad againe"[49]—in which the character acknowledges that he will assume the guise of insanity to achieve his desired end. For Hieronymo, that desired end is revenge against those who killed his son, while the persona of "The Waste Land" is set on the quest for personal salvation, believing that source of salvation will "set my lands in order" regardless of what the mass of humanity may do. Kierkegaard left the Church because he felt that the institution had strayed from the path of truth and Ignatius follows a similar pattern.

Kierkegaard's consideration of faith exerts a clear influence on *Confederacy*. In his journal, the philosopher wrote,

> Faith therefore hopes also for this life, but, be it noted, by virtue of the absurd, not by virtue of human understanding, otherwise it is only practical wisdom, not faith. Faith is therefore what the Greeks called the divine madness.[50]

Kierkegaard advocated a life of self-examination in which the human being is not content to be resigned to things as they are but is rather committed to saving the soul. This attempt "to save my soul," he argues, is what makes one a knight of faith who may be forced to wear "the motley of the fool" but will not be deterred from his quest.[51] Through recognizing the absurdity and paradoxical nature of the world, one is set upon the right path. "The Christian heroism," he insists, "is to venture to be oneself, as an individual man, this definite individual man."[52] Abraham was Kierkegaard's greatest hero because he was capable of putting aside conventional ethics and heed the voice of God when it told him to slay his own son.

Throughout *Confederacy*, Toole hints that he was familiar with Kierkegaard, most notably in Ignatius's commitment to the absurd and his insistence on acting by his own lights, regardless of how foolish or even mad he may appear to others. In a reference to Original Sin, Ignatius tells Myrna Minkoff that he refuses to believe in the positive and eschews optimism as a philosophy. Humanity, since the fall of man, is doomed to suffering. When Myrna replies that she is not miserable, Ignatius assures her that she is though she may not know it, reflecting Kierkegaard's belief that most human beings live in despair and that "the specific character of despair is precisely this: it is unaware of being despair." Significantly, Walker Percy uses the quotation for the epigraph of his first novel, *The Moviegoer*.

For Kierkegaard, despair is the natural state of the human being. Living any sort of meaningful life is impossible unless the state of despair is recognized. Similarly, Walker Percy's characters struggle to free themselves from the malaise that everyday life imposes upon their existence. None of Percy's characters behave in a manner quite as outrageous and unorthodox as does Ignatius Reilly, and yet in their recognition of the absurdity of the world in which they live, they reflect many of the ideas Toole developed. Binx Bolling in *The Moviegoer* withdraws from active participation in much that was held sacred by his family because he felt it forced an identity upon him. In *The Last Gentleman*, Will Barrett ponders the fact that life in the modern world has become progressively more meaningless, so his ancestors beliefs and the actions they take seem impossible to him. In *Lancelot*, the protagonist, after discovering that his wife is unfaithful and that his child was fathered by another man, commits murder and is confined to a mental hospital in New Orleans, where he concludes that, in an insane world, only the insane man is at home. All Percy's protagonists, in short, recognize the confederacy of dunces, and although their reaction to the vicissitudes of modern existence are not as drastic as that of Ignatius, they are nevertheless alienated by the absurdity of the world around them.

Although attributing the belief of any character in a novel to its author, clearly Toole shared the faith of his creation, Ignatius, even if he was not so vehement in expressing his own views. Emilie Dietrich Griffin wrote about the time she spent in New York with the novelist: "Ken was a Catholic. In those days, I wasn't. We didn't talk much about religion, yet I knew being Catholic meant something to him—as a cultural stance if not on the level of belief." She recalled that he once wrote on the blackboard at Hunter College, "Anticatholicism is the antisemitism of the liberal," obviously having sensed some prejudice against his religion among the students, many of whom were Jewish. Griffin notes that Catholics were automatically considered nonintellectual in New York, whereas in New Orleans, quite the opposite was true: "I knew Ken cared about being Catholic, enough to get mad when he was patronized for it; enough to defend Catholicism as an intellectual stance; enough to write defensive slogans on the blackboard at Hunter." On the other hand, Griffin believed that Toole was not committed to religion: "Perhaps the only act of faith that Ken was capable of making was to write. I'm sure that writing is an act of faith." Griffin's analysis of her friend's relation to religion is valid, but I would argue that both intellectually and spiritually, the novel *Confederacy* demonstrates that he felt himself, consciously or unconsciously, to be a part of the church in which he had grown up and to share in the faith it espoused.

NOTES

1. *Confederacy*, 120.
2. *Confederacy*, 300.
3. *Confederacy*, 40.
4. *Confederacy*, 40.
5. *Confederacy*, 40.
6. *Confederacy*, 40.
7. *Confederacy*, 41
8. *Confederacy*, 371
9. Percy, vi.
10. *Confederacy*, 40.
11. It is obvious that these are the actors and the movies that Ignatius is watching, although Toole does not specifically name them.
12. Percy, vii.
13. *Confederacy*, 241.
14. The streetcars that ran on the Desire line were removed in 1948, and the "bus" seems an acknowledging nod on the part of John Kennedy Toole to Tennessee Williams, who is the one writer most responsible for creating the literary myth of the French Quarter.
15. *Confederacy*, 238.
16. *Confederacy*, 131.
17. *Confederacy*, 238.
18. *Confederacy*, 139.
19. *Confederacy*, 266–267.
20. *Confederacy*, 240.
21. *Confederacy*, 241.
22. *Confederacy*, 42.
23. Boethius, 179–181.
24. *Confederacy*, 87.
25. *Confederacy*, 281.
26. *Confederacy*, 300.
27. *Confederacy*, 351.
28. *Confederacy*, 13.

29. *Confederacy*, 224.
30. *Confederacy*, 125.
31. Coles, 8.
32. Coles, 7.
33. Coles, 3.
34. Coles, 9.
35. *Confederacy*, 20.
36. *Confederacy*, 65.
37. *Confederacy*, 72.
38. *Confederacy*, 213–214.
39. *Confederacy*, 205.
40. *Confederacy*, 89.
41. *Confederacy*, 273.
42. Personal interview between Joel Fletcher and Thelma D. Toole.
43. *Confederacy*, 64.
44. *Confederacy*, 136.
45. *Confederacy*, 112.
46. *Confederacy*, 136.
47. *Confederacy*, 152.
48. Barzun, 95.
49. Eliot, *Waste*, II.
50. Kierkegaard, 10.
51. Kierkegaard, 60.
52. Kierkegaard, 142.

BIBLIOGRAPHY

Barzun, Jacques. *From Dawn to Decadence: 1500 to the Present: 500 Years of Western Cultural Life*. New York: HarperCollins, 2001.

Brown, Calvin et al. *The Reader's Companion to World Literature*. New York: Penguin, 1956.

Coles, Robert. "Gravity and Grace in the Novel *A Confederacy of Dunces*." The Flora Levy Lecture in the Humanities. Lafayette: U of Southwestern Louisiana, 1981.

Eliot, T. S. "The Waste Land." In *Chief Modern Poets of Britain and America*. London: The Macmillan Company, 1970.

Fletcher, Joel. Letter to author. 2 July 2003.

Griffin, Emilie Dietrich, "Style and Zest: Remembering John Kennedy Toole." *Image* 24 (Fall 1999).

Kierkegaard, Soren. *Fear and Trembling and the Sickness Unto Death*. Trans. Walter Lowrie.

Garden City: Doubleday, 1954.

Percy, Walker. *The Moviegoer*. New York: Farrar, Straus and Giroux, 1961.

Percy, Walker. *The Last Gentleman*. New York: Farrar, Straus and Giroux, 1966.
Percy, Walker. *Lancelot*. New York: Farrar, Straus and Giroux, 1977.
Toole, John Kennedy. *A Confederacy of Dunces*. New York: Grove Press, 1987.

Chapter 7

John Kennedy Toole's Queer Carnivalesque in *A Confederacy of Dunces*

Tison Pugh

"That's what's so wonderful about New Orleans. You can masquerade and Mardi Gras all year round if you want to," Dorian Greene informs Ignatius J. Reilly in *Confederacy*, with his words highlighting the city's perennial carnivalesque pleasures.[1] Ignatius, in contrast, acknowledges his hometown merely as a cesspool of depravity, as "that sinkhole of vice."[2] Despite Ignatius's sourpussing, the carnivalesque, a comic mode predicated upon a topsy-turvy world order, pervades New Orleans and its annual hedonistic rituals surrounding Mardi Gras—an environment that John Kennedy Toole, a native New Orleanian, could hardly have avoided during his many years in the city. Given these conditions, it is not particularly surprising that a carnivalesque spirit spins throughout the inspired lunacy of his masterpiece, and reading this novel through the lens of the carnivalesque, particularly in its focus on the grotesque human body, its overturning of social rituals, and its lunatic humor, illuminates Toole's comedy by placing it in the context of such masterworks as Rabelais's *Gargantua and Pantagruel*.

At the same time, *Confederacy*, truly a sui generis work, expands upon previous iterations of the carnivalesque to construct an anti-procreative, anti-erotic, and uniquely queer version of this longstanding tradition. To date, few studies of Toole's work acknowledge his likely homosexuality as a key factor in interpreting his literature, yet in creating a queer version of the carnivalesque, *Confederacy* merges the reproductive possibilities of the carnival season with an anti-utopian underbelly, thereby severing comedy from its regenerative aspects yet ironically, paradoxically, and comically aligning it with tragedy's death drive. The distinction between comedy and tragedy, a longstanding but ultimately arbitrary division of artistic modes, crumbles in Toole's queer carnivalesque, which reorders the assumed telos of these literary genres in their disparate treatment of laughter and dying, instead framing the possibility of a comic gestation without end.

TOOLE AND THE LITERARY CARNIVALESQUE

In his seminal *Rabelais and His World*, Mikhail Bakhtin defines the carnivalesque and places it in its social and historical context, as he also establishes its broad contours and focuses on its particular enactments, paying close attention to its place in medieval folk culture: "As opposed to the official feast, one might say that carnival celebrated temporary liberation from the prevailing truth and from the established order; it marked the suspension of all hierarchical rank, privileges, norms, and prohibitions."[3] As Bakhtin's title indicates, Rabelais's *Gargantua and Pantagruel* models this carnivalesque spirit both of hierarchies overturned and of the grotesque, excessive body as a site of humor. The key to this suspension of ideological hierarchies, Bakhtin argues, emerges in the disruptive force of laughter, which implicitly, and often explicitly, questions a community's social structures: "Laughter is essentially not an external but an interior form of truth; it cannot be transformed into seriousness without destroying and distorting the very contents of the truth which it unveils."[4] Bakhtin also affirms that "exaggeration, hyperbolism, excessiveness are generally considered fundamental attributes of grotesque style."[5] As a whole, carnival seasons and carnivalesque literature enable a new view of the prevailing social order, one in which established truths are reassessed, if only during the carnival's duration.

Although the carnivalesque represents an escape from the quotidian structures of normalcy, laughter requires seriousness as its counterbalance, for we could not recognize carnival without temporal markers positioning it as the utopic break it is purported to be. In this light, some scholars locate in the carnivalesque an ultimate conservatism, as in Terry Eagleton's observation that

> carnival, after all, is a *licensed* affair in every sense, a permissible rupture of hegemony, a contained popular blow-off as disturbing and relatively ineffectual as a revolutionary work of art. As Shakespeare's Olivia remarks, there is no slander in an allowed fool.[6]

Given this tension between laughter and seriousness, between carnival's revolutionary potential and the ideological structures that allow it, Kobena Mercer states that in the carnivalesque "laughter's relationship to seriousness is one of antagonistic interdependence rather than logical incompatibility,"[7] an apt phrasing for the humor of *Confederacy*, in which Ignatius both unwittingly solicits the subversive comedy of his misadventures and stands in staunch opposition to humor in its various guises: in one of the text's defining ironies, he is the humorless center of an outrageously humorous novel.

Critics broadly agree that the carnivalesque, grotesque, and Rabelaisian themes running throughout *Confederacy* illuminate and elevate its humor, storyline, and characters. William Bedford Clark declares that "its comedy is unfailingly earthly, sometimes scatological, and frequently obscene. Toole's humor is not merely grotesque; it is at times unabashedly gross."[8] In a similar vein, John Lowe reads the novel as exemplifying "ethnic carnival," which he describes as a "liberating process [that] disrupts boundaries of all sorts, upending hierarchical structures and, ultimately, building new possibilities for community, thereby countering separation, scapegoating, and typecasting."[9] In more generally comic terms, David McNeil suggests that the novel is a "reverse satire" because Ignatius "embodies the very perversions against which he rages,"[10] and Wesley Britton, reading the novel for its allegorical structure and themes, proposes that its allegorical form "see[s] ideological conflicts in terms of medieval topology" and concludes, in contrast to the novel's Boethian themes, that "the consolation is not in philosophy but in the force of laughter."[11]

Beyond the general theme of the world turned upside-down, Bakhtin specifies the human body's role in carnivalesque humor, particularly in its grotesque, exaggerated, and earthly incarnations: "The grotesque body . . . is a body in the act of becoming. It is never finished, never completed; it is continually built, created, and builds and creates another body." Bakhtin also proposes that the bowels and the phallus "play the leading role in the grotesque image, and it is precisely for this reason that they are predominantly subject to positive exaggeration, to hyperbolization."[12] This body, as incarnated in Ignatius Reilly, is represented through its insistent earthiness—as a farting, belching, excreting body freed from any sense of civilization or decorum. Ignatius continually focuses on his digestive "valve" (*"Everyone has a valve!* . . . I am trying to open a passage which you have succeeded in blocking," he cries),[13] and Toole often foregrounds the demands of Ignatius's body, as when his protagonist attempts to convince his mother that he need not converse with Mr. Levy: "Mother, I must attend to my bowels."[14] Toole also foregrounds Ignatius's phallic pleasure in his frequent masturbating, such as when he turns to self-pleasure to console himself after the tumultuous and climactic events at Lana Lee's Night of Joy: "Ignatius spent the day in his room napping fitfully and attacking the rubber glove during his frequent, anxious moments of consciousness. . . . He lunged at the glove, deflowering it, stabbing it, conquering it."[15]

In recognition of these and other such scenes, various readers overwhelmingly concur on Ignatius's carnivalesque and grotesque aspects, thus cementing the novel's place in carnivalesque traditions. Elizabeth Bell identifies him simply as a "grotesque anti-hero,"[16] Andrei Codrescu sees him as a "gargantuan slob,"[17] and Lloyd Daigrepont agrees that "in Ignatius the child and the man are grotesquely combined."[18] Robert Rudnicki, turning his attention to key literary authors, traditions, and genres that influenced Toole, explores Ignatius's verbosity as reflective of John Lyly's *Euphues: The Anatomy of Wit*, while also acknowledging the ways in which Ignatius "is informed by the Rabelaisian tradition."[19] Noel Harold Kaylor views Ignatius as a "grotesque caricature of a medieval monk in his mother's home."[20] Richard Patteson and Thomas Sauret align Ignatius's exaggerated physicality to the novel's comic themes: "Hyperbolic descriptions of Ignatius's physique . . . give the novel a mock-epic dimension, but they also emphasize his gluttony, his grotesqueness, and his physical alienation from people."[21] William Nelson links the novel's comic mode with Ignatius's alienating demeanor—"the comic grotesque mode presents a topsy-turvy universe in which even the absurd hero is only remotely sympathetic"[22]—and, indeed, Robert Regan assesses not only Ignatius but all of the novel's characters as grotesques: "*A Confederacy of Dunces* is filled with characters of all varieties: each is a grotesque, but each is recognizably real."[23] In sum, critics have spoken with near unanimity of Toole's carnivalesque themes and grotesque characterizations.

The carnivalesque spirit of *Confederacy* merges surprisingly well with Ignatius's favorite book, Boethius's *The Consolation of Philosophy*, for both the novel and the philosophical tome are structured on Fortune's reversals. As Ignatius writes, in one of his Big Chief tablets, "Fortuna's wheel had turned on humanity, crushing its collarbone, smashing its skull, twisting its torso, puncturing its pelvis, sorrowing its soul. Having once been so high, humanity fell so low,"[24] and he similarly proclaims, "Since man's fall, his proper position in the universe has been one of misery."[25] Although on many levels thematically and stylistically opposed, both tragedy and comedy can be narratologically structured upon reversals—from high to low for tragedy, from low to high for comedy—with Toole exploiting this overlap. Certainly, as Northrop Frye notes, "The tragic hero is typically on top of the wheel of fortune, halfway between human society on the ground and the something greater in the sky"[26]—an apt expression of Ignatius's view of his circumstances. When Mancuso, apprising *The Consolation of Philosophy*, determines that "it wasn't the kind of book that exactly made you look up to the brighter side,"[27] Toole's ability to wring wry humor from Boethius's philosophical musings testifies to the power of the carnivalesque in his fiction.

Still, as much as the outrageous revelries of Mardi Gras define New Orleans's character for much of the popular imaginary, and as much as Boethius's *The Consolation of Philosophy* can be adapted to a comic framework in its attention to the turning wheel of Fate, it is also worth questioning any simple correlations between the carnivalesque and Ignatius's adventures. After all, Ignatius himself does not celebrate the city's revelries, instead praising his hometown for its lackadaisical, if not desultory, ethos, declaring that "New Orleans is . . . a comfortable metropolis which has a certain apathy and stagnation which I find inoffensive."[28] Moreover, in some readings of *Confederacy* as a carnivalesque novel, critics overstate the influences of this theme, such as when John Lowe exaggerates Ignatius's carnivalesque spirit, declaring that "Ignatius is the perfect king of Carnival, a fact signified by the name of his much-beloved, now-deceased collie, Rex, the title of the most legendary of the Mardi Gras krewes."[29] The "perfect king of Carnival" might inhabit one of two rules—the true king who allows the carnival to occur or the mock king who assumes this role for the day and leads the festivities—yet both of these positions appear inapt for Ignatius. Certainly, Ignatius does not lead the carnivalesque events of *Confederacy* as much as he leaves them in his wake. Furthermore, while Lowe is correct to identify Rex as one of the leading Mardi Gras krewes, Ignatius's deceased dog more specifically symbolizes his lost faith after this pet died, with the name alluding to the heavenly Rex/King and Miss Annie articulating this connection for readers: "Then the dog dies. . . . The priest says no [about a funeral for Rex], and I think that's when Idnatius left the Church."[30]

Thus, while it is surely true that Ignatius incarnates a grotesque body, it is less clear that he personifies the carnivalesque as a whole, particularly because he aligns himself with the authority figures against whom the carnivalesque celebrates. He vehemently endorses monarchies over democracies: "What I want is a good, strong monarchy with a tasteful and decent king who has some knowledge of theology, geometry, and to cultivate a Rich Inner Life."[31] In another such moment, Ignatius condemns any possibility that the Catholic Church would loosen its dogmas or hierarchies: "I do not support the current Pope. He does not at all fit my concept of a good, authoritarian Pope. Actually, I am opposed to the relativism of modern Catholicism quite violently."[32] These words do not reflect their speaker's carnivalesque attitude, and thus they suggest the limitations to the carnivalesque as indicative of Toole's comic ambitions in *Confederacy*.

Further along these lines, Ignatius rails against cinema's carnivalesque potential, again displaying his hostility toward comedy in its various guises. Moviegoing need not necessarily be a carnivalesque entertainment, depending largely on the subject matter of a given film, yet in most instances the journey to the theater entails the decision to leave the everyday world and to enter a space of recreation. At the theater, Ignatius thunders against any movie he views. "What degenerate produced this abortion?" he shouts, and "thank God that scene is over," he sighs after a musical's chorus number. Following its love scene, Ignatius pronounces disgustedly of the actors, "They probably have halitosis. . . . I hate to think of the obscene places those mouths have doubtless been before."[33] Richard Patteson identifies this film as *Billy Rose's Jumbo* (1962), a musical comedy starring Doris Day, Jimmy Durante, and Martha Ray, noting that it "played the Prytania Theatre (where Ignatius sees it) from February 22 to February 28, 1963."[34] A musical set in a circus, *Billy Rose's Jumbo* depicts a carnivalesque storyline, and so it exemplifies Ignatius's virtually masochistic relationship to carnival in that he obsessively returns to the theater only to engage with the scopophilic "pleasures" that he finds so offensively distasteful. Later Ignatius proclaims to Mr. Clyde, the proprietor of Paradise Vendors, "Actually, I have seen every film that is playing downtown, and since they are all offensive enough to be held over indefinitely, next week looks particularly bleak."[35] He soon reiterates his anti-carnivalesque stance against comic films, again in conversation with Mr. Clyde: "The film I saw last night was especially grueling, a teen-age beach musical. I almost collapsed during the singing sequence on surfboard."[36] On a similar note, Miss Trixie, Ignatius's compatriot against humor, rejects the carnivalesque: "if this is some sort of an April Fool, I don't think it's funny,"[37] she tells Mr. Levy after learning that her beloved friend "Gloria" has been fired. An anti-carnivalesque, carnivalesque novel, *Confederacy* celebrates this tradition through its comedy while Ignatius condemns the world turned upside-down for its lack of "any theological and geometrical standards,"[38] resulting in a novel that posits a uniquely queer version of the carnivalesque.

TOOLE'S QUEER CARNIVALESQUE

Throughout critical discussions of Toole and *Confederacy*, a surprising hush surrounds his potential homosexuality and its likely influence on his writing. Of course, this very issue generates controversy. In their biography *Ignatius Rising: The Life of John Kennedy Toole*, René Pol Nevils and Deborah George Hardy speak with acquaintances who recall the ambiguity of Toole's erotic life and point to incidents suggestive of his homosexuality, yet their work has been harshly criticized for its presumptive use of evidence.[39] Leslie Marsh denounces *Ignatius Rising* as suffering from "low-grade psychological speculation,"[40] and Cory McLaughlin concludes in his biography of Toole, *Butterfly in the Typewriter: The Tragic Life of John Kennedy Toole and the Remarkable Story of a Confederacy of Dunces*,

> It is possible, as it is for any human being, that Toole had desires other than het-
> erosexual ones, but there is no firsthand evidence and no credible testimony to
> the fact. . . . Delving into such murky waters offers little more than sensational-
> ism to the story of his life. And . . . because it is mere conjecture, the suggestion
> has no bearing on the merit of his artistic work.[41]

Further along these lines, one could well argue that authors' sexualities bear little influence on the reception of their literature, citing the bromide of the "death of the author" as a subject of critical inquiry.[42]

The primary problem with any such contention that Toole's potential homosexuality would have borne little consequence to his literature, however, is that it is little short of ludicrous, particularly in considering the careers of mid- to late twentieth-century gay and lesbian Southern authors, including Tennessee Williams, Truman Capote, Rita Mae Brown, and Alice Walker. To propose that any of these authors' sexualities did not measurably affect their literary output overlooks the ways in which sexuality figured determinatively in their lives and figures as well in their narratives' meanings. It is difficult to conceive of such characters as Tennessee Williams's Blanche Dubois in *A Streetcar Named Desire*, Truman Capote's Joel Harrison Knox in *Other Voices, Other Rooms*, Rita Mae Brown's Molly Bolt in *Rubyfruit Jungle*, and Alice Walker's Celie in *The Color Purple* without their authors' unique comprehension of social and sexual otherness. These overarching conditions hold equally true for John Kennedy Toole and the bizarrely yet humorously anti-erotic Ignatius Reilly, as evident in his determined evasions of Myrna Minkoff's advances, which are recalled by his neighbor Miss Annie: "'Put down that skirt.' and 'Get off my bed.' And 'How dare you? I'm a virgin.'"[43]

And so, to strike a middle path between Nevils and Hardy's presumption of Toole's homosexuality and McLaughlin's dismissal of it due to the lack of incontrovertible evidence, one can posit that, while it is unclear if Toole were gay, he was certainly queer in his erotic life, with the critical term *queer* fracturing the binary between gay and straight. Certainly, like Ignatius, Toole appeared disinclined to pursue romantic relationships with women; at the very least, no record attests to a long-term relationship that moved beyond rather chaste good-night kisses.[44] Moreover, Toole aligned himself with his protagonist, declaring in a letter to editor Robert Gottlieb that "this book became more real to me than what was happening around me: I was beginning to talk and act like Ignatius. No doubt this is why there's so much of him."[45] Suzanna Danuta Walters posits the radical potential of queerness to reassess prevailing codes of gender, theorizing it "as somehow beyond gender, a vision of a sort of transcendent, polymorphous perversity deconstructing as it slips from one desiring/desired object to the other," and also affirming that "*queer* is not gender specific" and so it seeks "to dethrone gender as the significant marker of sexual identity and sexual expression."[46] In this light, queerness offers a viable means of discussing Toole's sexuality in relation to his literature, for it avoids the taxonomic clarity of homosexuality in favor of a broader, more protean sense of the erotically non-heteronormative in its myriad permutations.

Like Toole himself, Ignatius can be definitively labeled neither gay nor straight, yet he appears queer in his decidedly unique sexual desires. For the most part, he appears stringently anti-erotic, and Mrs. Reilly, perplexed by his asceticism, frequently encourages her son to take a sexual interest in women: "They got strippers in here at night, huh?" she wheedles suggestively at the Night of Joy.[47] Ignatius, however, affirms his anti-erotic stance, telling his mother, "You know how I feel about touching other people."[48] As mentioned previously, Ignatius repeatedly rebuffs Myrna Minkoff's sexual advances, testifying to his predominant anti-eroticism, yet counterbalancing these scenes, he feels the flame of heteroerotic desire when gazing at Lana Lee's pornographic photograph: "A nude woman was sitting on the edge of a desk next to a globe of the world. The suggested onanism with the piece of chalk intrigued Ignatius." Upon noticing the copy of *The Consolation of Philosophy* in her hand, he stammers in excitement, "Do I believe what I am seeing? What brilliance. What taste. Good grief."[49] Building on this moment, Toole adumbrates the likelihood that Ignatius's anti-eroticism merely cloaks his deep-seated anxieties concerning his lack of sexual experience: "He would describe every lush moment with this scholarly woman. With her background and Boethian worldview, she would take a very stoic and fatalistic view of whatever sexual gaucheries and blunders he committed."[50]

Furthermore, while these episodes suggest that Ignatius's queer sexual desires fall primarily within the realm of the anti-erotic and of the anxiously heteronormative, a key passage indicates as well the necessity of allowing for Ignatius's occluded homosexuality. When Santa Battaglia advises Mrs. Reilly on her love life, admonishing her to accept Mr. Robichaux's advances, she declares pointedly, "What you need is a man in that house, girl, to set that boy straight,"[51] a scene of which Michael Hardin proposes, "We should allow for the possibility that Toole is teasing us about Ignatius's sexuality."[52] And while Ignatius does not express any homosexual desires personally, he views himself as arousing such affections, such as when denounces the French Quarter as a "Sodom and Gomorrah" and declares, "I will probably be kept very busy every moment protecting my honor against those fiends who live down there."[53] Myrna alludes to the possibility of Ignatius's homosexuality in her pointed comment that "Freud linked paranoia with homosexual tendencies,"[54] and George blatantly identifies Ignatius as gay: "You big crazy fruit. . . . Who wants to eat anything your fruity hands touched?"[55]

Viewing Ignatius as a queer protagonist, one who eludes the homosexual/heterosexual binary, illuminates the various contradictions of his character while attuning readers to the ways in which queer potential permeates the novel's comic form. As he does with his queer protagonist, Toole encodes *Confederacy* not with a standard version of the carnivalesque but a queer incarnation that smashes normative boundaries. Limning a key aspect of the medieval carnivalesque, Bakhtin connects the festival season to rebirth:

The gaping mouth, the protruding eyes, sweat, trembling, suffocation, the swollen face—all these are typical symptoms of the grotesque life of the body; here they have the meaning of the act of birth. . . . [A] highly spiritual act is degraded and uncrowned by the transfer to the material bodily level of childbirth, realistically represented.[56]

Carnival is in many ways a season of rebirth and rejuvenation, and thus this theme is germane to the comic spirit that pervades *Confederacy*, yet a key argument of queer theory emphasizes the rebellious power inherent through an anti-reproductive stance. Gay people cannot reproduce without external assistance (e.g., sperm or egg donors, surrogate mothers), and their inability to do so has long opened a key line of attack against homosexuality and gay marriage, based on the (specious) argument that the covenant of marriage is designed for child-raising.[57] Yet rather than seeing this anti-reproductive allegation simply as a shameless denigration to the sanctity of gay lives and loves, some queer theorists have taken this slur as a provocative challenge for rethinking the ideological promotion of childbirth and its implicit embrace of futurity. As Lee Edelman explains, "the death drive names what the queer, in the order of the social, is called forth to figure: the negativity opposed to every form of social viability."[58] In these iterations, queerness aligns with the death drive, advancing a revolutionary, if ultimately moribund, vision of the future freed from the shackles of reproductive optimism. For *Confederacy*, these dynamics result in a carnivalesque in which the riotous humor is accompanied by a subversive, alienating deprecation of the future's very possibility—an encoding of the ultimate tragedy of humanity's demise within the framework of riotous humor.

In his queer framing of the carnivalesque, Toole continually degrades images of maternity and childbirth, contaminating them with images of feces and stillbirth. Lana Lee sullies the cultural ideal of the expectant mother awaiting her baby's birth, opining instead that "mothers are full of shit,"[59] an image she builds upon by referring to Mrs. Reilly and Ignatius as an "old lady and a fat turd."[60] The social importance of reproduction divides Mrs. Reilly and Ignatius, with the former hoping that the latter will embrace both a wife and future fecundity. Reminiscing over Myrna, Mrs. Reilly proposes, "Maybe you shoulda married her. You two might of settled down and had a nice baby or something."[61] Ignatius's stance on reproductive eroticism shifts in various moments of the novel, as evident in the "pile of articles he had once written with an eye on the magazine market," which include the opposing titles "Children, the Hope of the World" and "Abstinence, the Safest Method of Birth Control."[62] Of these two positions, however, he appears to lean decidedly in the direction of the latter. He informs his mother of his fervent hope that the current generation will be the last: "I also told the students that, for

the sake of humanity's future, I hoped that they were all sterile."[63] After Ignatius begins his job at Levy Pants, Mrs. Reilly asks him expectantly, "They
got any cute girls working there?," and Toole recounts her son's response:
"Ignatius thought of Miss Trixie and said, 'Yes, there is one.'"[64] The line is
certainly humorous, yet because Ignatius often fulminates at his mother yet
rarely jokes with her, it seems at least possible that Ignatius is serious in his
reply. Is Ignatius attracted—intellectually, sexually—to Miss Trixie? The
question falters at the moment of its enunciation, for Ignatius's stringent
asexuality admits of few attractions except in such bizarre moments as this
one, which broach the potential of eroticism only to link it to the impossibility of reproduction. Further along these lines, Ignatius expresses his hope that
the uprising at Levy Pants will cause jealousy to "gnaw at Myrna's musky
vitals"[65]—an envisioning of her reproductive organs not as a site of desire or
fecundity but of barrenness and despair.

Both of Ignatius's planned revolts against the current world order are
predicated upon nonreproductive eroticisms—the solipsistic masturbatory
pleasures evident in the Levy Pants uprising and the homosexual revolution
planned at Dorian Greene's French Quarter party. In regard to the former,
Ignatius's masturbatory habits are detailed throughout the novel, with an
early indication appearing in Toole's description of Mrs. Reilly's fingers as
"chafed from many years of scrubbing her son's mammoth, yellowed draw-
ers";[66] the reader later sees "Mrs. Reilly hanging a spotted and yellowed sheet
on a line that ran through the bare fig trees."[67] Fig trees symbolize infertility
and sterility in numerous artworks, alluding to Jesus's curse of a fruitless tree:
"When he came to it, he found nothing but leaves, for it was not the season
for figs. He said to it, 'May no one ever eat fruit from you again'" (Mark
11.13–14).[68] The narrator details Ignatius's skills in this ultimately fruitless
endeavor: "At one time he had almost developed it into an art form, practicing
the hobby with the skill and fervor of an artist and philosopher, a scholar and
gentleman."[69] An emblem of his masturbatory desires, Ignatius's bed sheets
assume another symbolic cast when he uses them as part of his rebellion at
Levy Pants: "Ignatius was at last vertically atop the long table, holding the
bundled bed sheet over his pelvis to hide from his audience the fact that
during the process of being lifted, he had become somewhat stimulated."[70]
Ignatius's erect penis at this moment of rebellion testifies to his desires not
for reproductive sexual congress but to dismantle the current political order,
as further evident in the bed sheet symbolizing his past erotic pastimes.
Toole then bolsters the scene's anti-erotic humor, noting that "among the
yellow stains the word FORWARD was printed in high block letters in red
crayon. Below this *Crusade for Moorish Dignity* was written in an intricate
blue script."[71] In response, the workers ironically begin to protest not the
working conditions at Levy Pants but the stains on Ignatius's bed sheets. "I

ain putting my hand on that," one employee declares, with another crying out, "I wonder who been sleepin on that old thing."[72] The narrator discreetly adds, "Several other prospective rioters expressed the same curiosity in more explicitly physical terminology."[73] Explaining the bed sheet's signification, Ignatius attempts to rally his troops, yet his words are contradicted by its imagery: "'Sheet? What sheet!' Ignatius replied. 'I am holding before you the proudest of banners, an identification of our purpose, a visualization of all that we seek.'"[74] Whereas the bed sheet's words urge united action, its semen stains tacitly advocate solitary and anti-reproductive pleasures, a queer resignification of Ignatius's purported aims that, much like his masturbatory indulgences, lead to nowhere.

Following the failure of the Levy Pants rebellion, Ignatius soon identifies a new means of overthrowing the contemporary ideological order, yet one that is likewise predicated upon the rejection of reproduction. Determining that gay men are "the hope for the future"—a comically ironic line, in terms of their likely reproductive potential—Ignatius sighs, "There certainly doesn't seem to be anything else very promising on the horizon."[75] Dorian Greene also stresses the anti-reproductive element of Ignatius's planned revolution—"We would also help to end the population explosion," he declares,[76] a mordant assessment of the queer carnivalesque world that Ignatius seeks to inspire. Certainly, Ignatius agrees with Dorian's assessment while also disclosing his hope for anti-reproductive heterosexuals as well: "Your method would probably be more satisfying and acceptable than the rather stringent birth control tactics which I have always advocated."[77] In lines dripping with irony, Ignatius declares to Dorian, "Although I had never considered it before, you may hold the key to the future,"[78] yet a "future" with an expiration date coupled to it in the loss of reproduction. Ignatius writes in his journal, "Degeneracy, rather than signaling the downfall of a society, as it once did, will now signal peace for a troubled world. We must have new solutions to new problems."[79] Surely one could label this a carnivalesque image, one that highlights Toole's propensity for inverting the standard ideological order throughout Ignatius's adventures, yet it is a carnivalesque image that explicitly imagines not only the end of carnival but also the end of the entire social order that enables carnival. At the climactic moment of this storyline, as Ignatius hopes to incite Dorian Greene's guests to action, he cries out, "The challenge . . . is placed before you. Will you turn your singular talents to saving the world, or will you simply turn your backs on your fellow man?"[80] Given that these words are spoken to a room of gay men, who "turn their backs on their fellow man" during their most intimate encounters, the scene's comic excesses are coupled with a vivid rendering of the anti-reproductive nature of sodomy.

Still, as much as Ignatius's anti-eroticism and anti-futurism infuse the carnivalesque impulses of *Confederacy* with a queer frisson and a tragic underbelly of sterility, Toole balances these themes through his treatment of Mr. Levy's rebirth. In many ways, Mr. Levy models the anti-reproductive potential of heterosexuality in his strained relationship with his wife and his daughters Susan and Sandra. When Mrs. Levy upbraids him, "You've never been a father figure to Susan and Sandra," Mr. Levy answers, "The last time Sandra was home, she opened her purse to get cigarettes and a pack of rubbers falls on the floor right at my feet."[81] This brief exchange condemns Mr. Levy for his paternal failings, with Sandra's condoms stressing the potential for anti-reproductive eroticism to prematurely end Mr. Levy's paternal line. In another such exchange, Mrs. Levy again chastises Mr. Levy for his failings: "The least that you've always given them has been material comfort. Susan and Sandra will hate to know that they could have ended up as prostitutes or worse," to which Mr. Levy replies, "They might at least have made some money at it. As it is, they're all for free."[82] Certainly, readers know to distrust Mrs. Levy's pop-psychology diagnoses of her husband's failings, as the narrator reports her dismal performance in a correspondence course, "The final examination of which she had failed resoundingly. The correspondence school had even refused to give her an F";[83] however, when she tells Mr. Levy. "Now I know why you've drifted, why you don't have any ambition, why you've thrown a business down the drain. . . . You have the death wish,"[84] she appears to have struck upon a key aspect of his psyche.

Rehabilitating Mr. Levy from his death wish thus allows Toole to spin from the novel's anti-reproductive and queer carnivalesque to its normative counterpart, as Mr. Levy is symbolically reborn. Evident in the novel's imagery of childbirth, Mr. Levy's house is described as a womb: "the interior was a successful attempt at keeping the rustic out entirely, a permanently seventy-five-degree womb connected to the year-round air-conditioning unit by an umbilicus of vents and pipes."[85] In short, Mr. Levy suffers from arrested development, of ensconcing himself in the maternal womb, so as to avoid life's challenges. Ignatius's plans for Levy Pants include inspiring Mr. Levy into his rebirth—"I, for one, will eventually make Mr. Levy decide to put his heart and soul in the firm"[86]—and by the novel's end, Mr. Levy realizes the symbolic value of Levy Pants:

> A neglected Levy Pants was like a neglected child: it could turn out to be a delinquent that created all sorts of problems that a little nurture, a little care and feeding could prevent. The more you stayed away from Levy Pants, the more it plagued you. Levy Pants was like a congenital defect, an inherited curse.[87]

In aligning Levy Pants with neglected children, Toole leavens his anti-erotic carnivalesque with a comic emphasis on marriage and reproduction. The queerly carnivalesque world of *Confederacy* comes to the reluctant conclusion that children are necessary for the future, but with the grim vision of them as a "congenital defect, an inherited curse." And so this storyline ends as Mr. Levy realizes, "That Reilly kook had really been worth saving after all. He had saved himself, Miss Trixie, and Mr. Levy, too, in his own kook way"[88]—a statement of the necessity of kooks both for the saviors and the saved.

At the novel's conclusion, Toole's queer carnivalesque escapes the temporal binary that structures carnival pastimes, for in most instances, it is either carnival time or it is not, with the clock striking midnight on Mardi Gras signaling the party's end. Instead, Toole imagines a carnivalesque in which potential riotousness might emerge at any moment. Myrna earlier admonishes Ignatius, "Get out of that womb-house for at least an hour a day,"[89] and Ignatius appears to be heeding this advice when he flees with her from New Orleans. Still, his wooing words to her—"The scent of soot and carbon in your hair excites me with suggestions of glamorous Gotham. . . . I must go flower in Manhattan"[90]—collapse under their inherent ridiculousness. It is likewise difficult to hear true romantic ardor as he presses forward: "Quickly. To a motel. My natural impulses are screaming for release."[91] Noting the novel's interest in images of children and childbirth, William Bedford Clark admonishes that "it is worth remembering that [Ignatius] assumes the fetal position upon entering Myrna's car,"[92] as the novel's final image shifts from his mother's attempt to commit him to a mental hospital to the perpetual stasis of gestation: what could possibly be born next, as he travels in Myrna's car? In Lana Lee's words, as quoted previously, "Mothers are full of shit," but the novel appears to end with the potential of autonomous reproduction, as Ignatius will birth himself in the undepicted moment when he emerges from Myrna's vehicle.

At the very least, this ending complicates the traditional markers of comedy and death, in the former's fecundity (marriage, children, and celebration) versus the latter's fatalism (notably, the protagonist's death). As Northrop Frye explains of comedy, "The ritual pattern behind the catharsis of comedy is the resurrection that follows death, the epiphany or manifestation of a risen hero."[93] Whether we imagine the future of the novel beyond its ending as optimistic in Ignatius's rebirth or as pessimistic in the likelihood that Fortune will prepare a new round of torments for him, any possibility of Ignatius's future must allow for the likelihood of a queer carnivalesque to follow this moment of self-reproduction. Myrna tells Ignatius, "You have a brain that could really grow and flower here in [New York],"[94] but readers never witness the blossom, only the buried seed.

Given the general acclaim *Confederacy* has garnered since its publication, as evident in its legion of devoted fans and the 1981 Pulitzer Prize for fiction, it is somewhat disconcerting that its obvious merits still generate controversy. Jefferson Humphries and John Lowe summarize this critical impasse: "And still the debate rages on about John Kennedy Toole's *Confederacy*; can such a popular, wildly funny book really be any good?"[95] Latent in Humphries and Lowe's provocative query is the longstanding privileging of tragic and dramatic modes over comic and carnivalesque ones, of denigrating humor as essentially inferior to the moral seriousness of drama. The carnivalesque, as a literary mode and as a social practice, in particular invites such critical snobbery through the dismissive view that anything so fun cannot be good in itself, nor can it be good for its participants. Aesthetic judgments reflect not objective truths but subjective assessments, but those that rely on offhand dismissals of the carnivalesque for its burping, farting, shitting, and other such antics risk being blinded by this mode's fecundity, even in its most anti-fecund enactments. The carnivalesque allows Toole to create in New Orleans an apt yet outrageous setting for Ignatius's comic misadventures, and the queerness that he uncovers in this form allows his protagonist to triumph while simultaneously imagining the inherent tragedy of a world without a future.

NOTES

1. *Confederacy*, 220.
2. *Confederacy*, 181.
3. Bakhtin, *Rabelais*, 10.
4. Bakhtin, *Rabelais*, 94.
5. Bakhtin, *Rabelais*, 303.
6. Eagleton, *Walter Benjamin*, 145–146; his italics. See also Eco, in *Carnival!* ed. Sebeok, 1–9.
7. Mercer, in *Laughing Matter*, 1–19, at 4.
8. Clark, "Toole's Children," 269–280, at 269.
9. Lowe, in *Louisiana Culture*, 159–190, at 160.
10. David McNeil, *A Confederacy of Dunces* as Reverse Satire, 35.
11. Britton, "Two Visions," 17–23, at 21, 23. For more on the novel's allegory, see "'It's prolly fulla dirty stories': Queer Masculinity and Masturbatory Allegory" in Pugh, *Queer*, 83–111.
12. Bakhtin, *Rabelais*, 317.
13. *Confederacy*, 42.
14. *Confederacy*, 313.
15. *Confederacy*, 324.
16. Bell, "Clash," 15–22, at 16.
17. Codrescu, "Introduction," v–ix, at viii.
18. Daigrepont, "Ignatius Reilly," 74–80, at 76.
19. Rudnicki, "Anatomy," 281–301, at 287. On Ignatius's speech patterns, see also Fennell and Bennett, "Sociolinguistic," 371–379.
20. Kaylor, "Fortune's Wheel," 73–81, at 75.
21. Patteson and Sauret, "Illusion," 77–87, at 83.

22. Nelson, "Comic," 36–40, at 36.

23. Regan, "Return," 169–176, at 175.

24. *Confederacy*, 25.

25. *Confederacy*, 52.

26. Frye, *Anatomy,* 207.

27. *Confederacy*, 163.

28. *Confederacy*, 103.

29. Lowe, "Voices," 161.

30. *Confederacy*, 309.

31. *Confederacy*, 183–184.

32. *Confederacy*, 45.

33. *Confederacy*, 49–50.

34. Patteson, "Ignatius," unpaginated, item 14.

35. *Confederacy*, 134.

36. *Confederacy*, 179.

37. *Confederacy*, 161.

38. *Confederacy*, 2.

39. Nevils and Hardy, *Ignatius Rising*.

40. Marsh, Review of *Butterfly*, 285–298, at 286.

41. MacLauchlin, *Butterfly*, 215.

42. On the "death of the author," see Barthes, *Image*, 142–143.

43. *Confederacy*, 309.

44. For example, see Nevils and Hardy, *Ignatius Rising*, 68 on Toole's relationship with Emilie Griffin.

45. Nevils and Hardy, *Ignatius Rising*, 139.

46. Danuta Walters, "Queer," 6–21, at 13.

47. *Confederacy*, 9.

48. *Confederacy*, 9.

49. *Confederacy*, 247.

50. *Confederacy*, 251.

51. *Confederacy*, 150.

52. Hardin, "Queer," 58–77, at 68.

53. *Confederacy*, 181.

54. *Confederacy*, 69.

55. *Confederacy*, 140.

56. Bakhtin, 308–309.

57. For an overview of arguments concerning gay marriage prior to the U.S. Supreme Court *Obergefell v. Hodges* decision, see Eskridge and Spedale, *Gay Marriage*. Concerning the issue of reproduction in arguments against gay marriage, Eskridge and Spedale summarize its historical reasoning as developed from Judeo-Christian traditions: "The only morally acceptable deployment is the union of a male body and a female body through procreative intercourse within a faith-sanctioned marriage. Thus, oral and anal sex can never be anything but 'disordered,' and the homosexual Christian must remain chaste" (p. 23).

58. Edelman, *No Future*, 9. See also Bersani, *Rectum*.

59. *Confederacy*, 21.

60. *Confederacy*, 29.
61. *Confederacy*, 46.
62. *Confederacy*, 85.
63. *Confederacy*, 45.
64. *Confederacy*, 68.
65. *Confederacy*, 120.
66. *Confederacy*, 4.
67. *Confederacy*, 34.
68. Coogan, ed. It should be noted that, in contrast, fig trees can also symbolize fertility, particularly in Greco-Roman mythology; see Impelluso, *Nature*, 180–186.
69. *Confederacy*, 28.
70. *Confederacy*, 118.
71. *Confederacy*, 119.
72. *Confederacy*, 119.
73. *Confederacy*, 119.
74. *Confederacy*, 119.
75. *Confederacy*, 216.
76. *Confederacy*, 216.
77. *Confederacy*, 216.
78. *Confederacy*, 217.
79. *Confederacy*, 232.
80. *Confederacy*, 275.
81. *Confederacy*, 84.
82. *Confederacy*, 242.
83. *Confederacy*, 159–160.
84. *Confederacy*, 306.
85. *Confederacy*, 81.
86. *Confederacy*, 66.
87. *Confederacy*, 306.
88. *Confederacy*, 223.
89. *Confederacy*, 185.
90. *Confederacy*, 331.
91. *Confederacy*, 332.
92. Clark, "Toole's Children," 276.
93. Frye, *Anatomy*, 215.
94. *Confederacy*, 156.
95. Humphries and Lowe, *Future*, 6.

BIBLIOGRAPHY

Bakhtin, Mikhail. *Rabelais and His World*. Trans. Hélène Iswolsky. Bloomington: Indiana University Press, 1984.
Barthes, Roland. *Image, Music, Text*. Trans. Stephen Heath. New York: Hill & Wang, 1977.

Bell, Elizabeth S. "The Clash of World Views in John Kennedy Toole's *A Confederacy of Dunces*." *Southern Literary Journal* 21, no. 1 (1988).

Bersani, Leo. *Is the Rectum a Grave? And Other Essays*. Chicago: University of Chicago Press, 2010.

Britton, Wesley. "Two Visions of Medievalism and Determinism: Mark Twain and John Kennedy Toole's *A Confederacy of Dunces*." *Southern Quarterly* 34, no. 1 (1995).

Clark, William Bedford. "All Toole's Children: A Reading of *A Confederacy of Dunces*." *Essays in Literature* 14, no. 2 (1987).

Codrescu, Andrei. "Introduction to the Twentieth-Anniversary Edition." *A Confederacy of Dunces*, v–ix, at viii.

Coogan, Michael D., ed. *The New Oxford Annotated Bible: New Revised Standard Version*. 3rd ed. Oxford: Oxford University Press, 2001.

Daigrepont, Lloyd. "Ignatius Reilly and the Confederacy of Dunces." *New Orleans Review* 9, no. 3 (1982).

Eagleton, Terry. *Walter Benjamin or Towards a Revolutionary Criticism*. London: Verso, 1981.

Eco, Umberto. "The Frames of Comic Freedom." In *Carnival!*, edited by Thomas A. Sebeok. Berlin, 1984.

Edelman, Lee. *No Future: Queer Theory and the Death Drive*. Durham, NC: Duke University Press, 2004.

Eskridge, William, and Darren Spedale. *Gay Marriage: For Better or for Worse? What We've Learned from the Evidence*. New York: Oxford University Press, 2006.

Fennell, Barbara, and John Bennett. "Sociolinguistic Concepts and Literary Analysis." *American Speech* 66, no. 4 (1991).

Frye, Northrop. *Anatomy of Criticism: Four Essays*. Princeton: Princeton University Press, 1957.

Hardin, Michael. "Between Queer Performances: John Kennedy Toole's *The Neon Bible* and *A Confederacy of* Dunces." *Southern Literary Journal* 39, no. 2 (2007).

Humphries, Jefferson, and John Lowe, eds. *The Future of Southern Letters*. New York: Oxford University Press, 1996.

Impelluso, Lucia. *Nature and Its Symbols*. Trans. Stephen Sartarelli. Los Angeles: Getty Museum, 2003.

Kaylor, Noel Harold. "Fortune's Wheel, *The Consolation of Philosophy*, Boethius, and Recent American and British Fiction." *Carmina Philosophiae* 10 (2001).

Lowe, John. "The Carnival Voices of *A Confederacy of Dunces*." In *Louisiana Culture from the Colonial Era to Katrina*, edited by John Lowe. Baton Rouge: Louisiana State University Press, 2008.

MacLauchlin, Cory. *Butterfly in the Typewriter: The Tragic Life of John Kennedy Toole and the Remarkable Story of* A Confederacy of Dunces. Boston: Da Capo, 2012.

Marsh, Leslie. Review of *Butterfly in the Typewriter: The Tragic Life of John Kennedy Toole and the Remarkable Story of* A Confederacy of Dunces." *Journal of Mind and Behavior* 34, no. 3–4 (2013).

McNeil, David. "*A Confederacy of Dunces* as Reverse Satire: The American Subgenre." *Mississippi Quarterly* 38, no. 1 (1984–85).

Mercer, Kobena. "Carnivalesque and Grotesque: What Bakhtin's Laughter Tells Us about Art and Culture." In *No Laughing Matter: Visual Humor in Ideas of Race, Nationality, and Ethnicity*, edited by Angela Rosenthal, David Bindman, and Adrian Randolph. Hanover, NH: Dartmouth College Press, 2015.

Nelson, William. "The Comic Grotesque in Recent Fiction." *Thalia: Studies in Literary Humor* 5, no. 2 (1982–83).

Nevils, René Pol, and Deborah George Hardy. *Ignatius Rising: The Life of John Kennedy Toole*. Baton Rouge: Louisiana State University Press, 2001.

Patteson, Richard. "Ignatius Goes to the Movies: The Films in Toole's *A Confederacy of Dunces*." *Notes on Modern American Literature* 6, no. 2 (1982).

Patteson, Richard, and Thomas Sauret. "The Consolation of Illusion: John Kennedy Toole's *A Confederacy of Dunces*." *Texas Review* 4, no. 1–2 (1983).

Pugh, Tison. *Queer Chivalry and the Myth of White Masculinity in Southern Literature*. Baton Rouge: Louisiana State University Press, 2013.

Regan, Robert. "The Return of *The Moviegoer*: Toole's *A Confederacy of Dunces*." *Delta* 13 (1981).

Rudnicki, Robert. "*Euphues* and the Anatomy of Influence: John Lyly, Harold Bloom, James Olney, and the Construction of John Kennedy Toole's Ignatius." *Mississippi Quarterly* 62, no. 1 (2009).

Toole, John Kennedy. *A Confederacy of Dunces*. Introduction by Andrei Codrescu. 1980. Baton Rouge: Louisiana State University Press, 2000.

Walters, Suzanna Danuta. "From Here to Queer: Radical Feminism, Postmodernism, and the Lesbian Menace." In *Queer Theory*, edited by Iain Morland and Annebelle Willox. Houndmills, Basingstoke: Palgrave Macmillan, 2005.

Chapter 8

Ignatius's Brain

Food and Sex in John Kennedy Toole's A Confederacy of Dunces

Olga Colbert

The present work examines *A Confederacy of Dunces*' discourse regarding food and sex, particularly the cognitive function of the protagonist's digestive system. Many critics have noted the less flattering traits of Ignatius Reilly's body (sloppiness, flatulence, and excess weight) ever present in Toole's novel. I will focus on the most salient aspect of Ignatius's body: his digestive system, particularly his (pyloric) valve. This valve, mentioned thirty-nine times in the novel, seems to have a regulatory function, regulating not only digestion but also action. Ignatius seems to think with his gut, and therefore, his pyloric valve functions as a form of "brain" in the text. Ignatius's discourse regarding his body is consistent with his persona as a medievalist who despises modern society: it seems to fall within the Galenic paradigm still in vogue during medieval times. However, when Ignatius discusses other characters' consumption of food or their sexual behavior in particular, his discourse moves clearly within the Freudian paradigm that was current when the novel was written. To add yet another scientific paradigm, Ignatius's own behavior regarding food or sex, when closely examined, can be best understood within the parameters of the latest research in neuroscience, particularly that which falls within the umbrella of chemical and genetic approaches. I will delve on the state of scientific discourse in the three periods, discussing the work of Galen (and its medieval and Renaissance influences in anatomists such as Montaña de Monserrate and Maimonides), Freud's theory of the instincts and drives, and modern studies on chemical food addiction and neurological conditions that affect impulse control. Recent neurological studies regarding the enteric nervous system (a set of neurons running along the gastrointestinal tract) will also be incorporated into my analysis. The three paradigms overlap in the text and serve as a good case for examining the interplay between science and literature at any given time.

Confederacy tells the story of Ignatius Reilly, an eccentric medievalist who lives with his mother in a working-class New Orleans neighborhood in the early 1960s and who, despite his education, does not have a job and lives a limited existence which consists of watching movies at the Prytania movie theatre, eating junk food, and writing social commentary in notebooks he keeps under his bed. As the novel opens, Ignatius is standing outside of the D. H. Holmes department store in New Orleans' Canal Street, waiting for his mother, when a police officer, Patrolman Mancuso, attempts to arrest him for loitering, an event that sets the plot in motion. Ignatius, who wears a flannel shirt and the now iconic green cap with flaps, is described by Walter Percy in the foreword as a

> slob extraordinary, a mad Oliver Hardy, a fat Don Quixote, a perverse Thomas Aquinas rolled into one—who is in violent revolt against the entire modern age, lying in his flannel nightshirt, in a back bedroom on Constantinople Street in New Orleans, who between gigantic seizures of flatulence and eructations is filling dozens of Big Chief tablets with invective.[1]

Ignatius's body is large, loud, and sloppy. Descriptions of his anatomy, particularly his bodily functions, occupy a great deal of textual space in the novel. Among all this flesh, appetites, and organs there is a body part that takes central stage in the novel: his "valve." The pyloric valve is a conic-shaped muscle that regulates digestion, controlling the passage of digested food from the stomach into the small intestine. Ignatius's obsession with his pyloric valve is puzzling to the reader at best, not only on account of how frequently it is mentioned, but also regarding the valve's function. One could say that his valve is a kind of carnal conscience that guides his actions. There are numerous examples in the novel when Ignatius decides to initiate or abort action according to the indications his "valve" provides. For instance, when the atmosphere of the office at Levy Pants, a manufacturing plant where he interviews for a job, reminds him of his bedroom, "his valve opened joyfully" and Ignatius wishes vehemently to get the job.[2] Once he is hired, his visits to the factory are initiated or aborted in accordance to the valve's behavior, as shown in the following quote: "At last my valve seems to permit a visit to the factory. I must not pass up this opportunity."[3]

The way Ignatius views his digestive system falls within the parameters of the science of medicine proposed by Galen, a Greek physician who lived in the second century AD (AD 129–210) and whose views were still considered mainstream during the Middle Ages. As Owen Powell states in his Introduction to Galen's seminal work *On the Property of Foodstuffs*, "For one and a half millennia Galen of Pergamum influenced the practice of medicine in the Western world, and for rather longer in some parts outside it."[4] A medievalist, Ignatius favors an orderly universe, consistent with his medieval worldview. He often describes himself as an anachronism, as a man from a different age, out of synch with modern times. Ancient and medieval anatomists saw the stomach as an active, almost thinking part of the body. Galen states that "[nature] has granted the stomach alone and particularly to the parts of it near its mouth the ability to feel a lack which rouses the animal and stimulates it to seek food."[5] Centuries later Bernardino Montaña de Monserrate, a Renaissance doctor who was personal physician of Emperor Charles I, published *El Libro de la Anathomía del Hombre* in 1551, the first known treatise on anatomy written in Spanish. His work is fundamentally a compendium of Galenic knowledge, although according to M. Vicente Pedraz, it "contains the basic ingredients of the urban utopias of the moment"[6] by incorporating the work of the urban guilds. This medical treatise is structured as a dialogue between a nobleman, the Marquis of Mondéjar, and his physician, who is entrusted with the task of interpreting a mysterious, allegorical dream the marquis had. In this dream, a pregnant woman depicted as a home is in charge of building a fortress inside her home, which represents the fetus of her unborn child. Despite the existence of more modern medical treatises published before Montaña's work, Montaña's description of the digestive process is clearly galenic: in this home, the kitchen represents the stomach, and the "mouth" of the stomach is the kitchen door. It is worth noting that in Spanish the pit of the stomach is still called "the mouth" of the stomach ("*la boca del estómago*"), recalling its ancient characterization as an animal. It is consistent with the Galenic notion of digestion as a kitchen in which "the stomach is like a kettle, the gallbladder is the cook, and the liver is the fire."[7]

In Toole's novel, Ignatius's stomach and digestion are clearly portrayed in galenic terms: On one occasion, his pyloric valve closed "filling his stomach with trapped gas, gas which had character and being and resented its confinement":[8] as we see, his stomach is characterized as an animal: it screams, it has personality and feelings. And he adds, "He was wondering whether his pyloric valve might be trying, Cassandralike, to tell him something."[9] The invocation of Cassandra, a Greek mythological figure who had the gift of prophecy, shows the metonymic relationship Ignatius has with his valve, the part of his body that is more like him: prophetic, judgmental, and controlling.[10]

Another medieval medical belief makes its way into Ignatius's worldview, linking his respiratory system to the circumstances of his conception; he protests:

Please, blow your smoke elsewhere. My respiratory system, unfortunately, is below par. I suspect that I am the result of a particularly weak conception on the part of my father. His sperm was probably emitted in a rather offhand manner.[11]

This is consistent with the medieval view that the horoscope at birth or conception was important to determine a person's constitution. Pietro d'Abano, a thirteenth- to fourteenth-century physician, subscribed to the notion that

> in addition to the general influence of the heavenly bodies, the horoscope at conception or birth was also considered to signal or predispose the physical and mental constitution of each individual down to the most minute detail, such as food preferences.[12]

The crucial importance of digestion to maintain general health, and particularly the importance of a bath before bed to aid digestion is another Galenic influence in *Confederacy*. Maimonides, a twelfth-century Sephardic Jew, says of Galen that "he believed that a healthy regimen protects a person against disease" and he refers to Galen's belief that "no one who avoids improper digestion will fall ill."[13] According to Davidson, Maimonides was a firm believer in Galen's theories on digestion, quoting Galen as having stated, "You should know that there is nothing as effective as sleep after a bath for maturing what needs to be matured [in the digestive system] and for destroying noxious humors."[14] Ignatius Reilly is often depicted as soaking in the bathtub in *Confederacy*, to his mother's chagrin. The following quote shows the rationale for Ignatius's bathing as having a positive effect on his digestive system: "The trauma of having found employment had affected his valve negatively and he was waiting until the warm water in which he wallowed like a pink hippopotamus had a calming effect upon his system."[15] This happened after he has eaten dozens of hot dogs while working as a vendor and refusing to sell hot dogs to a teenager. Ignatius does not consider his unhealthy diet as having any bearing on the episode and instead faults his job-seeking experience. This passage also shows the medieval prejudice of working with his hands as having a negative effect on his self-image.

The location of the pyloric valve is relevant, as it sits precisely on the spot where food becomes waste. According to John Wilkins, "Galen was particularly concerned with the points where the esophagus joined the stomach and where the stomach joined the duodenum,"[16] that is exactly the pyloric valve or "the valve" in Ignatius narrative. The clean becomes unclean, food turns into excrement. The novel pays a lot of attention to Ignatius's lack of hygiene. His body and clothing are presented as ostensibly unkempt and dirty, making a connection to the concept of the "clean and proper body" unavoidable. Ignatius is aware of this and appropriates the concept: while working as a hot dog vendor, he mentions that his smock signals him as untouchable.[17] This is not a far-fetched assumption, as he is selling a foodstuff made from animal discards and casing (tripe), which clearly falls within the unclean category. The hot dogs are indeed presented as "impure" food. Chapter 7 introduces

Ignatius trailing a Paradise vendor while attracted by the foul stench of the hot dogs: "I would like to buy one of your hot dogs. They smell rather nasty."[18] That the foul smell is a great part of the food's appeal is shocking to the reader; furthermore, the description of the ingredients used to produce the hot dogs provided by Mr. Clyde, the Paradise Vendors manager, further highlights their undesirability as food and clearly places them as impure: "Rubber, cereal, tripe. Who knows? I wouldn't touch one of them myself."[19] Tripe, as the casing of the intestine that contains food waste in an animal body, would be considered impure. Therefore, the hot dogs are inedible and untouchable (even by the vendor) and Ignatius will acquire "untouchable" status once he is working as a hot dog vendor.

On another occasion, at the beginning of chapter 9, Mr. Clyde is upset about a complaint from the Health Department against Ignatius, who was seen picking up a cat from the gutter while selling hot dogs. When confronted, Ignatius responds, "Tell me, what archaic sanitary taboo have I violated?" as he vigorously defends the cleanliness of the cat: "It has apparently been taken for granted that the cat was unclean. How do we know that? Cats are notoriously sanitary."[20] In her study on the concepts of purity and impurity in medieval penitentials, Julia Helmus writes that ambiguity is at the center of abjection in the medieval mind, resulting "from the blurring and transgression of boundaries between cosmological categories that seem to be a fixed feature of life."[21] Helmus asserts that domestic animals and animals who live in the house, such as "dogs and cats, but also mice, are intrinsically impure and therefore could pollute clean food and liquid."[22] While mice can be seen as polluting food and drink by coming in contact with it, the reason for considering dogs and cats "polluting" or "unclean" were different; their abjection comes from living in close proximity to humans: by living "relatively intimately with humans," they "crossed a certain cosmologically determined boundary, which made them ambiguous."[23] In this theological context, one gains greater clarity about Mr. Clyde's affirmation that they are talking about Ignatius, not the cat. Ignatius protests that his nails are clean, but this argument seems insufficient and weak. He does not defend himself from the accusation of uncleanliness with the same passion with which he had defended the cat. However, the same ambiguity that had deemed the cat unclean plagues Ignatius. In his case, it is sexual ambiguity. Ignatius is subsequently given another chance and sent to work in the French Quarter, an area he describes as "Sodom and Gomorrah" highlighting homosexuality and connecting it textually to the unclean taboo.[24] In the case of sodomy, "the polluting effect arises from the fact that the boundaries between certain cosmological categories are violated."[25] Helmus' work echoes Julia Kristeva's classic essay on abjection in which liminality, the blurring of borders, was also the main reason something became abject. However, for Kristeva, in the contemporary context, this liminality mostly entailed the blurriness of the border between object and subject (between alive and dead), while in the medieval worldview analyzed by Holmes it is the crossing of fixed/static cosmological boundaries that produces an abject effect.

Mary Douglas in her 1966 classic study *Purity and Danger: An Analysis of the Concepts of Pollution and Taboo* ponders why saliva is nonpolluting while most fluids or solids shed from the body are and concludes that it is because tears are not related to the bodily functions of digestion or procreation. The novel includes a barrage of bodily fluids and foul smells which contribute to produce an experience of disgust in most readers. They are all connected to digestion or sex. Two infamous examples are the bedsheet stained with his semen used as a political placard by the factory workers of Levy Pants,[26] and the mention of the digestive byproduct of his hot dog binge-eating episode, what is called "Paradise gas" in the novel.[27]

In addition to impurity, hot dogs have obvious erotic undertones in *Confederacy*. Not only the hot dogs are archetypal phallic symbols, but there is a comic exaggeration of their phallic quality ("12 inches of Paradise"), and their connection to homoerotic desire, as thoroughly noted by Michael Hardin in his excellent article "Between Queer Performances: John Kennedy Toole's *The Neon Bible* and *Confederacy*."[28] When Ignatius follows the hot dog vendor, we are told he is "analyzing, cataloguing, categorizing, and classifying the distinct odors of hot dog, mustard, and lubricant."[29] *Paradise Vendors, Incorporated* was located in a former auto repair shop, so the lubricant smell referred to in the previous quote is, at surface level, the stench of automobile lubricant. However, in the next description of hot dogs, he refers to one of the main components as "rubber" as we just saw. Sandwiched between these two excerpts is the description of "the boiling water the frankfurters swished and lashed like artificially colored and magnified paramecia," a clear reference to penises and sperm.[30] Shortly after the previous quotes, Ignatius gloats satiated upon the consumption of four hot dogs in a row: "After his fourth hot dog, Ignatius ran his magnificent pink tongue around his lips and up over his moustache and said to the old man, 'I cannot recently remember being so totally satisfied.'"[31] The quote is almost a textbook example of Freud's vision of sexual desire. Ignatius derives intense pleasure from the consumption of the hot dogs, and the scene is told with unmatched sensuality, in contrast with potential sexual encounters with Myrna Minkoff, his college friend, whose advances fill Ignatius with dread and repugnance. Furthermore, when we look at the previous excerpts in the context of homoerotic desire, the orality of the previous quote is hard to miss and fits well with Freud's consideration of homosexuality as a perversion, or at least a borderline condition, one in which the individual's growth is arrested in the oral stage. This is further accentuated when in the same paragraph Ignatius speaks of himself as lacking a "perversion." In the typical equivocal nature of Ignatius's speech, the "perversion" he is referring to is connected to job seeking and, though it seems to allude to his lack of interest on getting a job, he literally says, "Apparently I lack some particular perversion which today's employer is seeking."[32] This episode links food and sex, specifically, food cravings and homoerotic sexual desire. In Ignatius's own words, "human desire for food and sex is relatively equal."[33] However, in the novel Ignatius is depicted as having a conflicted sexuality. While every encounter with a willing female sexual partner provokes Ignatius's disgust, there are countless textual examples that suggest others see Ignatius as gay. I agree with Michael Hardin's argument that Ignatius feels compelled into a performance of heterosexuality, while drawn to a queer identity.[34] Myrna often discusses Ignatius sexuality and she accuses him of having unacknowledged homosexual tendencies. She thinks Ignatius has blocked regular sexual channels, and suggests his sexual impulses are going into the "wrong" channels: "Your normal sexual outlets have been blocked for so long that now the sexual overflow is seeping out into the wrong channels."[35] She views Ignatius's urge to recruit sodomites (to fight) as a normalization of Ignatius natural impulses. She also believes that the story of his arrest is a paranoid fantasy; and let's not forget that Freud linked paranoia to homosexual tendencies.

It should be noted that this clearly Freudian discourse is mainly centered on food. While Ignatius sees his body as a food consumption and disposal machine, in Galenic terms, his approach to food slides the discourse towards the Freudian paradigm in vogue at the time the novel was written, in the 1960s. The fashion enjoyed by Freudian ideas at the time is made explicit by the references to Freud by the best educated characters in the novel: Myrna Minkoff, Ignatius, and Mr. and Mrs. Levy (the owners of Levy Pants). Mrs. Levy and her friends practice psychoanalysis, and Mrs. Levy accuses Mr. Levy of having a personality type that is not even in psychology books, pointing out that Mr. Levy could make his psychiatrist famous, "just like that crippled girl or whoever it was put Freud on the map," and adding, "they'd be inviting him to Vienna to speak."[36] Sublimation is the most frequently used Freudian concept in the novel, usually to great effect. In Freudian terms, sublimation is an ego defense mechanism in which the libido is diverted into noninstinctual channels. Socially unacceptable impulses are unconsciously transformed into socially acceptable behaviors. It involves a *"desexualization of the drives,"* according to L. Todesqui Tavares.[37] At the end of the novel, when Myrna unexpectedly appears to take Ignatius away from home to New York City, he explains his food consumption and resulting weight gain as a form of sublimation: "I've gained pounds by lying continuously in bed, seeking surcease and sublimation in food. Now we must run. I must leave this house. It has terrible associations."[38] While Myrna attributes his weight gain to lifestyle ("I can tell how inactive you've been from your weight"), Ignatius, as we saw, attributes his weight gain to psychological factors.[39] While Ignatius's use of the concept of sublimation in the above quote was obviously Freudian, let's not forget that sublimation has another, more ancient, meaning: an alchemical process by which solids are transformed into vapors without passing through the liquid phase. That seems oddly consistent with Ignatius's digestion processes.

However, Ignatius's most unequivocally unapologetic use of Freudian theories appear to explain other characters' eating habits, and it is here where the connection between food and sexuality reaches its highest comical notes. Ignatius is forced by his mother to get a job and he holds a succession of menial ones that culminate in his working as a hot dog vendor in New Orleans' French Quarter, as stated earlier. On one occasion he ate most of the hot dogs but lied to his boss about it, accusing a teenager boy of stealing the missing food: "Perhaps some vitamin deficiency in his growing body was screaming for appeasement. The human desire for food and sex is relatively equal."[40] While starting his argument with a vitamin deficiency, a chemical condition known since the early twentieth century, he quickly turns to Freud's theory of the instincts and drives outlined in *Beyond the Pleasure Principle*, in which the impulse to eat and to copulate are bundled as part of the Eros, the life instinct, in opposition to self-destruction instincts, which would be part of the death drive, Tanatos.[41] When the unconvinced hot dog owner responds: "You are full of bullshit," Ignatius deepens his Freudian explanation indicating that the youth must have been stimulated ("crazed" is the word he uses) by "suggestive television programs and lascivious periodicals," and at the same time rejected "by some rather conventional adolescent females who refused to participate in his imaginative sexual program. His unfulfilled physical desires therefore sought sublimation in food.'"[42] He tells the incredulous business owner that they both must be grateful the youth "turned to food for an outlet. Had he not, I might have been raped right there on the spot."[43] Curiously, the Freudian explanation convinces the old man who, in one of the funniest dialog exchanges in the novel, retorts: "That son of a bitch, I wonder how he could carry all them hot dogs away."[44]

What is inescapable to the modern reader but couldn't possibly have been in the radar of the author at the time of the creation of the novel in the early 1960s, or even to its earliest readers in the 1980s, is the strong evidence the text provides to support the most recent theories of chemical dependency or genetic linkage to explain Ignatius's excessive consumption of food. The current paradigm of food addiction and impulse control might be more useful to explain Ignatius gluttony and his mother's implied alcoholism. This is quite new: as late as the 1990s there was no evidence of physical basis for food cravings, and therefore no consensus in the medical community. It was

believed that the causes for overconsumption of food were mostly psychological or environmental. This is also what the novel's characters claim: that
they eat or drink because they are stressed. For instance, Mrs. Reilly, after
finishing a drink insists "I'm gonna make me another one, if you don't mind,
sugar. I got problems."[45] And, on another occasion: "I gotta have my little
drink. It relieves the pressure. You know?"[46] She is referring to the stress
of living with Ignatius. Ignatius seems to feel that living with his mother is
emotionally taxing as well, as the following quote suggests: he "prepared a
hot dog for himself and ravenously ate it. His mother had been in a violent
mood all week, refusing to buy him a Dr. Nut."[47] It is obvious throughout
the novel that Ignatius binges on sweets (cakes, doughnuts, and sugary soft
drinks) and hot dogs. Irene Reilly aptly summarizes her son's eating habits
and cravings: "Ignatius just likes to eat junk, anyways. You give Ignatius a
few bottles of Dr. Nut and plenty bakery cakes, and he's satisfied."[48] Dr. Nut
was a soft drink that was produced in New Orleans between 1930 and the
late 1970s. It was advertised as "nutritious, high in food value" in a company
poster and was almond flavored, similar to Amaretto liquor, although it was
non-alcoholic. Tom Lowenburg blogs that "the taste was like a Dr. Pepper but
instead of leaving your mouth just with a coating of sugar it had a nutty finish, therefore making you want another drink, genius, really."[49] Dr. Nut was
Ignatius's favorite drink, as Mrs. Reilly explained: "I gotta buy it by the case.
Sometimes he sits himself down and drinks two, three Dr. Nuts at a time."[50]
In addition to the cultural significance of the drink and its sugary content, the
sexual connotation of the name needs to be acknowledged, as it supports the
novel's homoerotic undertones. These quotes show not only Ignatius's food
and drink preferences, high in carbohydrates and sugar, but also the excess
with which he consumes them and the intensity of his cravings: "Ignatius
says to me this morning, 'Momma, I sure feel like a jelly doughnut.' You
know? So I went over by the German and bought him two dozen. Look, they
got a few left."[51] In addition to Ignatius's sugar compulsion, the quote shows
Irene's enabling role in her son's excessive consumption of junk food: she
bought two dozen cakes, which he almost finished in a few hours. When she
offers the doughnut box to Mancuso, it looked "as if it had been subjected
to unusual abuse during someone's attempt to take out all the doughnuts at
once."[52] His consumption of candy in his frequent visits to the Prytania movie
theater is also marked by excess, eating three Milky Ways and two bags of
popcorn.[53]

Food addiction is now often seen as a chemical dependency. Phil Werdell,
a pioneer in food addiction, contends that there is new research that concludes
that excessive consumption of sugar can produce an endogenous opioid
dependency, with the brain of a food addict creating its own opium-like drug.
"Often they will identify sugar, flour or fat as a substance that is acting in

their bodies as a narcotic."[54] Although not supported by all, another recent line of research on chemical dependency contends that the bodies of alcoholics produce a chemical called tetrahydrolsoquilnoline (THIQ) during the digestion of alcohol that nondrinkers do not. The discovery of the role of THIQ in the "pathogenesis of chronic alcoholism" dates from the late 1970s.[55] This mammalian alkaloid "is considered to account for the neurobehavioral abnormalities associated with alcoholism and may act as a neurotransmitter."[56] Furthermore, "In 1994, Nobel et al at UCLA discovered that obese adults who were' bingeing on dense carbohydrates' and who were neither alcoholic nor drug addicted had the same D2 dopamine gene marker that distinguishes alcoholism and other drug addictions."[57] Consequently, it is now understood that there is a genetic link, a genetic predisposition to food addiction as well as to alcoholism. The novel characterizes Ignatius's mother, Irene, as someone who consumes alcohol in excess. She has a few beers at The Night of Joy bar right after Ignatius's failed arrest at the beginning of the novel. The text describes her drunken gait once they leave the bar: "three quick steps to the left, pause, three quick steps to the right, pause."[58] She is clearly inebriated, as noted by the narrator while describing her "somewhat beery courage."[59] She subsequently crashes her Plymouth into a post supporting a balcony, an event that has serious financial consequences for the family. In fact, having to pay compensation to the owner of the building prompts Irene to force Ignatius to get a job in order to keep her home. Ignatius repeatedly characterizes her as an alcoholic, at one point demanding "between wine breaks, bring me a snack of some sort. My valve is screaming for appeasement."[60] This quote links both his galenic view of his digestive system (the valve as an animal who screams) and his view of his mother as alcohol dependent. But it is not only Ignatius who comments on Irene's excessive drinking. Her new friend, Santa Batagglia, Patrolman Mancuso's mother, who is in the process of fixing Irene with Mr. Robicheaux, tries to prevent Irene from drinking her third drink while waiting for the arrival of her gentleman caller: "Irene! You gonna be on the floor, girl. I ain't gonna introduce no drunk to this nice old man."[61]

In *Confederacy*, there is a clear textual link between alcohol and food addictions. Ignatius's mother hides her bottle from view in the oven. Early in the novel Ignatius protests that when he opened the oven "to put in my frozen pizza, I was almost blinded by a bottle of broiled wine that was preparing to explode."[62] When he suggests Irene stops supporting the liquor industry, she protests that she only spends money on "a few bottles of Gallo muscatel."[63] On another occasion, as Irene is nagging Ignatius about getting out of the bathtub, he retorts, "Don't you have a bottle of muscatel baking in the oven? Now let me alone. I'm very nervous."[64] On yet another occasion, to deflect attention away from himself, Ignatius tells his mother, "Get your bottle out of the oven. It must be done by now."[65] The textual displacement from alcohol into food is significant: a bottle of muscatel takes the place of food inside the oven, which seems comical in the context of the novel, but it is not very far from the truth: alcohol is high in sugar, much like the doughnuts and cakes Ignatius consumes all the time. The sweet wines Irene favors (muscatel) in particular contain as much as 20–150 grams of sugar per liter. A study by Nicole Avena, Pedro Rada, and Betty Hoebel concludes that "sugar is noteworthy as a substance that releases opioids and dopamine and thus might be expected to have addictive potential."[66]

The other connection is genetic. Ignatius may have inherited his mother's predisposition to addiction; according to the National Center on Alcohol Abuse and Alcoholism, "research shows that genes are responsible for about half of the risk for AUD."[67] The same source indicates that Alcohol Use Disorder often seems to run in families. Therefore, although Ignatius sees his mother's addiction to alcohol in moral terms, the novel's text supports the current view of addiction (both to alcohol and food) as dopamine receptor, opioid production, and genetic issues. On another note, it should be noted that Ignatius is addicted to carbohydrates (bread) while his mother is addicted to wine. Since they are Catholic, the connection between bread and wine and their transformation into the body and blood of Christ during mass is hard to miss. Particularly, since Ignatius sees addiction as a moral flaw and the novel discusses Ignatius rejection of formal Catholic religion (ever since the priest refused to hold a funeral for his beloved deceased dog), while the mother is a devout, practicing Catholic. While her faith is not particularly discussed, the novel mentions her attendance to traditional Catholic devotionals, such as novenas, even though it provides clues to reassess Irene's level of devoutness when she uses the novena as a cover to attend a party at Battaglia's home to meet Robicheaux.

Phil Werdell insists that food addicts experiment three experiences that he calls "euphoric recall," "obsessions of the mind," and "mental blank spots."[68] Remembering the good experiences of taste and mitigation of pain and forgetting negative consequences would constitute euphoric recall, while obsessions of the mind consists of rationalizing eating based on irrational thoughts. If we examine Ignatius's behavior in *Confederacy*, we find a good example of this at the beginning of chapter II; while Ignatius is writing on his tablets, the narrator states he feels bloated, a bloating he attributes to his disgust over the fall of Western Civilization:

> He often bloated while lying in bed in the morning contemplating the unfortunate turn that events had taken after the Reformation. Doris Day and Scenicruisers, whenever they came to mind, created an ever more rapid expansion of his central region. But since the attempted arrest and the accident, he had been *bloating for almost no reason at all.*[69]

This quote shows an erroneous rationalization, by not recognizing food consumption as the real cause of his discomfort. The reader later learns that he had consumed almost two dozen donuts that morning, the real reason why he is feeling bloated. Later in the story Ignatius mentions that his recent weight gain, discomfort, and fatigue are caused by his malfunctioning valve. As he sits on the steps of the cathedral, there is no mention of his overeating as part of the problem, "his recently increased weight and the bloating caused by the inoperative valve made any position other than standing or lying down somewhat awkward."[70]

Werdell includes mental blank spots, what he describes as "unexplained absences of logical thinking that would serve to prevent one from engaging in behaviors known in the past to inflict pain" as the third trait of those suffering from food addiction.[71] The novel insists on Ignatius uncomfortable seating at the Prytania movie theater, where he consumes several candy bars and "two auxiliary bags of popcorn," resulting in "his body filling the seat and protruding into the adjoining ones."[72] The previous experiences do not deter him from consuming excessive candy and popcorn each time. The same could be said of most of the excessive food consumption in the novel (hot dogs or sweet cakes) resulting on digestive issues commonly addressed as his valve acting up.

One would be remiss, in a novel so dominated by the workings of the body, if an attempt wasn't at least made to incorporate the current field of embodied cognition to shed light on Ignatius obsession with his valve. According to George Lakoff in his classic study *Metaphors We Live By*, metaphors of digestion have to do with understanding, with knowledge. Both food and ideas "can be digested, swallowed, devoured, and warmed over."[73] In a more recent work, "Mapping the Brain's Metaphor Circuitry: Metaphorical Thought in Everyday Reasoning," Lakoff includes digestion as one of the "four special case conceptual metaphors."[74] The entire chain would be "Thinking Is Eating; Ideas Are Food; Communication is Feeding; Understanding is Digesting." The problem is, in Toole's novel, we rarely find metaphors of digestion when discussing ideas, whether the acquisition of ideas, or the sharing or understanding of ideas, and so on. An exception is a comment Ignatius makes of Dr. Talc, a professor "renowned for the facile and sarcastic wit and easily digested generalizations that made him popular . . . and help conceal his lack of knowledge about almost everything in general and British history in particular."[75] In this case "digestive" is used to indicate easy to understand, simply articulated ideas. Ignatius also calls his Big Chief tablets, where he writes his thoughts about the perils of civilization, "the fruits of my brain."[76] While in the previous passages we find uses of the digestive metaphor consistent with Lakoff's ideas, the vast majority of the references to digestion or to the consumption of food in the novel (verbs like "digest," "bake," etc.,) are used literally (not figuratively) within the context of the sentence in which they appear. However, as Peter Norvig notes, Hobbs and Rumelhart insist on the importance of metaphor to language understanding, adding "it should be indistinguishable from literal language interpretation," since the interpretation process is almost the same, arguing "there is no sense having separate mechanisms for 'literal' and 'metaphorical' interpretations."[77]

The fact is, *Confederacy* is a novel about knowledge: about formal knowledge acquired through reading and studying, and about self-knowledge. Ignatius is highly educated, with a master's degree that cost Irene her inheritance, as she does not tire of telling Ignatius. Ignatius quotes Boetius and is conversant with the classics. However, he was professionally unsuccessful and writes convoluted invectives in the Big Chief tablets he keeps under his bed. The essays, while elegantly written in terms of grammar and style, often contain confusing, half-baked ideas. To continue with the digestion metaphor, he does not seem to have digested well all the knowledge provided by his expensive education. While his writings are tirades against the modern world, perhaps the real object of his criticism is the education system. Overeducated in his neighborhood and household, as well as in the workplace, his education has alienated him from his family and neighbors, who truly speak a different language than he does. The language usage of his mother, Santa Battaglia, Patrolman Mancuso, his neighbor, and all the other characters in the working-class neighborhood where he grew up shows more eloquently than any study the pitiful state of public education in the state of Louisiana for working class children and the added disadvantages of poverty. Despite his privileged access to formal education, Ignatius lacks sufficient self-knowledge. There is a significant gap between how Ignatius is perceived by others (sloppy, lazy, crazy, selfish, and boorish) and how he perceives himself (superior and moral). I would say that Ignatius's most blatant lack of self-knowledge has to do with his sexuality. Myrna harasses him by letter and in person trying to get Ignatius "to clarify (his) sexual inclinations" by asking him "pointed questions" since they first met.[78] This is a blatant and inexcusable attempt to out a possibly gay person. The reader, however, has the impression Ignatius is not so much concealing his sexual identity, but unwilling or unable to explore it at this point, perhaps succumbing to the pressure of a society so intensely bent in maintain a heteronormative sexual behavior.[79]

Nevertheless, however unaware Ignatius is of his public image/perception, including his body image, he is clearly more attuned to the internal workings of his body: noticing sensations, having an internal body consciousness, and being aware of internal organs and their functioning in ways that escape most individuals. We had mentioned earlier that Ignatius's valve functioned almost as a form of brain within the text. It is in this space that Ignatius's medievalist views and modern science intersect. In 1907, Byron

Robinson wrote a book entitled *The Abdominal and Pelvic Brain*, discovering the enteric nervous system, what he called "the abdominal brain." At about the same time, Johannis Langley noticed that it worked independently from the central nervous system. The enteric nervous system is a set of neurons running along the gastrointestinal tract. However, not until the late 1970s a connection was established between the enteric nervous system and some neurological conditions: Edgard Cayce, one of the early advocates of an abdominal nervous system, believed that certain neurological syndromes had an abdominal etiology, such as epilepsy and migraines. The enteric nervous system (ENS) "contains 200-600 million neurons, distributed in many thousands of small ganglia."[80] According to Adam Hadhazy, It is now believed that significantly more information goes from the intestines to the brain than the other way around: 90% of the fibers in the primary visceral nerve, the vagus, carry information from the gut to the brain and not the other way around.[81]

He asserts that the ENS uses more than thirty neurotransmitters, with 95 percent of the body's serotonin found in the bowels.[82]

To conclude, a reflection is in order: was Ignatius's view of his digestive system anachronistic or, on the contrary, truly visionary, giving the gut a central role in his body's cognition? When Ignatius was questioning whether his valve was, "Cassandralike," trying to tell him something, the real answer may be yes. The enteric nervous system positions the gut as a second brain, a transmitter of information. However, the message the valve was trying to communicate, by virtue of his food addiction, may have been lost in translation.

NOTES

1. Percy, Foreword to *Confederacy*, viii.
2. *Confederacy*, 67.
3. *Confederacy*, 110.
4. Powell, 1.
5. Stanford web, "A History of the Stomach and Intestines," https://web.stanford.edu/class/history13/earlysciencelab/body1/stomachpages/stomachcolonintestines.html.
6. Pedraz, "El cuerpo de la república. La metáfora organicista en tres discursos médicos del Siglo de Oro español," *Brocar*. My translation.
7. Stanford web.
8. *Confederacy*, 30.
9. *Confederacy*, 30.
10. For a characterization of Ignatius as a prophet, see Colbert, "Apocalypse."
11. *Confederacy*, 295.

12. Siriasi, *Medieval*, 111.

13. Davidson, *Maimonides*, 72.

14. Davidson, *Maimonides*, 72.

15. *Confederacy*, 175.

16. Wilkins and Hill, *Food*, 229.

17. *Confederacy*, 164.

18. *Confederacy*, 153.

19. *Confederacy*, 153.

20. *Confederacy*, 208–209.

21. Helmus, *Amorous Adventures*, 91.

22. Helmus, *Amorous Adventures*, 40.

23. Helmus, *Amorous Adventures*, 40.

24. *Confederacy*, 211.

25. Helmus, *Amorous Adventures*, 78.

26. "Among the yellow stains the word FORWARD was painted in high block letters and red crayon." *Confederacy*, 136.

27. *Confederacy*, 177.

28. Hardin, 58–77.

29. *Confederacy*, 152.

30. *Confederacy*, 153.

31. *Confederacy*, 154.

32. *Confederacy*, 154.

33. *Confederacy*, 164.

34. Hardin, 1.

35. *Confederacy*, 303.

36. *Confederacy*, 357.

37. Tavares and Hasimoto, "Sublimation."

38. *Confederacy*, 388.

39. *Confederacy*, 388.

40. *Confederacy*, 164.

41. Freud, *Pleasure Principle*.

42. *Confederacy*, 164.

43. *Confederacy*, 164.

44. *Confederacy*, 164.

45. *Confederacy*, 195.

46. *Confederacy*, 44.

47. *Confederacy*, 160.

48. *Confederacy*, 263.

49. Lowenburg blog. Consulted December 21, 2003.

50. *Confederacy*, 10.

51. *Confederacy*, 39.

52. *Confederacy*, 39.

53. *Confederacy*, 55.

54. Werdell, "Craving," 6.

55. Suhr and Kim, "Neurotoxic," 63.

56. Suhr and Kim, "Neurotoxic," 63.
57. Suhr and Kim, "Neurotoxic," 1.
58. *Confederacy*, 24.
59. *Confederacy*, 25.
60. *Confederacy*, 217.
61. *Confederacy*, 196.
62. *Confederacy*, 49.
63. *Confederacy*, 49.
64. *Confederacy*, 178.
65. *Confederacy*, 213.
66. Avena, Rada, and Hoebel, "Evidence," 19–20.
67. "Genetics of Alcohol Use Disorder," *National Center on Alcohol Abuse and Alcoholism*, www.niaaa.nih.gov.
68. Werdell, *Bariatric Surgery*.
69. *Confederacy*, 29 (my emphasis).
70. *Confederacy*, 245.
71. Werdell, *Bariatric Surgery*.
72. Werdell, *Bariatric Surgery*, 55.
73. Lakoff, *Metaphors*, 147.
74. The other three are: Thinking is Moving, Understanding is Seeing, and Thinking is Object Manipulation.
75. *Confederacy*, 127.
76. *Confederacy*, 47.
77. Norvig, Book Review, *Metaphors*. Norvig argues that

Rumelhart considers the interpretation of sentences like 'The policeman raised his hand and stopped the car.' This uses no metaphors, but it requires a complex interpretation process that must identify knowledge structures having to do with traffic cops, drivers, brakes, and cars. This interpretation goes well beyond a simple composition of the literal meanings present in the words and is similar to the type of interpretation that is done in processing metaphors.

78. *Confederacy*, 177.
79. The so-called Lavender scare, which involved the massive firing of gay government workers, had taken place in the 1950s, and Toole committed suicide in 1969, three months before the continued persecution of the LGBT community erupted in the Stonewall riots in New York City.
80. Furness, Callahan, Rivera, and Cho, "Enteric," 39–71.
81. Hadhazy, "Think Twice."
82. Hadhazy, "Think Twice."

BIBLIOGRAPHY

Avena, Nicole M., Pedro Rada, and Bartley G. Hoebel. "Evidence for Sugar Addiction: Behavioral and Neurochemical Effects of Intermittent, Excessive Sugar Effects." *Neuroscience Biobehavioral Review* 32, no. 1 (2008): 20–19.

Colbert, Olga. "Apocalypse and A-Bomb: States in Consciousness in John Kennedy Toole's A Confederacy of Dunces." In *Novelistic Inquiries into the Mind*, edited by Grzegorz Maziarczyk. Cambridge: Cambridge Scholars Publishing, 2016.

Davidson, Hubert. *Moses Maimonides: The Man and His Works.* Oxford: Oxford University Press, 2010.

Douglas, Mary. *Purity and Danger: An Analysis of the Concepts of Pollution and Taboo.* Routledge, 2002.

Freud, Sigmund. *Beyond the Pleasure Principle.* New York: Norton Library, 1961.

Furness, J. B., Callahan, B. P., Rivera, L. R. and Cho, H. J. "The Enteric Nervous System and Gastrointestinal Innervation: Integrated Local and Central Control." *Advances in Experimental Medicine and Biology* 817 (2014): 39–71.

Hadhazy, Adam. "Think Twice: How the Gut's 'Second Brain' Influences Mood and Well-Being." *Scientific American*, February 12 (2010).

Hardin, Michael. "Between Queer Performances: John Kennedy Toole's *The Neon Bible* and *A Confederacy of Dunces.*" *The Southern Literary Journal* 39, no.2 (Spring 2007): 58–77.

Helmus, Julia. *Amorous Adventures and Questionable Meals: Concepts of Impurity and Pollution in Early Medieval Penitentials.* Master's Thesis. University of Utrecht, 2013.

Lakoff, George. "Mapping the Brain's Metaphor Circuitry: Metaphorical Thought in Everyday Reasoning." *Frontiers in Human Neuroscience.* Published online December 16, 2014.

———. *Metaphors We Live By.* Chicago: University of Chicago Press, 1980.

Lowenbug, Tom. Blog. Consulted December 21, 2003.

Norvig, Peter. *Metaphors We Live By.* Book Review. Norvig.com.

Ohlms, David L. "The Disease Concept of Alcoholism." Mental Health America.

Pedraz, Vicente M. "El cuerpo de la república. La metáfora organicista en tres discursos médicos del Siglo de Oro español." *Brocar: Cuadernos de Investigación Histórica* (2016): 47.

Percy, Walter. Foreword. *A Confederacy of Dunces.* New York: Grove Press, 1980.

Powell, Owen. *Introduction* to *On the Property of Foodstuffs (De alimentorum facultatibu*s). Cambridge: Cambridge University Press, 2009.

Siriasi, Nancy. *Medieval and Early Renaissance Medicine.* Chicago: Chicago University Press, 1990.

Stanford Web. "A History of the Stomach and Intestines." https://web.stanford.edu/class/history13/earlysciencelab/bodyd1/stomachpages/stomachcolonintestines.html.

Suhr, Young Joon, and Hyun-Jung Kim. "Neurotoxic Effects of Tetrahydroisoquinolines and Underlying Mechanisms." *Experimental Neurobiology* 19 (September 2010): 63–70.

Todesqui Tavares, Leandro Anselmo Tavares and Francisco Hasimoto. "Sublimation as a Paradigm of the Psyche Constitution: Metaphysiology and Theoretical-clinical Developments." *Ágora: Estudios em Teoría Psicanalítica* 19, no. 2 (2016).

Toole, John Kennedy. *A Confederacy of Dunces.* New York: Grove Press, 1980.

Werdell, Phil. "Physical Craving and Food Addiction: A Scientific Review." Food Addiction Institute. Foodaddictioninstitute.org. 2009.

———. "The Science of Food Addiction." https:/foodaddiction.com/resources/scien ce-of-food addiction.

Wilkins John M., and Shaun Hill. *Food in the Ancient World.* Oxford: Blackwell Publishing, 2006.

Chapter 9

Dunces and Dialogue

Ignatius J. Reilly's Menippean
Misreadings and Onanistic Annotations
of Boethian Philosophy

Anthony G. Cirilla

The following pages present the argument that *A Confederacy of Dunces* is a semi-allegorical meditation upon the corollary between masturbation and marriage and monological versus dialogical dispositions of communication. The four components of the argument are presented briefly here. First, Ignatius's incomplete understanding of Boethius is mirrored by his masturbatory sex life.[1] Just as he brings no satisfaction to a meaningful sex partner (Myrna Mynkoff chief among them) and therefore also fails to satisfy himself, he is unable to sustain a thorough relationship even with the text for which he professes so ardent an affection. Second, however, it is not mere masturbation, as is contended below, in which Ignatius engrosses himself. Instead, Ignatius is specifically engaged in onanism (self-gratification at the expense of reproductive responsibility)—a word he applies with intrigue to the chalk in faux-Lady Philosophy's hand.[2] It is this failure of responsibility, whether to his mother, his employers, or even to his own intellectual labors, which is permitted by his pernicious misreading of Boethius's discourse on Lady Fortuna. This locks his mode of discourse into a monological style which prevents him from entering into true conversation with others throughout the novel (except, perhaps, in a few rare moments—such as when he attempts to share his copy of the *Consolation of Philosophy*). And so, third, because Ignatius's intellectual labors began in college, we can draw a legitimate parallel between the philosopher's weeping complaint at the opening of *Consolation* and Ignatius's belching protests: education and its promises have failed them both, or at least as they perceive it. Boethius's *Consolation* was informed by his own role as a writer of textbooks on the seven liberal arts: grammar, logic, rhetoric, arithmetic, geometry, astronomy, and music. Indulging in rhetoric divorced from the love of learning upon which it thrives, the mind of Ignatius is thus understandably, by his own admission, a morality play of conflict[3] Fourth and finally, however, it must be recognized that, just as Toole was too sophisticated to be inexorably trapped by the urge to caricature himself as some would have it, he was likewise too sympathetic and perceptive to merely create a character at whom we are simply intended to sneer. Although Ignatius is a fool who is frustratingly too wise in his own estimation to see it, manipulating others to avoid the responsibilities implied by and represented by his sexuality with a perverted imitation of genuine eloquence, if we scrutinize ourselves with the Boethian honesty which Toole's infantile Boethian so desperately lacked, we will see the Ignatius bellowing within our own discourse when it grows masturbatory. Just as the imprisoned Boethius broke the homological discourse of his own grief with the voice of Lady Philosophy, Toole, a master at imitation because a deft listener, presents in the centrifugal whirl of Ignatius's self-absorbed, Fortune-obsessed onanism a glimpse into the space provided by a divorce from the sound of our own voices where listening can truly take place.

MENIPPEAN MASTURBATION AND
IGNATIUS REILLY'S BIG CHIEF TABLETS

When told that a main character of a novel ardently loves the work of Boethius, Ignatius J. Reilly is not the figure one might expect if familiar with the work of the so-called last of the Romans and first of the scholastics. Boethius was a high-powered politician, an influential theologian and philosopher, a translator and transmitter of Greek thought to his Roman peers, and, to the Middle Ages, a great example of a noble soul tragically persecuted, imprisoned, and then executed by a barbaric, heretical tyrant.[4] The carnivalesque Ignatius J. Reilly, whose antics prevent him from holding a job for more than a few weeks and a devouring son who oppresses his continually nonplussed mother, seems more fitting as a humorous character from *The Canterbury Tales* or a Dickens novel than a disciple of Boethian thought.[5] The failure on the part of Ignatius to recognize his own foolishness is precisely the Menippean release of satisfaction readers of the wildly hilarious text are time and again denied.

Direct humor is sparse in *Consolation*, but the one true joke in the text is at the expense of a philosopher who thinks himself wise. Another philosopher challenges him to endure insults to prove his wise patience: "For a time he did assume patience and after accepting the insults asked with a sneer whether the other now agreed that he was a philosopher. 'I would,' came the reply, 'if you had not spoken'" (2.7).[6] This moment, as well as others, has been regarded by some scholars (such as Joel Relihan and John Marenbon) as an indication that Boethius is not always quite so serious in the presentation of Lady Philosophy's arguments—that he is engaged in fashioning a Menippean satire,[7] a genre of mixed form where *a man who thinks himself wise discovers he is in fact a fool*.[8] This attack on the legitimacy of an intellectual's claim to the title is made by Ignatius against Dr. Talc in a typically, farcically belligerent letter:

> Your total ignorance of that which you profess to teach merits the death penalty. I doubt whether you would know that St. Cassian of Imola was stabbed to death by his students with their styli. His death, a martyr's honorable one, made him a patron saint of teachers.
>
> Pray to him, you deluded fool, you "anyone for tennis" golf-playing, cocktail-quaffing pseudo-pedant, for you do indeed need a heavenly patron.
>
> Although your days are numbered, you will not die as a martyr—for you further no holy cause—but as the total ass which you really are.[9]

Ignatius actually seems to be accurate in his assessment of Dr. Talc, yet his vitriol against the inept professor is decidedly out of keeping with the Boethian teaching about sympathy toward men who fail in virtue:

> There is no reason at all for hating the bad . . . weakness is a disease of the body, so wickedness is a disease of the mind . . . since we think of people who are sick in body as deserving sympathy rather than hatred, much more so do they deserve pity rather than blame who suffer an evil more severe than any physical illness (Boethius 4.iv.101).

In spite of Ignatius's pseudonym, Dr. Talc knows exactly who is threatening him, and so Ignatius breaks the philosopher's capacity for silence in the face of another's provocations; likewise, Ignatius fails to make peace with Dr. Talc's shortcomings, which are annoying to the intellectually curious student but rather harmless (except perhaps to his female students). College age Ignatius was arguably more accurate in the target of his disdain, yet it remains expressed in a manner clearly at variance with the teachings of *Consolation*.

Perhaps when Ignatius penned that note he had not yet read Boethius, but when we meet him in the novel he is "matured" into his worldview and continues to misread his idolized author. In the opening of the second chapter of *Confederacy*, where the explicitly Boethian matter is first introduced, we find Ignatius using the wheel of Fortune as a motif by which he rails against the degradation of society since the Middle Ages. Unable to sustain the vision of his plaintive intellectual history, Ignatius moves to his despondent, Boethian lamentation, and then into a bizarre, disappointing session of masturbation. In limited third person omniscience, the narrator tells us that

"Ignatius believed in the *rota Fortunae*, or wheel of fortune, a central concept in *Consolation*, the philosophical work which had laid the foundation for medieval thought".[10] Correctly adjudicating the legacy of Boethius, Ignatius's reported stream of consciousness turns to an almost encyclopedic account of the Roman senator's life: "Boethius, the late Roman who had written the *Consolation* while unjustly imprisoned by the emperor, had said that a blind goddess spins us on a wheel, that our luck comes in cycles."[11] Recalling his intellectual hero's signature contribution to medieval poetic imagery, Ignatius goes on to lament, in hyperbolic Boethian style, his own mistreatment at the hands of Fortune: "Was the ludicrous attempt to arrest him the beginning of a bad cycle? Was his wheel rapidly spinning downward?"[12] In this self-pitying and hilariously self-ignorant lamentation, however, Ignatius elides a crucial component of Philosophy's teaching on Fortuna—she is not a real force, but merely a product of human ignorance in the face of complex circumstances:

> If chance is defined as an event produced by random motion without any causal nexus, I would say that there is no such thing as chance, and that apart from signifying the subject matter of our discussion it is a completely meaningless word (Boethius 5.i.117).

It seems possible, given Ignatius's misunderstanding of Boethius's doctrine concerning the ontological status of Fortune, that he never himself finished the very book he is so adamant in telling others to read. He prays, "Oh, Fortuna, blind, heedless goddess, I am strapped to your wheel. . . . Do not crush me beneath your spokes. Raise me on high, divinity".[13] Only metaphorically would Boethius ever refer to Fortuna as "divinity," and never would he seriously recommend praying to her—she does not exist except as a useful fiction for collating the existential frustration of the individual's inability to fully comprehend reality's numerous, unpredictable causes. Toole was perfectly aware of the authentic understanding of Boethian philosophy, as is clear from a statement he made as recorded by MacLauchlin: "Fortune and nature are, together, on the bottom rung of what might be called the Boethian hierarchy. . . . Destiny directs God's will directly through them to man".[14] As Lady Philosophy teaches Boethius at the close of the *Consolation*, Ignatius should be praying to God rather than Fortuna, and Toole is well aware of this.[15]

Toole is thus in control of Ignatius's personality in a way that undercuts the critical tendency to read Ignatius as merely an avatar or mouthpiece of his philosophy.[16] It is more likely that, as a discerning observer of personality plopped among professors and students (a crowd which desires desperately to be deemed wise much like the philosopher in Boethius's humorous anecdote), Toole perceived the Ignatian tendency to project greater confidence in one's knowledge than was always appropriate and then, even, to rest one's perspective and identity upon that imperfect information. Introspective as he was, Toole likely saw that self-aggrandizing tendency in himself (unavoidably so given his mother's tireless adulations of him), and perhaps in his fellow professor and Boethius scholar Byrne, the model for Ignatius Reilly. But Ignatius is that tendency writ large, into a caricature who does not even seem to notice or be bothered by his disorienting transition from sympathetic meditation on Boethius, to an irate exchange with his mother, to an underwhelming session of masturbation. His masturbatory habit, brought to the reader's attention as it is in the same scene where Ignatius identifies for the first time Boethius as the source of his perspective and where we first see him at work at what is in his view his primary vocation (writing), suggests itself as a hermeneutic, so to speak, at work in Ignatius's interpretive strategies. His reading of *Consolation* is incomplete, just as any object of masturbatory fantasy is incomplete—for it is a fantasy and not engaged with the actual object (or subject) of desire. Once, Ignatius had labored to compensate for this deficiency in masturbation by means of a more thorough make-believe: "At one time he had almost developed it [masturbation] into an art form, practicing the hobby with the skill and fervor of an artist and philosopher, a scholar and gentleman."[17] It seems almost oxymoronic to envision masturbation as gentlemanly, while the terms artist, philosopher, and scholar all seem to refer back to Ignatius's identification with Boethius, whose *Consolation* was the result of intense scholarly learning and artistic capability.

But literal gentlemanliness is one thing that is precluded in self-pleasuring, for there is no other person to be treated with dignity and earnest attentiveness as can occur in partnered sexual activity (whether heterosexual or otherwise). Of course, one's masturbatory fantasies could be more or less gentlemanly—the startling turn of Ignatius's mind to his collie Rex is less, especially given that Rex is, in the fantasy, tricked into performing imagined assistance to his release. The fact that Ignatius does not even bother to imagine a human suggests just how masturbatory his masturbation has become—he does not even pretend to attract another's sexual interest or someone who could verbally respond to his presence. "Woof! Woof! Arf!" says Rex, innocent of sexual interest in the game of chase.[18] There is no other human voice in this example of Ignatius's sex life, which mirrors the descent into animality by the vicious human soul as imagined by Boethius: "[Y]ou cannot think of anyone as human whom you see transformed by wickedness. . . . A wild and restless man who is for ever exercising his tongue in lawsuits could be compared to a dog yapping" (4.p.iii.92). Certainly wild and restless, Ignatius also frequently threatens to summon his non-existent army of lawyers at the least offense or to protect himself from incrimination.[19] The constant shouting from his neighbor Miss Anne to keep it down reduces Ignatius to little more than an annoying dog whose voice must be silenced. Indeed, given his unboethian devotion to the metaphysical reality of Lady Fortuna, Ignatius has consigned himself to a silenced voice. Lady Philosophy tells Boethius, "If Fortune herself had been speaking, she would have left you without a single syllable you could utter by way of reply" (Boethius 2.p3.27). Boethius himself lamented Fortune's ways at the outset of his *Consolation* as she turned her favor away from him, and yet the purpose of Lady Philosophy's personification of the fickle goddess is to lift him *out* of contemplation of Fortuna, whereas Ignatius instead devotes himself to her (just as masturbation may come to replace the pursuit of intimacy rather than serve as a private longing for it).

This is why Ignatius's sessions of masturbation have grown unsatisfactory: "He thought somewhat sadly that after eighteen years with his hobby it had become merely a mechanical physical act stripped of the flights of fancy and invention that he had once been able to bring to it."[20] Lady Philosophy promises just that capacity of mental flight, but away from attachment to worldly goods rather than toward momentary, ultimately unsatisfactory pleasure: "I will give your mind wings on which to lift itself; all disquiet shall be driven away" (Boethius 4.p1.86). But Ignatius's lonely orgasms, rather than dispelling disquiet, have begun to produce it: "There were still hidden in his room several accessories which he had once used. . . . Putting them away again after it was all over had eventually grown too depressing."[21] Mirroring his efforts at sensual relief are his efforts at composing his criticism of the age, which far from consoling the mind assure it of the decadence of modern society: "Fortuna's wheel had turned on humanity, crushing its collarbone, smashing its skull, twisting its torso, puncturing its pelvis, sorrowing its soul."[22] The amusingly redundant and macabre imagery, including as it does damage to the reproductive region, can lead nowhere except dissatisfaction. And it is precisely when Ignatius's composition turns to the idea of having to be productive, for his sake and his mother's, that he loses his writerly stamina: "And a vicious fate it was to be: now he was faced with the perversion of having to GO TO WORK. His vision of history temporarily fading, Ignatius sketched a noose at the bottom of the page."[23] Boethius thought of death when he found himself thrown unjustly into prison; Ignatius thinks of death because he needs to get a job. The bathetic imagination necessary to contain both Ignatius and Boethius may seem incredible, but unburdened as he is by an interest to interpret *Consolation* apart from his own concerns removes this challenge.

Like his perpetually clinching valve, Ignatius's ontologically reified interpretation of Fortuna's wheel permits him to forge a masturbatory understanding of Boethius which is then the perspective from which he interprets reality itself. Ignatius pleases himself with the thought that "what had once been dedicated to the soul was now dedicated to the sale. 'That is rather fine,' Ignatius said to himself and continued his hurried writing."[24] There is no other voice or perspective who he has to worry about pleasing in this thought—no intellectual equal who can challenge his understanding either of the Middle Ages or his own time—and so his latest mental ejaculation joins the "yellowed pages and wide-ruled lines" of "the dozens of Big Chief tablets" which Ignatius "thought smugly . . . were the seeds of a magnificent study in comparative history."[25] He hopes it will be his seminal work—yet it is hard to tell apart from the other work he performs on paper in the room where he hopes he has "some Kleenex."[26] The problem is of course not that Ignatius masturbates, but that masturbation has become the dedicated site of his sexual imagination, closing him off from the vulnerable, yet what would be for him more satisfying, experience of true intimacy. With no external voices in his pursuit of sexual pleasure, Ignatius likewise truncates the possibility of real dialogic encounters in his perspective—even with Boethius, whom he reduces to a fatalistic philosopher of random chance, ignoring Boethius's discourse on free will to the end (whether intentional or not) of limiting his own access to personal responsibility (implied in the despair over his need to "GO TO WORK"). Ignatius regards himself as a wise, marginalized Boethian prophet indicting his age, yet he is as isolated from the thought of Boethius as he his from a real lover. Without Boethian empathy toward the failures of others or recourse to the Boethian rationale for some measure of hope in life, his writing is thus unsurprisingly unproductive in spawning much more consolation than the solace that he is surrounded by a confederacy of dunces, unable to quite fathom the core joke of the Menippean hero's journey—that he was the fool, who thought himself wise.

THE ONANISTIC RAPE OF PHILOSOPHY

Ignatius's refusal of financial productivity, manifested in his self-sabotage as an employee at Levy Pants and Paradise Vendors and his unfulfilled attempt to compose his medievalist's commentary on the modern age, both represent the unfulfilled consummation of his potential to the perennial frustration of Mrs. Reilly. While supposed to be working to assist his mother manage their desperate household financial situation, Ignatius finds himself in conversation with the street urchin George, and so finds the rare, if unintended, fruit of his Boethian seed in the form of Lana Lee's illegal pornographic merchandise:

"Oh, my God!" Ignatius stared at what he saw. Once in high school someone had shown him a pornographic photograph, and he had collapsed against a watercooler, injuring his ear. This photograph was far superior. A nude woman was sitting on the edge of a desk next to a globe of the world. The suggested onanism with the piece of chalk intrigued Ignatius. Her face was hidden behind a large book. While George evaded indifferent slaps from the unoccupied paw,

> Ignatius scrutinized the title on the cover of the book: Anicius Severins Manlius Boethius, *The Consolation of Philosophy.* "Do I believe what I am seeing? What brilliance. What taste. Good grief."[27]

Certainly, onanism can simply mean masturbation, and perhaps that is all that Ignatius intended in the word, communicated as it is via the third person narrator. But as Leighton points out, Genesis was on Toole's mind when he composed *Confederacy*, with Abelman a plausible yet obvious portmanteau of "Abel" and "man," and Ignatius a brother-despising Cain figure (it should be remembered that Grendel, a monster descended from Cain in *Beowulf*, emerged from his lair to destroy innocent lives because he was annoyed by the noisy productions of his culture, not entirely unlike Ignatius). Much later in the Book of Genesis, when a man with the allegorically poignant name Er dies, his brother Onan is tasked with the responsibility of seeing to it that neither his brother nor his wife are left without a legacy:

> Then Judah said to Onan, "Go in to your brother's wife and perform the duty of a brother-in-law to her; raise up offspring for your brother." But since Onan knew that the offspring would not be his, he spilled his semen on the ground whenever he went in to his brother's wife, so that he would not give offspring to his brother. What he did was displeasing in the sight of the Lord, and he put him to death also. (Genesis 38: 8-10, NRSV)

God does not kill Onan in Genesis because he masturbated, but because he employed coitus interruptus to shirk his duty to his deceased brother's wife. If God is, at minimum in the register of the hero's journey, the individual's manifest duty to the wellbeing of the community and the consequences which descend upon that individual when those responsibilities are shirked, Ignatius has certainly angered God as well. Ignatius levied his own critique of society when admonishing Mancuso for bothering him when he is merely waiting for his mother:

> This city is famous for its gamblers, prostitutes, exhibitionists, Antichrists, alcoholics, sodomites, drug addicts, fetishists, onanists, pornographers, frauds, jades, litterbugs, and lesbians, all of whom are only too well protected by graft. If you have a moment, I shall endeavor to discuss the crime problem with you, but don't make the mistake of bothering me.[28]

Ignatius not only hypocritically elevates himself above the members of this list; he is engaged in his social onanism even as he shiftlessly waits for his mother to come from the grocery store (with no plans to help her carry, let alone to pay for, those groceries). Shortly thereafter we learn that his own repeated call for "theology and geometry" is itself a social obligation he leaves unsatisfied: "The last time that she had forced him [Ignatius] to accompany her to mass on Sunday he had collapsed twice on the way to the church and had collapsed once again during the sermon about sloth."[29] And unlike Lady Fortuna, except to reiterate "oh, my God!" any number of times, Ignatius never prays to him—only asserts that he must not be questioned (unlike Abraham, who questions God directly, and Jacob, who is renamed Israel for his willingness to wrestle with the Lord). Even God is but a mono-logical tool in Ignatius's theological browbeating of society—unquestioned and, so, unheard.

The mockery of education in Lana Lee's smut, furthermore, coincides with Ignatius's own cerebral onanisms, her chalk as reminiscent of Ignatius's own invective-spurting pen (which at times he struggles to operate properly) as it is of his wayward erections. That Ignatius is titillated rather than horrified at the onanistic use of his intellectual hero underscores that he sees here a reflec-tion of his own employment of Boethian philosophy. In its own way, pornog-raphy, too, could be seen as a sort of onanistic emission of sexual potential without anything produced from it—except an invitation of young men like George to an onanistic lifestyle with the same obstacles to connection with which Ignatius must contend. In opposition to the masturbatory fantasies of Ignatius, *Consolation* is centered around conjuring imagined women (Lady Philosophy, Lady Fortune, and the Muses) for the end of producing dialogue. Lady Philosophy banishes the Muses because, instead of helping Boethius to find his voice, they "slay the rich and fruitful harvest of Reason with the barren thorns of Passion" (Boethius 1.1.4). Lady Philosophy is herself the object of an intellectual assault rendered more distressing by her feminine personification:

> After that the mobs of Epicureans and Stoics and the others each did all they could to seize for themselves the inheritance of wisdom that he left. As part of their plunder they tried to carry me off, but I fought and struggled, and in the fight the robe was torn which I had woven with my own hands. (1.3.7)

In his onanistic reading of *Consolation* as a book merely about Fortune's wheel, Ignatius has made himself one of the mob of the pseudo-philosophers. His mother's dress is torn, which he scornfully mocks: "I dare you to come out in that shredded nightgown and get me!"[30] After his first genuine sexual arousal at the image of the faux-Lady Philosophy Lana Lee, Ignatius attends a movie where he demands the rape of an apparently virginal actress: "How dare she pretend to be a virgin. Look at her degenerate face. Rape her!"[31] In this vile comment, bellowed to the dismay of his fellow movie goers, he has called for the same treatment to which Lady Philosophy would have been sub-jected if she had not been capable of defending herself. However hyperbolic or intended for comic effect, Ignatius crosses a line here in language that seems causally connected to the awakening of his pseudo-Boethian, onanistic appetite. Where Boethius uses personification to imbue thought with voice, Ignatius's preference for Lee's hidden face and onanistic chalk transforms his passive objectification of sexuality into violent objectification.

IGNATIUS'S DIALOGIC DYSFUNCTION AND THE COPULATIVE NATURE OF BOETHIAN COMMUNICATION

It is no accident that the pseudo-Lady Philosophy is aping an educational "posture" in her pornography created for children. Lady Philosophy's goal was to recover for Boethius her program of education: "[T]his man has been nourished on the philosophies of Zeno and Plato. . . . be gone, and leave him for my own Muses to heal and cure" (Boethius 1.1.5). Through alternating prose and poetry, Lady Philosophy reminds Boethius of the education in the life of the mind he had received under her tutelage. As a pedagogue, Boethius had written on the seven liberal arts, including rhetoric, which concluded the sequence of the Trivium (grammar, logic, and rhetoric), and in fact he connects his discourse on Fortune to the province of rhetoric:

> I know the many disguises of that monster, Fortune. . . . If you can recall to mind her character . . . Let us bring to bear the persuasive powers of sweet-tongued rhetoric, powers which soon go astray from the true path unless they follow my instruction. (Boethius 2.i.22)

Rhetoric is the tool which exposes Fortuna, but also shares in her erratically persuasive nature. Ignatius's wildly eloquent tongue exhibits rhetoric's capacity for persuasion, yet remains uncoupled with the sapient *telos* Lady Philosophy requires of Fortune-transcending rhetoric.[32] As Miriam Joseph puts it in *The Trivium*, a textbook modeled on the same language curriculum in which Boethius operated, "Communication, as the etymology of the word signifies, results in something possessed in common; it is a oneness shared. Communication takes place only when two minds really meet."[33] Through philosophy, Boethius escapes the onanism of Fortune's masturbatory silence and achieves eloquent union with the love of learning—a love which Ignatius was so disappointed to find lacking in Dr. Talc (and which he, admittedly eloquently if brutishly, condemns).

With his volatile changes in mood, Ignatius is a mercurial figure in the literal sense of the word, but also represents eloquence—or rather, an onanistic, abortive parody of eloquence. Indeed, it is perhaps precisely Ignatius's verbal alacrity which makes him so amusing for the reader to "listen to" in spite of the often wretched nature of his utterances. Rhetoric is, unlike grammar and logic, marked by sensitivity to the tempo of the concrete utterance, the lack of which sensitivity is established as utterly absent in Ignatius when he tells his bus story to his mother at the Night of Joy: "Mrs. Reilly's attention wavered between her son and the beer. She had been listening to the story for three years."[34] Rather than detecting her desire to talk about something else, "Ignatius continued, mistaking his mother's rapt look for interest."[35] Unlike Lady Philosophy who uses language to marry Boethius's mind to comforting truths, Ignatius uses his language to uncouple himself from others, either from his written professions of a divorce from modern society's values or to the self-pleasuring way in which he communicates with others even when they have no interest in hearing him. "Oneness shared" is hardly the result of Ignatius's words—he professes to share his story of the bus with his mother to give her insight into one of his formative moments, and yet is unable to interest her. Darlene finds Ignatius engaging because he offers the rhetorical spice of narrative and because of the educated manner in which he speaks. She says, "I like good stories. You got a spicy one?,"[36] initiating the conversation because of Ignatius's storytelling capacity, and then noting, "You got a good education" when she hears him use big words such as "atrophy."[37] But the lack of good will (a failure of ethos, one of the essential appeals of successful rhetoric) he exhibits toward his mother renders his eloquence off-putting rather than admirable to Darlene:

> "'Graduated smart,' Ignatius repeated with some pique. 'Please define your terms. Exactly what do you mean by 'graduated smart'?'
> 'Don't talk to your momma like that,' Darlene said."[38]

The rhetorical triangle, that is, the speaker, listener, and shared message, is treated to a sort of eloquent hand grenade every time Ignatius speaks. As his off-putting accomplice in tormenting Dr. Talc at college and as the one attempting to push his impractical elocutions into a more active life, Myrna is a parody of Lady Philosophy. Tison Pugh comments insightfully that "if Ignatius is ever to see a woman as a woman and not as an obstacle, it must be Myrna who will educate him"[39]—educate him out of his masturbatory hermeneutics, one might add. But whereas Ignatius cannot help but accrue audiences everywhere he goes (even when standing outside of the grocery waiting for his mother let alone while fainting onanistically before what Ignatius himself terms the allegorically named *Desire* bus), Myrna, in her passionate desire to give transforming lectures (a love of learning however comically perverted by her pseudo-Freudianism) is frustrated by her inability to maintain an audience. She writes Ignatius, "The lecture was not exactly a success, I'm afraid. It went over all right—right over the people's heads. . . . Just as I suspected, I was a little too advanced for the neighborhood audience."[40] Myrna is just as guilty as Ignatius in using her (even if relatively more modern) ideology to circumvent actually listening to his perspective and instead provide him a psychoanalytical diagnosis:

> Are you hanging around with some queers? I could have guessed that this would happen. . . . Your normal sexual outlets have been blocked for so long that now the sexual overflow is seeping out into the wrong channels.[41]

Myrna understands even less of what Ignatius is up to than his own distorted letters could suggest; his speech is homophobically stripped away as Myrna views Ignatius as an interesting scientific subject for her and her friends to condescendingly mull over. But this deafness to Ignatius's voice, not only from Myrna but from his own mother as well as many others, is made inexorable by his own inability to undergo Boethius's journey to marry articulated speech to good will.

Because he has misread Philosophy's discourse on Fortune, Ignatius has adopted a worldview that actually militates against the communicative perspective of central importance to Boethius: "When you speak, your whole voice fills the ears of many hearers to an equal extent, but your riches cannot in the same way be shared equally among many without diminution" (2.v.33). Boethius mentions the power of voice as being greater than the power of wealth, but this power can only bring order to the individual (the theology and geometry Ignatius often references but never elucidates upon) when the heart of the individual is married to the Love which orders the cosmos: "If Love who rules the sky/Could rule your hearts as well!" (2.viii.45-46). Far transcendent to the wheel of Fortune, which is merely a metaphor for psychological attachment to worldly goods, it is love by which cosmic harmony can manifest itself in true communication. Ironically enough, however, Ignatius has indeed been a force of Fortuna; his bumbling presence helped Mancuso to uncover Lana Lee's illicit and revolting capitalization on children, Mr. Levy to escape the devouring Freudianism of his wife, and Burma Jones to become gainfully employed.[42]

Indeed, Mr. Levy is one of the few characters in the novel whose efforts at listening are actually depicted (excepting Burma Jones and, to a lesser extent, Darlene)—he really listens to Ignatius, to Miss Anne, and even to Trixie. For all of the wild dialogue surrounding Ignatius, it is only Levy whose internal processing of what Ignatius had to say, and what others had to say about him, allows him to find a sympathetic vantage point from which the giant Boethian can be understood:

"Don't hit him again," Mr. Levy said. The kook's head was already bandaged. Outside of the prizefighting ring, violence made Mr. Levy ill. This Reilly kook was really pitiful. The mother ran around with some old man, drank, wanted the son out of the way. She was already on the police blotter. That dog was probably the only thing that the kook had ever really had in his life. Sometimes you have to see a person in his real environment to understand him.[43]

In fact, even though it ultimately displeases her, Mrs. Levy is even listened to by the nonplussed factory owner. Mr. Levy had listened so carefully to Ignatius, furthermore, that simply by remembering his vocabulary, he realizes that Ignatius had deceived him into blaming Mrs. Trixie—and yet he carries through with letting her take the fall because it is the best for all involved, Mrs. Trixi included.[44] Likewise, even Myrna, in spite of her tendency towards mono-logical thinking, has at least listened enough to detect sickness in Ignatius. And he tells her, "If only I had listened to you earlier".[45] In a manipulative sort of way, Ignatius capitulates to her ideology, but admits he regrets not listening to her. Myrna had written, "I need immediate communication from you,"[46] liter-ally meaning correspondence, but true communication, the marriage of the spo-ken word with the listening ear, is precisely what they both desperately needed.

AUDIENCE AWARENESS AND IGNATIUS AS TOOLE'S NEGATIVE, YET SYMPATHETIC, EXEMPLUM

Rudnicki aptly observes that "one of the many reasons Ignatius Reilly makes readers laugh is that his speech is entirely inconsistent with the situ-ation in which he finds himself".[47] But underneath the humor of his antics, there is a profound tragedy in Ignatius. He is a man who falls down, whose grief was never answered over the death of his dog, whose confidence was legitimately shattered in school, whose mother excessively coddled him and empowered him to become the leech she could no longer tolerate, whose health unsurprisingly fails due to his obesity, and whose intellec-tual appetites were stymied by an incompetent professor who, instead of being an example to Ignatius, rendered odious the one profession he might have sought. Imagine the potent force Ignatius could have been if he had adopted Mr. Levy's attentiveness and Myrna's interest in the truth (however momentary): if he had actually listened to his mother, and spoken to her with a listening, dialogic word. The centripetal force of successful com-munication never occurs because of the whirring, circular, centrifugal force which, when it connects, creates centripetal crashing instead of centripetal connection. Just as at the failed party at Dorian Greene's apartment, despite all of his bellowing, Ignatius never speaks because he never listens. And what could he have to listen to, if the words of others are but the offshoots of Fortuna's wheel? Toole emerges in his biography as someone who was an incredibly capable listener. Meanwhile, Ignatius scoffs at the "exemplum" the children on his television program are supposed to provide,[48] but a negative exemplum is precisely his function in the adroit narrative hands of Toole as he portrays Ignatius's noisy eructations (whether literal belches or his belch-like words). More eloquence can be found, rather, in silence—as Boethius is silent at the end of the *Consolation of Philosophy*, and as Ignatius is finally quiet as Myrna takes him away from a dungeon fashioned in no small part by his hyper-verbal, onanistic misreading of his own Menippean folly. The consolation to be found in *Confederacy* is in the recognition that Ignatius is the dunce of dialogue and so is the reader who judges him to be so, and therefore as depicted with Mr. Levy, masturbatory hermeneutics and onanistic discourse can be abandoned in favor of adopting the radical responsibility of opening our own speech to the space of outside vocalization. Parties like those at Dorian Greene's apartment, "where the other guests were attacking one another with conversation"[49] can be exchanged for the car-ride conversation, where can be breathed "the salt-air blowing in over the marshes from the Gulf."[50] Ignatius might still be waiting expectantly on Fortuna's "new cycle," but he "breathed again, this time more deeply";[51] he has ceased oppressing his mother and begun to hear others—however distorted, manipulation at least requires genuine listening. Affectionately pressing Myrna's pigtail against his lips and leaving behind his pseudo-Boethian tomblike womb-room, Ignatius is not too wise for dialogue anymore.

NOTES

1. *Confederacy*, 30–31.
2. *Confederacy*, 288.
3. *Confederacy*, 270–271.
4. For a comprehensive examination of Boethius's life, work, and times, see Chadwick, 1981.
5. Toole was well aware, of course, of Chaucer's deep indebtedness to Boethius. See Leighton, 2014.
6. 42–43. I use throughout the 1999 translation of *Consolation* by Watts.
7. Payne, *Chaucer*, has been particularly influential in asserting the interpretation of Boethius's *Consolation* as part of the genre, and thus the Boethian impact upon Chaucer in that regard:

> I shall analyze the Menippean qualities of the *Consolation*, for to judge by Chaucer's use of it . . . . he saw Boethius' work not only as a textbook for classical philosophy but also, and much more important, as the culmination and fulfillment of an ironical mode of containing and assessing the realities of human thought and experience. (p. 58)

8. Relihan offers the most rigorous reading of Boethius's *Consolation* as a Menippean satire, arguing that a

> constant theme in the genre is that those who presume to observe the world from some superior vantage point, whether as moral critics (satirists) or intellectual critics (philosophers), cannot understand what they see, because human life and thought, inherently irrational, cannot be made to fit the logical categories of such observers; consequently, theorists are the butt of the humor of a Menippean satire (p. 5).

This theme is akin to the notion expressed by Paul of the worldly wise: "Claiming themselves to be wise, they become fools" (Romans 1:22, NRSV). Menippean satires expose such fools.

9. *Confederacy*, 28.

10. *Confederacy*, 30.

11. *Confederacy*, 30.

12. *Confederacy*, 30.

13. *Confederacy*, 30.

14. MacLauchlin, *Butterfly*, 50. However, I should add that, as Lady Philosophy claims that she loves to sing about nature in Book III of the *Consolation*, fortune occupies an even lower place than nature in the Boethian hierarchy.

15. Leighton, 90–100, provides a diagram from this same assignment, commenting, "Byrne was not the sole source of Toole's knowledge of Boethius. Toole clearly understood the Boethian idea that an apparently malevolent, worldly Fortune could be under the control of Destiny, the temporal agent of God's beneficent Providence." Ignatius's misreading of Boethius is thus an artistic choice on Toole's part.

16. This can be seen, for example, in Britton, p. 17, who argues that Toole and his maligned literary forebearer Twain "use major characters as voices for their own philosophical bents." The irony of Ignatius's disdain for Twain and his similarity to Twain's knack for idiosyncratic characterization alone complicates this mouthpiece thesis, although I certainly do not deny that Toole saw something of himself in his characters—only that one must proceed with caution when trying to infer from any character what Toole thought, especially the satirically drawn Ignatius J. Reilly.

17. *Confederacy*, 31.

18. *Confederacy*, 31.

19. When Lana Lee tries to collect the money for the drinks Ignatius and his mother had at the Night of Joy, Ignatius thunders, "This is highway robbery! . . . You will hear from our attorneys," *Confederacy*, 23. When Irene tells Ignatius that the man whose building was damaged by their accident is asking for a thousand dollars for damages, he replies, "A thousand dollars? He will not get a cent. We shall have him prosecuted immediately. Contact our attorneys, mother," *Confederacy*, 41. After falling from a stool provided by Mr. Gonzolez at Levy Pants, Ignatius threatens, "I am preparing to contact my attorneys and have them sue you for making me get on that obscene stool," *Confederacy*, 85. To a bewildered Dorian Greene he unleashes his most lavish threat of lawsuits:

> My corps of attorneys will contact you in the morning wherever it is that you carry on your questionable activities. I shall warn them beforehand that they may expect to see and

hear anything. They are all brilliant attorneys, pillars of the community, aristocratic Creole scholars whose knowledge of the more surreptitious forms of living is quite limited. They may even refuse to see you. A considerably lesser representative may be sent to call upon you, some junior partner whom they've taken in out of pity. *Confederacy*, 249.

In the midst of this exchange Dorian calls him an "awful, terrible animal" and a "revolting beast," which, along with the narrator's oft-repeated appellation of "paws" for Igantius's hands (as well as his chosen masturbatory fantasy of Rex and his memory of the dog's death) link him to canine animality befitting Boethius's allegorical taxonomy of beasts.

20. *Confederacy*, 31.
21. *Confederacy*, 31.
22. *Confederacy*, 28.
23. *Confederacy*, 29.
24. *Confederacy*, 28.
25. *Confederacy*, 29.
26. *Confederacy*, 31.
27. *Confederacy*, 288.
28. *Confederacy*, 3.
29. *Confederacy*, 8.
30. *Confederacy*, 307.
31. *Confederacy*, 290.
32. Kline, 290, elucidates the role of rhetoric in Toole's *Confederacy*:

The odd cohabitation of the irreducibly incompatible with the causally conclusive is explained by the structural pattern of disruptive metonymic processing. While rhetorical patterns may not account for every comic effect, the deep structure of humor creation in Toole's novel may be explained by this coexistence of the grotesque with sequentiality.

Kline here means the rhetorical structure of the text, but his point extends as well to the rhetoric of the characters themselves, especially Ignatius, whose words are as much events creating further sequentiality as any action undertaken by the characters.

33. Joseph, 19.
34. *Confederacy*, 11.
35. *Confederacy*, 11.
36. *Confederacy*, 19.
37. *Confederacy*, 21.
38. *Confederacy*, 22.
39. Pugh, 110.
40. *Confederacy*, 304.
41. *Confederacy*, 303.
42. The symbolism of "Ignatius as Wheel" of Fortune has been noted by other scholars, as well as the Fortunesque manner in which he "disrupts the lives of others and changes their fortunes." (See Leighton, "Evidences," 27–28). It is fitting that, as an agent of blind Fortuna, Ignatius is himself blind to the impact left in his impressive wake.

43. *Confederacy*, 367.
44. *Confederacy*, 377.
45. *Confederacy*, 388.
46. *Confederacy*, 304.
47. Rudnicki, 282.
48. *Confederacy*, 42.
49. *Confederacy*, 315.
50. *Confederacy*, 394.
51. *Confederacy*, 394.

BIBLIOGRAPHY

Bakhtin, M. M. *The Dialogic Imagination: Four Essays*. Trans. Caryl Emerson and Michael Holquist. Austin, TX: University of Texas Press, 1983.
Boethius. *The Consolation of Philosophy*. Trans. Victor Watts. Penguin Books, 1999.
Britton, Wesley. "Two Visions of Medievalism and Determinism: Mark Twain and John Kennedy Toole's *A Confederacy of Dunces*." *The Southern Quarterly* 34, no. 1 (1995): 17–23.
Hardin, Michael. "Between Queer Performances: John Kennedy Toole's *The Neon Bible* and *A Confederacy of Dunces*." *Southern Literary Journal* 39, no. 2 (2007): 58–77.
Kline, Michael. "Narrating the Grotesque: The Rhetoric of Humor in John Kennedy Toole's *A Confederacy of Dunces*." *The Southern Quarterly* 37, no. 3/4 (1999): 283–291.
Leighton, H. Vernon. "Evidences of Influences on John Kennedy Toole's *A Confederacy of Dunces*, including Geoffrey Chaucer." Version 2.1. 2 June 2014, accessed August 28, 2018, http://course1.winona.edu/vleighton/toole/Leighton_Toole_Chaucer.pdf.
———. "The Dialectic of American Humanism: John Kennedy Toole's *A Confederacy of Dunces*, Marsilio Ficino, and Paul Oskar Kristeller." *Renascence* 64, no. 2 (2012): 201–215.
Lerer, Seth. *Boethius and Dialogue: Literary Method in The Consolation of Philosophy*. Princeton, NJ: Princeton University Press, 1985.
Lewis, C.S. *The Discarded Image*. Cambridge, UK: Cambridge University Press, 1964.
MacLauchlin, Cory. *Butterfly in the Typewriter: The Tragic Life of John Kennedy Toole and the Remarkable Story of A Confederacy of Dunces*. Da Capo Press, 2012.
Marenbon, John. *Boethius*. Oxford, UK: Oxford University Press, 2003.
McCluskey, Peter M. "Selling Souls and Vending Paradise: God and Commerce in *A Confederacy of Dunces*." *Southern Quarterly* 47, no. 1 (2009): 7–22.
Payne, F. Anne. *Chaucer and Menippean Satire*. Wisconsin University Press, 1981.
Potrc, Julija. "Feast of Fools: The Carnivalesque in John Kennedy Toole's *A Confederacy of Dunces*." *UDK* 821, no. 111 (2010): 83–92.

Pugh, Tison. "'It's prolly fulla dirty stories': Queer Masculinity and Masturbatory Allegory in John Kennedy Toole's *A Confederacy of Dunces*." In *Queer Chivalry: Medievalism and the Myth of White Masculinity in Southern Literature*, 83–111. Louisiana: Louisiana State University Press, 2013.

Relihan, Joel C. *The Prisoner's Philosophy: Life and Death in Boethius's Consolation*. Chicago, IL: Notre Dame University Press, 2007.

Rudnicki, Robert. "*Euphues* and the Anatomy of Influence: John Lyly, Harold Bloom, James Olney, and the Construction of John Kennedy Toole's Ignatius." *The Mississippi Quarterly* 62, no. 1/2 (2009): 281–301.

Toole, John Kennedy. *A Confederacy of Dunces*. New York, NY: Grove Press, 1980.

Chapter 10

The Representation of Speech in *A Confederacy of Dunces*

Connie Eble

The epigraph to *A Confederacy of Dunces* consists of two quotations: the first about language and the second about culture. It aptly lays the foundation of the novel, for it is the fusion of language and culture that creates the palpable world of New Orleans in the late 1950s and early 1960s, in which the hero, Ignatius J. Reilly, makes his way. How the characters sound—their "odd speech," as Walker Percy calls it[1]—permeates the reading experience. Beginning with Mrs. Reilly's first words on page four, the representation of the speech of New Orleanians in the novel proves more than important: it is essential. Hardly a reviewer of the novel when it was published or since fails to comment on Toole's ability to evoke the perception of accurate local dialect. Even natives of the city, who rarely feel that imitators of New Orleans speech get it right, hear themselves and their neighbors. According to John Lowe, "I have yet to meet a New Orleanian who has read *Confederacy* and *doesn't* believe that Toole got the city and its citizens exactly right, including the ethnic voices."[2] This essay examines how John Kennedy Toole effectively uses selected features of varieties of New Orleans speech to construct images of fictional characters inextricable from their city.

First, he establishes at the outset by means of the epigraph the expectation that New Orleans has a peculiar accent for a city located in the Deep South, one like the area around New York City rather than like other southern cities.

> There is a New Orleans city accent . . . associated with downtown New Orleans, particularly with the German and Irish Third Ward, that is hard to distinguish from the accent of Hoboken, Jersey City, and Astoria, Long Island, where the Al Smith inflection, extinct in Manhattan, has taken refuge. The reason, as you might expect, is that the same stocks that brought the accent to Manhattan imposed it on New Orleans.

Early in the novel, on page four, the narrative voice repeats this information the first time Ignatius's mother Mrs. (Irene) Reilly speaks: "Oh, Miss Inez, Mrs. Reilly called in that accent that occurs south of New Jersey only in New Orleans, that Hoboken near the Gulf of Mexico. Over here, babe."[3] Toole brings up the issue of dialect directly two additional times, both in the voice of Ignatius.

> Please! Ignatius shouted furiously. I'm not in the mood for a dialect story.[4]

> Noticing me, they paused and, in sharp Midwestern accents which assailed my delicate eardrums like the sounds of a wheat thresher (however unimaginably horrible that must sound), begged me to pose for a photograph. [Lance, Your Besieged Working Boy][5]

The opening chapter immediately confirms the importance of the way characters sound and use language. It contains the greatest amount of dialog and exemplifies almost all of the means that Toole uses to prompt the impression of authentic local speech that lasts through the reading of the novel. The first conversation involving Mrs. Reilly sets her up as the major conveyor of the accent throughout the novel. Only some of the other characters are *dialect carriers*: Mrs. Reilly's neighbor Miss Annie and her gentleman friend Claude Robichaux, Police Sgt. Angelo Mancuso, Angelo's aunt Santa Battaglia, the owner of Paradise Vendors, the owner of the Night of Joy night club, the bargirl Darlene, and the African American Burma Jones. Furthermore, the combined dialog of these characters constitutes less than half of the book.

Toole depicts the phonology (sounds) of the dialect carriers in a limited way. He mainly uses conventional spellings of spoken forms, for example, *gimme, hasta, wanna, gonna, shoulda*, and so on. Here are a few instances of such misspellings representing the speech of Mrs. Reilly.

Look, you wanna gimme half a dozen wine cakes, too?
   Ignatius gets nasty if we run outta cake.[6]
Ignatius hasta help me at home.[7]
You musta done something while you was waiting
   for me, Ignatius. I know you, boy.[8]
You wanna go back on the street?[9]
What I'm gonna do with a boy like that?[10]
I shoulda guessed Ignatius was wrong all along.[11]

These represent colloquial language, certainly not distinctive to New Orleans or to any other region. However, only the dialect carriers use them—even though other characters in the novel speak informally as well. For example, chapter three, section three, is devoid of dialect indicators. Mr. Gonzalez and

Miss Trixie converse in informal but grammatically standard speech, and Toole records their speech entirely in conventional spelling.[12] A later conversation among Gus Levy, Mrs. Levy, and Miss Trixie[13] is likewise informal but lacking in any indicators of how the characters sound.

Other than the conventional renderings of the kind illustrated above, nonstandard spellings are used sparingly to indicate local pronunciation.

In the opening conversation between Mrs. Reilly and Miss Inez, Toole records the first of a tiny set of local pronunciations—the spelling *er* for the diphthong /oi/, which occurs in such words as *oil, toilet,* and *appointment.* Miss Inez, the bakery clerk at D. H. Holmes, says, "We make him go set himself in a tub fulla berling water."[14] Mrs. Reilly uses the same pronunciation in "that was the one knocked a pot of berling water on her arm when she was a child."[15] Later Santa Battaglia says *ersters* for *oysters*: "I just finished opening four dozen ersters out in the backyard, Santa said in her rocky baritone. That's hard work, believe me, banging that erster knife on them bricks."[16] But this representation of a local stigmatized pronunciation occurs in only two vocabulary items fewer than ten times in the 400-page novel.

Toole records two additional words in their stigmatized local pronunciations associated in New Orleans with white working class speech. Mrs. Reilly says *wrench* for *rinse*, and both she and Santa Battaglia say *zink* for *sink*.

I wanna go wrench out my glass in the zink. [Mrs. Reilly][17]
Well, lemme go dump these dishes in the zink. [Santa Battaglia][18]

In the speech of Burma Jones, Toole shows the typical African American pronunciation *po-lice*[19] with stress on the first syllable and r-less *bobby-cue*[20] for *barbecue.*

Another feature of New Orleans speech—not exclusive to New Orleans to be sure—is simplification of final consonant clusters, as shown in the spellings *communis* for *communist(s)* and *arres* for *arrest.* Again, such spellings are confined to the speech of the dialect carriers and, except for the speech of Burma Jones, are concentrated in the opening chapter.

You better watch out who you calling a communiss. [Sgt. Mancuso][21]
I just got nervous. I got carried away. This policeman was trying to arres
    a poor boy waiting for his momma by Holmes. [Mr. Robichaux][22]
Poor old man. I bet nobody ast him out. [Santa Battaglia][23]

New Orleans speech has traditionally not pronounced /-r/ after vowels in some contexts, for example, pronouncing *artistic* and *autistic* alike and rhyming *water* and *quarter.* Toole uses this characteristic of New Orleans phonology sparingly. Loss of /-r/ shows up mainly in *they* for *they're* and *their* and *you* for *you're* and *your.*

Get a rag. One of the customers just spilled they drink. [Mrs. Reilly][24]
We know when we not wanted. [Mrs. Reilly][25]
They all operated by a bunch of bums. [Mrs. Reilly][26]
I think it's wonderful you praying, babe. [Mrs. Reilly][27]
They home, a woman[Miss Annie] screamed through
    the shutters of the house next door.[28]
You a fine boy with a good education. [Mrs. Reilly][29]

Toole knowingly puts *ax* for standard *ask* in the mouths of both the African American Burma Jones and three white dialect carriers.

And I know they somethin wron cause all of a sudden the Head Orphan
    stop showin up cause I'm axing plenty question. [Burma Jones][30]
Aw, relax, Irene. You making *me* nervous. I'm sorry
    I axt you over. [Santa Battaglia][31]
Ax that boy what he thinks of democracy some time. [Claude Robichaux][32]
If he was to ax me to marry him this very minute, I'd say,
    "Okay, Claude." I would, Ignatius. [Mrs. Reilly][33]

These five categories are the only ways that the *sounds* of the dialect are rendered in the novel. Instead, the impression of the dialect is achieved by grammar—nonstandard grammatical forms and sentence structure.

You was really sick when you got back home. [Mrs. Reilly][34]
I seen them downtown before. [Claude Robichaux][35]
You know, sweetheart, Mrs. Reilly said to the young man, me and
    my boy was in trouble today. The police tried to arress him.[36]
You was on radar. [Darlene][37]
He used to say to me, "Momma, I love you." He
    don't say that no more. [Mrs. Reilly][38]
Me and Mr. Mancuso here just having some coffee.
    You been nasty all afternoon. [Mrs. Reilly][39]
A few bottles of Gallo muscatel, and you with all them trinkets. [Mrs. Reilly][40]
They was nice to you at college, Ignatius. [Mrs. Reilly][41]
Well, you ain't gonna do too much damage to Paradise
    Vendors in one hour. [Mr. Clyde][42]
I never heard of nobody wanted a king. [Mrs. Reilly][43]
She the wife of that Lopez ran the little market over on
    Frenchman Street? [Santa Battaglia][44]
Claude ain't gonna want no Ignatius around, sweetheart. [Santa Battaglia][45]
"Ain't that awful," Mrs. Reilly said sadly.[46]

In addition to instances of incorrect grammar like these, Toole uses with great frequency two syntactic structures of spoken English that are usually avoided in careful writing: wh-questions without subject/auxiliary inversion and a construction I label *dative*. Almost all the dialect carriers use these constructions, with Mrs. Reilly the most frequent user. Of course, these sentence structures are not peculiar to New Orleans either.

In standard usage, a helping verb then the subject follows a question word, for example, *Where have you been?* or *What do you want?* In informal speech, the question word is simply placed before a statement, for example, *Why you went to the bank?*

Where you bought these nice wine cakes, lady? [Darlene][47]
What you mumbling about in there, boy? [Mrs. Reilly][48]
How you doing, Mr. Mancuso? What them people said? [Mrs. Reilly][49]
How much I gotta pay? [Mrs. Reilly][50]
What he said, honey? [Mrs. Reilly][51]
How I'm gonna pay that? [Mrs. Reilly][52]
What that girl wants? What she's doing nowadays? [Mrs. Reilly][53]
What she died from? [Santa Battaglia][54]
Where he came from? [Darlene][55]
How you like that, babe? How you like the way your
    grandson Angelo made good? [Santa Battaglia][56]
Where I gonna fin me another job? [Burma Jones][57]

Toole particularly favors an informal sentence structure that states an unnecessary indirect object pronoun co-referential with the subject of the clause (in earlier English a function of the dative case). Again, this construction is used mainly by Mrs. Reilly.

I think I could drink me another beer, Ignatius. [Mrs. Reilly][58]
Ignatius graduated from college. Then he stuck around there for four
    more years to get him a master's degree. [Mrs. Reilly][59]
Now that I think of it, I oughta get me some commission for what
    them people drank up in here last night. [Darlene][60]
Come on in the house, and we'll have us a nice cup of coffee. [Mrs. Reilly][61]
Thank you anyway, Miss Reilly. I had me a big lunch. [Sgt. Mancuso][62]
I had me a real estate agent offered me seven thousand last year. [Mrs. Reilly][63]
I wish I had me a hobby like that. [Mrs. Reilly][64]
Nobody else got him a valve but you. *I* ain't got no valve. [Mrs. Reilly][65]
Tomorrow we looking at the want ads in the paper. You
    gonna dress up and find you a job. [Mrs. Reilly][66]
You can get you a good job. [Mrs. Reilly][67]
We sure had us some hard times down on Dauphine Street. [Mrs. Reilly][68]
Almost every other club on the street's got them an animal. [Darlene][69]

Another marker of local speech is distinctive vocabulary items. Toole uses many accurate place and product names like *Constantinople St., D. H. Holmes, Fazzio's* bowling alley, the *Prytania* movie theater, and *Dixie 45* beer. However, aside from proper nouns, the number and variety of local words and phrases in the novel are surprisingly small. I notice only the ten listed below.

"Hey, how you making?" Miss Inez asked. "How you feeling, darling?"[70]
Me, I always like some good cake after I finish eating. [Mrs. Reilly][71]
I can get a thousand dollars over by the Homestead. [Mrs. Reilly][72]
I'll go stay by a old folks' home. [Mrs. Reilly][73]
She got knocked down by a streetcar over on Magazine Street early one
  morning when she was on her way to Fisherman's Mass. [Mrs. Reilly][74]
Until he was five years old and had finally managed to walk in an almost normal
  manner, he had been a mass of bruises and hickeys. [narrative voice][75]
I was right there with them ersters banging away
  on the banquette. [Santa Battaglia][76]
Mr. Watson, the quiet, tan, café au lait owner had sole authority
  over the restricted merchandise. [narrative voice][77]
What's them bo-bos on your hand? [Mrs. Reilly][78]
You know that poor old colored lady sells them pralines
  in front the cemetery? [Mrs. Reilly][79]

Two deserve comment. The locative *by*, as in "the family is celebrating Christmas by my cousin's," is unremarkable in the speech of all classes in New Orleans, and Toole's dialect carriers use it.

So I went over by the German and bought him two dozen. [Mrs. Reilly][80]
Next time I go by the alley, I'll let you know. [Sgt. Mancuso][81]
When I reconnized you down by the bowling alley with Miss Battaglia, I says
  to myself, "I hope I can meet her sometime." [Claude Robichaux][82]
I bought it by Lenny's. [Santa Battaglia][83]

The ordinary word for the public transportation that runs on tracks in New Orleans is *streetcar*. In the 1950s and 1960s, no one called it a *trolley*. Toole also shows a native's knowledge by referring to the two operators as the *motorman* and the *conductor*.[84] When Ignatius gets the rubber tire of his hot dog cart stuck in the groove of the track, the narrative voice calls the oncoming vehicle a *streetcar*, as does Ignatius.

What a promising day this appears to be. I am apparently to be run over by a
  streetcar and robbed simultaneously, thereby setting a Paradise record.[85]

Curiously, *trolley* is used by the narrative voice twice,[86] and Mrs. Reilly twice uses *trolley* to Ignatius.

Tomorrow morning you getting on that St. Charles trolley with the birds.[87]
. . . I said you getting on that trolley with the birds.[88]

Toole also uses two stereotypic features of New Orleans discourse, endearing nouns of address and the honorific *Miss* for adult women. In the novel, Mrs. Reilly and Santa Battaglia are the two dialect carriers who mainly use such endearments as *babe*, *honey*, and *precious*. As usual, Mrs. Reilly sets the pattern. In the first chapter, she addresses Miss Inez as *babe* and *sweetheart*; the young man in the Night of Joy as *babe*, *honey*, and *sweetheart*; and Sgt. Mancuso and Darlene as *honey*. Three minor characters bear in their names the honorific *Miss—Miss Inez*, *Miss Annie*, and *Miss Trixie*. Mrs. Reilley's opening words launch the representation of New Orleans dialect in the novel with these two readily recognized features.

"Oh, Miss Inez." Mrs. Reilley called in that accent that occurs south of New Jersey only in New Orleans, that Hoboken near the Gulf of Mexico. "Over here, babe."[89]

The New Orleans that Toole called home between 1937 and 1969 and that he depicts in *A Confederacy of Dunces* was racially segregated and had a complex class structure within the separate races. The novel has only one fully developed African American character, Burma Jones, one of the dialect carriers. Jones's dialect is distinct. Although Jones shares some characteristics with other dialect carriers, his speech is more fully and obviously represented by departures from conventional grammar and spelling. When Toole was writing *A Confederacy of Dunces*, the scholarly study of African American Vernacular English was still in its infancy. Linguists had not yet demonstrated that the dialect is a systematic variety of American English with its own patterns of phonology, vocabulary, and sentence structure. Most people considered the speech of African Americans randomly incorrect or poorly learned English. Toole's rendering of Burma Jones's speech, however, includes several of the characteristics that were later shown to be part of African American dialects. Foremost are the simplification of consonant clusters, the loss of final consonants, and the loss of /r/ after vowels and in final position. These characteristics Toole represents by the omission of letters, for example, *advertise* for *advertised, star* for *start*, *vagran* for *vagrant*, *color boy* for *colored boy*, *ain* for *ain't*, *wha* for *what*,[90] and *flo* for *floor*.[91] In addition, in Jones's speech the ending *–ing* is much more frequently spelled *–in* than in the speech of the white dialect carriers. The spelling *–in* is a common literary device to indicate lack of education, although the pronunciation is widespread in English universally in informal situations. A salient feature of African American phonology that is absent from Toole's representation is the substitution of *d* or *t* for the interdental fricative spelled *th* in words like *this*, *them*, and so on.

Two vocabulary items often cited as typical among African Americans are *police* with stress on the first syllable and *ax* for *ask*. In one instance, Jones uses both in the same sentence.

And you get off your stool and get on that phonograph before I call up the precinc and ax them po-lice mothers make a search for your orphan frien who disappear.[92]

His speech also contains a single instance of a derogatory term for whites, *ofay*.

You better tell your little ofay kid friend move along.[93]

Other characteristics of African American Vernacular illustrated sporadically in Jones's speech are *s*-less third person singular present tense (He tell me I better get my ass gainfully employ),[94] lack of the verb *be* (I starving to death in this cathouse),[95] and invariant *be* (I bet they be the firs orphan the po-lice be interes in ever).[96] These and other characteristics of Jones's speech are illustrated below.

How come they draggin in somebody like you? . . .
    Them po-lice mus be getting desperate.[97]
You don know? Whoa! That crazy. You gotta be here for
    somthin. Plenty time they pickin up color peoples for nothing,
    but, mister you gotta be here for something.[98]
I come about that porter job you got advertise in the paper.[99]
I ain exactly a character yet, but I can tell they gonna star that
    vagran no visible mean of support stuff on me.[100]
For twenty dollar a week, you ain running a plantation in here.[101]
You oughta tell your customer use they ashtray, tell them peoples you workin a
    man in here below the minimal wage. Maybe they be a little considerate.[102]
Times changin. . . . You cain scare color peoples no more. I
    got me some peoples form a human chain in front your door,
    drive away your business, get you on the TV news.[103]
You be lookin pretty junky with a Night of Joy broom stickin out your ass.[104]
When your little orphan frien comin here again? Whoa! I like to fin out what goin
    on with them orphan. I bet they be the firs orphan the po-lice be interes in ever.[105]
You got you a little business, got you a son teachin school probly
    got him a bobby-cue set, Buick, air-condition, TV.[106]

The language of the major character, Ignatius J. Reilly, gives no information about local speech and stands in contrast to that of the dialect carriers. Ignatius does not shift register. In all situations, he speaks and writes with school-approved grammar.

"I shall contact the mayor," Ignatius was shouting.[107]
Actually, Mother. I believe that it was he who started everything.[108]
I seriously doubt that he will permit me to elude him so easily.[109]

If anyone was ever minding his business, it was I.[110]
Leaving New Orleans also frightened me considerably. Outside of the
    city limits the heart of darkness, the true wasteland begins.[111]
That was the only time that I had ever been out of New Orleans in my life.[112]
No doubt they're more foxy than I.[113]

The register that Ignatius lives in is uncommonly formal and usually pompous. Here Ignatius explains his lack of hot dog sales to his employer.

[Mr. Clyde] You're full of bullshit.
    [Ignatius] I? The incident is sociologically valid. The blame rests upon our
society. The youth, crazed by suggestive television programs and lascivious
periodicals, had apparently been consorting with some rather conventional
adolescent females who refused to participate in his imaginative sexual program. His unfulfilled physical desires therefore sought sublimation in food. I,
unfortunately, was the victim of all of this. We may thank God that this boy has
turned to food for an outlet. Had he not, I might have been raped right there on
the spot.[114]

The same elevated diction and style is sustained in the large portion of the
novel consisting of Ignatius's writing. Here is one brief entry from a journal
entry signed *Lance, Your Besieged Working Boy.*

I quickly rolled my cart out of the garage and set out for the Quarter. Along
the way, many pedestrians gave my semi-costume favorable notice. My cutlass
slapping against my side, my earring dangling from my lobe, my red scarf shin-
ing in the sun brightly enough to attract a bull, I strode resolutely across town,
thankful tha I was still alive, armoring myself against the horrors that awaited
me in the Quarter. Many a loud prayer rose from my pink lips, some of thanks,
some of supplication.[115]

In sum, *A Confederacy of Dunces* is not filled with indicators of uniquely
New Orleans speech. What readers construe as typical, authentic dialect is
mainly the use of forms suppressed or eliminated in standard spoken or written English, a class dialect much more than a regional or local one. However,
accurate representation of speech is not the measure of what constitutes
effective dialect writing. A phonetic transcription of speech is accurate and
authentic but is tedious to read and does not enhance a work of literature.
Good dialect writing evokes in readers a culturally rich impression of authentic speech. *A Confederacy of Dunces* does that. The readers' experience of
hearing the characters is real and essential to experiencing the world of the
novel. Toole's accomplishment in creating that experience is no less real, and
is masterful.

NOTES

1. Percy, Foreword, vii.
2. Lowe, 188.
3. *Confederacy*, 4.
4. *Confederacy*, 216.
5. *Confederacy*, 231.
6. *Confederacy*, 4.
7. *Confederacy*, 6.
8. *Confederacy*, 8.
9. *Confederacy*, 9.
10. *Confederacy*, 42.
11. *Confederacy*, 43.
12. *Confederacy*, 63–70.
13. *Confederacy*, 184–188.
14. *Confederacy*, 4.
15. *Confederacy*, 175.
16. *Confederacy*, 91.
17. *Confederacy*, 199.
18. *Confederacy*, 266.
19. *Confederacy*, 14.
20. *Confederacy*, 351.
21. *Confederacy*, 5.
22. *Confederacy*, 16.
23. *Confederacy*, 194.
24. *Confederacy*, 17.
25. *Confederacy*, 23.
26. *Confederacy*, 25.
27. *Confederacy*, 30.
28. *Confederacy*, 38.
29. *Confederacy*, 50.
30. *Confederacy*, 131.
31. *Confederacy*, 196.
32. *Confederacy*, 203.
33. *Confederacy*, 363.
34. *Confederacy*, 11.
35. *Confederacy*, 16.
36. *Confederacy*, 19.
37. *Confederacy*, 20.
38. *Confederacy*, 43.
39. *Confederacy*, 45.
40. *Confederacy*, 49.
41. *Confederacy*, 51.
42. *Confederacy*, 157.
43. *Confederacy*, 213.

44. *Confederacy*, 267.
45. *Confederacy*, 299.
46. *Confederacy*, 300.
47. *Confederacy*, 21.
48. *Confederacy*, 30.
49. *Confederacy*, 38.
50. *Confederacy*, 39.
51. *Confederacy*, 40.
52. *Confederacy*, 40.
53. *Confederacy*, 216.
54. *Confederacy*, 267.
55. *Confederacy*, 333.
56. *Confederacy*, 345.
57. *Confederacy*, 350.
58. *Confederacy*, 13.
59. *Confederacy*, 22.
60. *Confederacy*, 34.
61. *Confederacy*, 38.
62. *Confederacy*, 39.
63. *Confederacy*, 42.
64. *Confederacy*, 44.
65. *Confederacy*, 48.
66. *Confederacy*, 50.
67. *Confederacy*, 52.
68. *Confederacy*, 92.
69. *Confederacy*, 105.
70. *Confederacy*, 4.
71. *Confederacy*, 21.
72. *Confederacy*, 42.
73. *Confederacy*, 45.
74. *Confederacy*, 43.
75. *Confederacy*, 84.
76. *Confederacy*, 91.
77. *Confederacy*, 130.
78. *Confederacy*, 213.
79. *Confederacy*, 216.
80. *Confederacy*, 39.
81. *Confederacy*, 44.
82. *Confederacy*, 203.
83. *Confederacy*, 262.
84. *Confederacy*, 287.
85. *Confederacy*, 286.
86. *Confederacy*, 212, 285.
87. *Confederacy*, 145.
88. *Confederacy*, 145.

89. *Confederacy*, 4.
90. *Confederacy*, 31–34.
91. *Confederacy*, 166.
92. *Confederacy*, 219.
93. *Confederacy*, 72.
94. *Confederacy*, 31.
95. *Confederacy*, 90.
96. *Confederacy*, 90.
97. *Confederacy*, 14.
98. *Confederacy*, 14.
99. *Confederacy*, 31.
100. *Confederacy*, 31.
101. *Confederacy*, 70.
102. *Confederacy*, 70.
103. *Confederacy*, 71.
104. *Confederacy*, 72.
105. *Confederacy*, 90.
106. *Confederacy*, 351.
107. *Confederacy*, 5.
108. *Confederacy*, 6.
109. *Confederacy*, 8.
110. *Confederacy*, 8.
111. *Confederacy*, 11.
112. *Confederacy*, 11.
113. *Confederacy*, 207.
114. *Confederacy*, 164.
115. *Confederacy*, 229.

BIBLIOGRAPHY

Lowe, John. "The Carnival Voices of *A Confederacy of Dunces*." In *Louisiana Culture from the Colonial Era to Katrina,* edited by John Lowe, 159–190. Baton Rouge: Louisiana State University Press, 2008.
Percy, Walker. Foreword. *A Confederacy of Dunces.* Rpt. Grove Press, 1987 [1980].
Toole, John Kennedy. *A Confederacy of Dunces.* Rpt. Grove Press, 1987 [1980].

Chapter 11

Thelma Toole

As Herself

Christopher R. Harris[1]

Walker had warned me. "I'm working with David on getting the Thelma Toole story in *People* (Magazine) . . . it's a great story." "Have fun . . . but don't linger!"

I had known Walker for only a short time. Walker was, of course, Walker Percy the literary giant who had identified the genius of John Kennedy Toole's manuscript for *A Confederacy of Dunces* and became its principal facilitator into publication, and David was the Pulitzer Prize winning, New Orleans based, old-hand reporter with *Life Magazine*, David Chandler. Big guns to be sure.

As was common at the time, David had written a general piece on Thelma and her brilliant son John on his own time, without my being there to take photographs. Instead, I would come in after the story was written—and without any knowledge of the flow or direction of his story—try to do a photographic take on my view of the subject that would work with his reporting. I had heard a basic story on how she contacted Walker as he taught a course a Loyola University in New Orleans, across Lake Pontchartrain from his home in Covington and he had championed its publication. But I was not ready for what would follow.

When I arrived at her small cottage—next to a funeral home—she met me dressed "to the nines" as my beloved Grandmother would say. Her hair was impeccable, with small curls set tight, and an application of precise bright red lipstick. She glowed.

Being a man of the South, I knew to carry some appropriate gifts with me to share—Petit Fours from an uptown bakery. We sat and shared some of the little delights and talked. I didn't take photos right away, we just continued to talk. Thelma was pleased to know I was from New Orleans and inquired about my family and background. I must have passed the test as she opened up to me about her life story. I started to photograph her in her small living room. She presented herself for her portrait and I shot from several angles, different lenses until she stopped suddenly. "Have you seen my John?" "He was such a pretty boy, and oh, so smart." And then, there it was, she slowly held up a wallet-size black and white print of her son. Tears welled-up as she shared the photo with me. I continued to shoot, perhaps to hide my embarrassment.

My raw film was sent to New York, the issue appeared and I called Thelma within a week or so of publication. Yes, she liked what was done and would love to see me again. So, suddenly, out of the blue she asked if I could come to take her "to make groceries." That phrase may be unique to New Orleans. It is a commoner's phrase—something Thelma always strived not to be. When we talked about her teaching in the city school system, she was very precise in telling me that she did not teach English to those "hellions,"—but rather she taught "e-l-o-c-u-t-i-o-n!" Having gone through the same public school system, I knew she must have suffered at the hand of the non-elocution masses. We made plans for my coming by and picking her up for the grocery trip. Her explanation to me was very precise, "I usually ask my brother"—who shared her house—"to pick-up what I need, but I want to go for myself."

I drove in from across Lake Pontchartrain to meet her precisely at 2:30, as was her request. Now I must say that at 2:30 on a summer day in New Orleans; it is hot and humid. I knew enough not to dress in shorts, for she was (and *needed* to be seen as) a lady!

When she responded to my knock on her door, I was not prepared. There she stood with a fresh hairdo, make-up, pearls, and best-of-clothes. Thelma, pulling-up her white cotton gloves, carrying her umbrella uttered "It's the sun, I just can't take the sun in the summer."

We bundled into my car stuffing her handbag and umbrella into crevices, all the time making small talk. I asked where she wanted to go. Thelma pointed across the street, directly across the street, and said, "there." Her finger jabbed verification, "across the street." She wanted to go to Schwegmann's, the working-man's grocery, in her finest.

I dutifully complied and delivered her to the front door. "No, just wait, I won't be long," she replied haughtily to my declaration that I would park the car and come in to assist her. So I waited by the store entrance in my car. Sure enough she popped her umbrella open from my car to the entrance, perhaps twenty feet, put it away, and went shopping. About fifteen minutes or so later she returned to the car, umbrella in full force. Whatever it was that she needed was held close to her in a partially filled bag that was wrapped down from the top as we returned across the street. I later found out it was homemade Hogshead cheese she carried. Hogshead cheese.

As I escorted her back to her house, she asked if I could come back at some time later so she could play some songs for me. She had earlier told me of her piano playing and how young John had loved her music. I agreed enthusiastically.

When I went to visit Thelma for her soirée she was dressed down, not like the elegance she had exhibited in going to the grocery, but rather in a common house dress. I felt it was a sign that she felt comfortable with me. She gave me a coke, pulled out a table chair for me to sit on and proceeded to sit at the piano, under a handmade banner spelling out "Thelma," and started playing. While I had expected something more casual, perhaps show tunes, or old classics, instead she started belting out bawdy songs of the mid-twentieth century. The classics she played were like what Moms Mabley might sing, or the dual piano singers at the piano bar at Pat O'Brien's. The cleaner songs were college-like fraternity songs, "Roll Me Over in The Clover" and such. I was stunned, but quickly responded to her talent and desire to sing these songs from her early life and leave behind the impression of a status-seeker she had so passionately conveyed to the public. Thelma was in her *other* element; she was the entertainer she always wanted to be, not just the mother of one of America's greatest writers. She played for several hours, looking more comfortable than I had ever seen her. Thelma was as eccentric as was needed. She could demand proper elocution in her finest dress or sing bawdy songs to a photographer whom she befriended.

Thelma was Thelma, and I enjoyed it all.

NOTE

1. See Christopher Harris' photographs of Thelma Toole located in the center of this book.

Index

addiction, 62, 123, 130–34, 136, 148; food, 8, 44, 47, 50, 123–27, 129–34, 136, 137n16, 167

aesthetics (taste), 6, 28, 40, 42–43, 48, 50, 55n17, 61, 65, 67, 70, 71nn1, 9, 72n22, 81, 93, 109–10, 112, 148

Aristotle, 65, 73n40, 86–88

Augustine, St., 24–26, 33nn11–12, 62, 68

Boethius (Boëthius). *See Consolation of Philosophy*

capitalism, 70, 74n68, 80

Catholicism (Catholic), xii, 30, 50, 94, 97–99, 101–2, 109, 133

Cervantes, Miguel de, 24, 29, 32–33nn4, 7, 55n17

Chaucer, Geoffrey, 18n52, 24, 26, 32, 33n15, 53n6, 64, 154nn5, 7

Christianity (Christian), 8, 11, 24–25, 29, 39, 66, 68, 70–71n11, 83, 85, 87, 96–100, 119n56

comedy (comedic), xiii, 1, 4–6, 9–12, 15nn4, 9, 16nn20, 23, 17nn24–25, 30, 18nn47, 54, 26, 28, 31, 95, 105–10, 117. *See also* humor; satire

Consolation of Philosophy (*De Consolatione Philosophiae*), 6, 17n31, 23, 25–27, 33n19, 34nn20–23, n25, 58n65, 61, 64, 66, 79, 81–87, 90, 96, 107–8, 112, 141–49, 154, 154nn6–7, 155nn8, 14

Dante, 24, 26, 33nn13, 14, 63, 95–96

decadence, 62–64, 72nn22, 24, 28, 73n47, 146

Enlightenment, 63, 69, 73n1, 74nn71, 79, 93

Fortuna/Fortune (Lady/Goddess), 8, 25–28, 30–32, 34n53, 37, 46, 50, 53n7, 64, 73n36, 81–87, 90–91, 93, 96, 108, 117, 118n20, 141–44, 146, 149–50, 152, 154, 155nn14, 15, 156n42. *See also* Philosophy (Goddess)

Freudian (Freud), 3, 15n13, 54n30, 112, 123, 128–30, 137n41–48, 151–52

God (gods), 8, 10, 13, 24–27, 29, 31–32, 33n11, 37, 40, 43, 45–45, 52n3, 58n65, 65–66, 69, 71n1, 72n22, 83–85, 93, 97, 100, 144, 148–49, 155n15, 167; atheism, 65–66, 84

About the Editor and Contributors

Leslie Marsh works in the Department of Pathology and Laboratory Medicine at The University of British Columbia Hospital. He has written on complexity, social epistemology, philosophical psychology, philosophical theology, political philosophy, philosophy of social science, and philosophical literature. Specifically, he has published on Michael Oakeshott, Friedrich Hayek, Adam Smith, Herbert Simon, and Walker Percy.

Anthony G. Cirilla is assistant professor of English at The College of the Ozarks. His research interests include old and middle English literature, Romantic and Victorian Medievalism, British fantasy literature (e.g., Tolkien, Lewis, and Rowling), and philosophy as literature, with a special emphasis on the reception and influence of Boethius. He is the associate editor of *Carmina Philosophiae: The Journal of the International Boethius Society*. He blogs at theboethianacolyte.com.

Olga Colbert is associate professor of Spanish at Southern Methodist University in Dallas. She is the author of *The Gaze on the Past: History and Popular Culture in the Novels of Antonio Muñoz Molina*. Her research interests include contemporary Spanish literature and culture, memory and exile, and cognitive approaches to literature.

Connie Eble is professor of Linguistics in the Department of English and Comparative Literature at the University of North Carolina-Chapel Hill. Her interests in philology and sociolinguistics have come together in her research on language variation in Louisiana, particularly on the dialects of New Orleans and the transition from French to English in the state.

Christopher R. Harris is a photojournalist and is represented by A Gallery for Fine Photography in New Orleans. His work has been published in *Time, Newsweek, Fortune, Forbes, Sports Illustrated, Life, Esquire, People, Playboy, Rolling Stone, GQ, Better Homes and Gardens, The New York Times*, Associated Press, United Press International, *Stern, Der Spiegel, Paris Match*, and *The Sunday Times* of London. He has photographed many of the literary greats including Tennessee Williams, Alice Walker, and Walker Percy, as well as Jimmy Carter and family and a "Who's Who" of local musicians and rock royalty passing through New Orleans.

Kenneth Holditch is emeritus professor of English at the University on New Orleans where he taught for 34 years. He has written extensively on Southern writers including six books on Tennessee Williams. It was Percy who introduced him to Thelma Ducoing Toole, mother of the author of *A Confederacy of Dunces*. He and Mrs. Toole became good friends; he ran errands for her, he typed for her, and she confided in him about her son and the Toole and Ducoing families. She bequeathed to him the manuscript and rights to her son's first novel, *The Neon Bible*, for which Holditch wrote the introduction to the Grove Press edition.

Jessica Hooten Wilson is an associate professor of humanities at John Brown University in Siloam Springs, Arkansas, where she also founded and serves as Chair of the Board for Sager Classical Academy. The author of three books, *Giving the Devil his Due: Flannery O'Connor and The Brothers Kara*mazov which received *Christianity Today's* book of the year award in Arts and Culture, *Walker Percy, Fyodor Dostoevsky, and the Search for Influence*, and *Reading Walker Percy's Novels*. Hooten-Wilson is currently preparing O'Connor's unfinished novel for publication. She was the 2017 Emerging Public Intellectual Award winner and the 2019 recipient of the Hiett Prize in the Humanities.

H. Vernon Leighton is coordinator of Liaison Services and Collections and Acquisitions Librarian for the Darrell W. Krueger Library at Winona State University. In addition to his work in library and information science, his interests include humor studies and evolutionary literary criticism. He has published and lectured extensively on Toole and *Confederacy*.

Kenneth B. McIntyre is professor of Political Science at Sam Houston State University. His research interests include the philosophy of history and social science, the philosophy of law, American political thought, and the political philosophy of the British idealists.

Tison Pugh is Pegasus professor of English at the University of Central Florida. His books include *Precious Perversions: Humor, Homosexuality, and the Southern Literary Canon* and *Queer Chivalry: Medievalism and the Myth of White Masculinity in Southern Literature.*

Stephen Utz is professor of Law at the University of Connecticut. He is a widely recognized expert in federal tax law, tax policy, and the philosophy of law. In addition to his central interest in philosophy he maintains an interest in Walker Percy and has some knowledge of French, German, Italian, Latin and Classical Greek.

www.ingramcontent.com/pod-product-compliance
Lightning Source LLC
Chambersburg PA
CBHW022316280326
41932CB00010B/1117